The Distance of Irish Modernism

Also available from Bloomsbury

Irish Modernisms, edited by Paul Fagan, John Greaney and Tamara Radak

The Distance of Irish Modernism

Memory, Narrative, Representation

John Greaney

BLOOMSBURY ACADEMIC
LONDON • NEW YORK • OXFORD • NEW DELHI • SYDNEY

BLOOMSBURY ACADEMIC
Bloomsbury Publishing Plc
50 Bedford Square, London, WC1B 3DP, UK
1385 Broadway, New York, NY 10018, USA
29 Earlsfort Terrace, Dublin 2, Ireland

BLOOMSBURY, BLOOMSBURY ACADEMIC and the Diana logo are trademarks of Bloomsbury Publishing Plc

First published in Great Britain 2022
Paperback edition published 2024

Copyright © John Greaney, 2022

John Greaney has asserted his right under the Copyright, Designs and Patents Act, 1988, to be identified as Author of this work.

For legal purposes the Acknowledgements on pp. viii–ix constitute an extension of this copyright page.

Cover image: 'Fall' © Cathal Ó Dubhláinn

All rights reserved. No part of this publication may be reproduced or transmitted in any form or by any means, electronic or mechanical, including photocopying, recording, or any information storage or retrieval system, without prior permission in writing from the publishers.

Bloomsbury Publishing Plc does not have any control over, or responsibility for, any third-party websites referred to or in this book. All internet addresses given in this book were correct at the time of going to press. The author and publisher regret any inconvenience caused if addresses have changed or sites have ceased to exist, but can accept no responsibility for any such changes.

A catalogue record for this book is available from the British Library.

A catalog record for this book is available from the Library of Congress.

ISBN: HB: 978-1-3501-2526-1
PB: 978-1-3503-2846-4
ePDF: 978-1-3501-2527-8
eBook: 978-1-3501-2528-5

Typeset by Newgen KnowledgeWorks Pvt. Ltd., Chennai, India

To find out more about our authors and books visit www.bloomsbury.com and sign up for our newsletters.

Contents

Preface	vi
Acknowledgements	viii
Introduction: The vicinities of Irish modernism	1
1 Samuel Beckett and the contexts of modernism	31
2 Brian, Flann, Myles and the origins of Irish modernism	63
3 Elizabeth Bowen's modernist history	91
4 Kate O'Brien's 'flawed' modernism	115
5 John McGahern and the limits of Irish modernism	141
Epilogue	169
Notes	175
Bibliography	213
Index	225

Preface

Do Irish modernist fictions constitute forms of cultural memory? Does the Irish modernist novel form a repository of Irish history? Do Irish literary modernisms offer imitative and referential representations of national and transnational histories?

In many of the recent studies of Irish modernism, it is rare to find one which calls for an examination of the relation between Irish modernism's affiliated literary texts and Ireland's history in modernity. Of those recent studies, the vast majority posit a homologous relationship between Irish modernism and Irish history, and emphasize that Irish modernism is most comprehensively understood in terms of its historical contexts. Indeed, postulations of modernist literatures doing anything near the opposite – as ambivalent to history or as autotelic structures cordoned off from the material and political world – have long since fallen from favour in Irish studies, modernist studies and literary studies more broadly. And it is not in favour of reviving such conceptualizations of modernist literature that the above questions are raised. Rather, these questions have arisen from the perception of a certain conundrum in recent definitions of Irish modernism: namely, the paradox through which Irish modernist fictions have become containers for national and transnational histories while such texts are often oblique and perverse in relation to the times and geographies from which they emerge. More specifically, these questions stem from an intuition that recent definitions of Irish modernism overlook, and are left unqualified by, the aesthetic practices of alienation, estrangement and non-representation prevalent to modernist literatures which distance and obscure extratextual historical realities. Animating this book, these questions are posed here in response to our contemporary critical and cultural moment: a moment replete with commemoration activity, in which literature plays the important role of providing different perspectives of the past; a moment in which historiographical methods dominate literary studies; and a moment in which Irish modernism and literary modernism have reached critical mass as historicist discourses. These questions thus serve to launch a metacritical interrogation of some of the finer assumptions of the modes of inquiry through which Irish modernism has been defined and has developed as a mode of narration and a structure of memory.

They simultaneously serve the purpose of opening Irish modernism to broader critical parameters than those usually deployed in the definition of the term.

The Distance of Irish Modernism: Memory, Narrative, Representation proposes a paradigm shift to reorient the way we think about Irish modernism and the literatures which shape its canon. It places literary representation at the forefront of how we conceptualize and define Irish modernism, an approach rarely assumed in Irish studies or modernist studies today given the archival, geopolitical and historicist impulses of these fields. In doing so, this book reverses the critical practice which has come to define Irish modernism: the process of considering modernist literary practice in and after material and political history. Building critically on the historicist impulses prevalent today in Irish studies and modernist studies, it analyses how and if the complex representational strategies of a host of Irish modernist literatures relate extratextual contexts and histories in languages and forms of equivalence and imitation. It thus interrogates whether modernist fictions still constitute an evidentiary form of cultural memory if we suspend the historicist assumption that such literatures referentially imitate and belatedly represent the actually lived world.

This change of vantage point implies a modification of the instruments and methodologies deployed to analyse and compare modernist texts. Close reading, formal analysis, narratology and philosophical accounts of literature are deployed here alongside historicist and materialist approaches as well as postcolonial and world literature paradigms to examine how, and by what aesthetic, formal and stylistic operations, modernist texts engage the cultural memories they supposedly transmit. The central hypothesis of this book suggests that while Irish modernist fictions maintain a certain proximity to historical and material realities, they also manifest an irreducible distance to the national and transnational histories of their periods and places. This argument is elaborated to raise an ethics of reading and interpretation at the intersections of Irish studies, memory studies and modernist studies, particularly concerning a critical tendency to posit a positive and homologous relation between literary experimentation and extratextual historical realities. The method and line of questioning pursued in these pages thus enables a new model for narrating Irish modernism, one shaped by the affinities and the tensions, and the proximity and the distance, between modernist aesthetic practice and the history of modernity in Ireland and beyond.

Acknowledgements

Thanks are due to many friends, colleagues and institutions who sustained this book through its early days up to the time of publication. It evolved from a PhD thesis written under the supervision of John Branigan at University College Dublin. I would like to thank John for his constructive insights on the work in its initial stages and for the example set by his intellectual generosity. Anne Fogarty and Colin Graham read and commented on my thesis, and their perceptive advice has guided my thinking in the years since. Barry Sheils, to whom I owe an intellectual debt, read most of these pages and made all of them better. The book was finished while I was a Fulbright-NUI postdoctoral scholar at the University of Pennsylvania where I was lucky to work under the mentorship of Jean-Michel Rabaté. Jean-Michel's intellectual rigour and *joie de vivre* provided fresh impetus for my thinking on Irish modernism and made life in Philadelphia inspiring and fun. At University College Dublin and the University of Pennsylvania, I joined great communities of scholars, many of whom offered spirited encouragement: Jed Esty, Margaret Kelleher, P. J. Mathews, Anne Mulhall, Emilie Pine, Cormac O'Brien and Paul Saint-Amour. I am grateful to all of them for questions and suggestions that helped me refine and redefine the project. Along the way, good friends and generous scholars shared their expertise and time with me: in Paul Fagan and Tamara Radak I found congenial collaborators in various Irish modernism-related pursuits; Nicholas Allen, Ruben Borg, Íde Corley, Patricia Coughlan, Christian Dupont, Astrid Erll, Patricia Gherovici, Maebh Long, Shane Mac an Bhaird, Stephen O'Neill and Michael Paye offered valuable advice. I would also like to express my gratitude to the Irish Fulbright Commission, the Irish Research Council and the National University of Ireland for providing vital support during the fruition and completion of this book. Thanks in particular are due to Dara Fitzgerald, Attracta Halpin, Emma Loughney and Sonya McGuinness.

Additional acknowledgements go to Lucy Brown at Bloomsbury for her editorial expertise, to the academic readers whose reports on my draft manuscript were insightful and to the artist Cathal Ó Dubhláinn for providing me with the cover image.

A portion of Chapter 2 of this book was published as 'Resisting Representation: Flann O'Brien and Ireland' in *Textual Practice* 34.4 (2020): 587–604, and a version of Chapter 3 appeared as '*The Last September*: Irish Modernism, Historical Determinism and Literary Deferral' in *Irish Studies Review* 27.2 (2019): 217–34. I acknowledge Taylor & Francis Group for permission to republish this work. I also thank the International Flann O'Brien Society in whose publication, *Flann O'Brien: Acting Out*, edited by Paul Fagan and Dieter Fuchs (Cork: Cork University Press, 2022), I rehearsed my thoughts on Brian O'Nolan's pseudonyms.

I have benefited immeasurably from the kindness and support of my family and friends: Clare, Róisín, Val, Niall, Tom and Cian have been influential at many distances; Helena taught me the difference between a setback and a catastrophe and showed the way through uncertain times; and for their buoyancy of spirit, which remains a constant source of inspiration, I would like to extend a special note of gratitude to my parents, Fergus and Bridget Greaney.

Introduction: The vicinities of Irish modernism

The venture

Few more than Ezra Pound have influenced and refereed the reception of literary modernism as an international phenomenon and a mode of aesthetic experimentation, an accomplishment which encompassed Irish modernist production. In 1915, in an article entitled 'The Non-Existence of Ireland', Pound set a particularly cosmopolitan and formalist tone for the institutionalization of modernist literature by Irish writers. Pound lauds James Joyce and J. M. Synge as European writers who were 'driven out [of Ireland] presumably by the local stupidity'[1] and claims they fled into the modern world to develop an art to which Ireland could not lay claim due to its inability to receive and understand it. The riots at the Abbey Theatre following the performance of Synge's *The Playboy of the Western World* and Joyce's lack of success in his home country prompted Pound to chart different trajectories for Ireland and the aesthetic achievements of some of its modernist writers. Joyce, particularly, for Pound is the 'only man calling himself Irish who is in any sense part of the decade'; and of that 'decade', Joyce and D. H. Lawrence are the 'only two writers of fiction' that 'anyone takes in earnest'.[2] Joyce 'writes as a European, not as a provincial', Pound suggests, 'all of which attests the existence of Mr. Joyce, but by no means the continued existence of Ireland'.[3] Writing as a European, Joyce writes with a 'clear hardness' and 'gauntness', a style which Pound casts in opposition to a 'mushy' new symbolism 'which has had more than its day in Ireland'.[4] Ireland is thus rendered as an obsolete category for measuring Joyce's achievements as he becomes an international and cosmopolitan writer partaking in an aesthetic and formalist modernism following Pound's delineations. And during the same period, Pound was pushing W. B. Yeats's poetry in a similar direction, encouraging the older poet to modernize his work by disbanding with symbolism and sharpening his meters and rhythms. Subsequently, Pound's position on literary modernism would be echoed, repeated and institutionalized by the scholars of New Criticism – from John Crowe Ransom to Cleanth Brooks and Robert Penn Warren to Hugh Kenner – in the process cementing modernism's identity in cosmopolitan and formalist terms, a narrative of modernism that would become a critical mainstay until the later decades of the twentieth century.

Over one hundred years on from Pound's 1915 declarations, the critical landscape concerning Joyce's and Synge's respective modernisms and how they relate to Ireland has changed dramatically. Most recently, Ireland's *Decade of Centenaries 2012–2022* has prompted, and coincided with, a turn to the study of cultural memory across the humanities and social sciences. Building on the interactions and successes of Irish studies and postcolonial studies, the rise of memory studies in the academy has produced yet another influential historicist lens through which Pound's European modernist writers can be regarded through the historical context of their nation, and their works can be investigated for how and what they remember of Ireland's past. Formalist definitions of modernism have thus given way to theorizations of literature as an expression of cultural memory, and so literary production can and has been read as a mode of representation which acts as a window on the actually lived world. As per the recent four-volume *Memory Ireland* series, Irish modernist literature 'contains', 'embodies' and 'forms a repository of' cultural memory, 'represents and unpacks the past', and 'is valuable ... as history itself'.[5] *Ulysses* (1922), *A Vision* (1925), *The Tower* (1928), *Finnegans Wake* (1939), *The Unnamable* (1953), *Waiting for Godot* (1953) – those oblique modernist achievements which uniquely liquefy Ireland's historical contours – are, in turn, increasingly investigated in the twenty-first century in terms of how they mediate their culture and time. Given the dominant historicist bent of literary studies over the last thirty years, and its ensuing implication of making Irish history far from irrelevant to the modernist productions of its literary citizens, Irish modernism has emerged in critical discourse as a mode of narration and a structure of memory for denoting and grouping modernist production relative to the social and political history of the nation state. At the culmination of Ireland's *Decade of Centenaries*, which coincides with the centenary of the publication of Joyce's *Ulysses*, modernism and Irish history are no longer on separate terrains; Pound's severing of Joyce from Ireland is now the obsolete paradigm.

Irish modernism is now a commonplace descriptor in both academic and public discourse for twentieth-century cultural production in, and in relation to, Ireland. The wide popularity of the term is in immediate evidence today in the academy and beyond: various publications, particularly edited collections of essays, deploy 'Irish modernism' as a titular term.[6] And in the public sphere, it is being used in exhibitions and galleries, as well as in media coverage of literary practice.[7] Tracking the rise of the term, Gregory Castle and Patrick Bixby, in their introduction to the recent *A History of Irish Modernism*, write that the first uses of Irish modernism appeared in publications in 1995, whereafter it appeared 'no more than twice a year until 2010' when its usage increased, 'later peaking at eighteen results in 2015'.[8] The critical ascendency of Irish modernism thus coincides with the interaction of various fields of study since the 1990s: the expansion of Irish studies (particularly its interaction with postcolonial studies) and the diversification of modernist studies into what has become 'the new modernist studies' have been significant to this end. These fields have corresponded where Irish studies has focused attention on the relationship between modernist production and imperial history, and where the new modernist studies has catered for looser understandings of modernist art and practice than what was once rigorously defined as an art of aesthetic autonomy, difficulty and formal experimentation. Moreover, the coincidence of modernist studies with area studies has expanded the remit of the modernist canon beyond, broadly speaking, a white, male, Eurocentric formulation, in turn catering for the relation of art to other domains of experience and knowledge, wider definitions of modernism, and different types of modernism. It has similarly led to the global and temporal expansion of the modernist canon to include multiple modernisms the world over, from Mongolian to Irish modernism and beyond.[9] As is thus evident by the term 'Irish modernism', a minimum condition of the institutionalization of (literary) modernism is no longer the necessity that it occupies an 'imaginary space beyond the political space of the nation through which literature can "happen"'[10] (notwithstanding, the scandal of its internationalism remains a concern of modernist discourse, despite the efficacies of materialist strategies focused on the local). In the production of an expanded modernist canon and remit – and because every national or transnational modernism does not have its own *Finnegans Wake* – a feature of scholarship in light of the new modernist studies has been a focus on cultural production in modernity rather than modes of modernism which compare to high modernism, or a difficulty of form in the respective styles of T. S. Eliot, Joyce, Pound or Virginia Woolf. The nation and its place in the world and world systems is now a formula by which modernism can be measured; as such, Irish history and Ireland's place in the geopolitical history of modernity have become determining factors in the definition of Irish modernism.

Irish modernism, in such terms, is an inclusive category, encompassing a range of artistic and aesthetic practices that can be made relative to the metanarrative of modernity in relation to Ireland, either locally or internationally, and functions to link artists as diverse as Joyce, Mary Swanzy, Brian Boydell and Eileen Gray. As Tom Walker suggests, 'material previously regarded as being too overtly political or nationalist to be categorised as such has come to be regarded as having some kind of relationship with modernism, while hitherto securely modernist works by Irish artists have been re-evaluated from more overtly political and nationalist perspectives'.[11] As an inclusive term, then, Irish modernism is also a capacious and positivist category, a result of which is that it includes works of literature which sit uneasily within, and pose problems to, its nationalist and statist parameters. Samuel Beckett's *The Unnamable*, for example, corresponds to the canon of Irish modernism given its author's biography; its narrative content, however, is uneasily made relevant to the metanarrative of Irish history and a specific modernity relative to Ireland, and thus presents problems to definitions of Irish modernism as bound up with Ireland's colonial history. Moreover, those quintessential works of Irish modernism – *Ulysses*, *A Vision*, *The Tower*, *Finnegans Wake*, *Waiting for Godot* – all maintain a perverse relationship to nationalist projects and projections, and, through their respective and unique aesthetic modes, leave the question of state formation and sovereignty open rather than enact and reinforce its enclosure. Such works thus prompt the paradox that Irish modernism's affiliated artworks maintain a divergence to the nationalist and statist discourses which underpin the term. This book attends to this paradox within discourses on Irish modernism to launch a metacritical interrogation of its governing criteria. It focuses on how some of the primary and marginal literatures of the Irish modernist canon remain untranslatable to the metanarrative of the nation state and thus establish an irreducible distance between literary representation and Ireland's history in modernity. In doing so, it recasts Irish literary modernism as a modernist concern as much as an Irish concern. It takes its cue from recent practices in the new modernist studies to build critically on the dominant paradigms of inquiry currently operative in that field.

Modernism/modernity

As per the new modernist studies, the study of modernist art and literature now relates to the concerns of the individual, the local, the national, the transnational and the ecological, as well as to questions of ability, affect, gender, race and sexuality. With this, the dominant trends of modernist studies currently concern transnationality and affect studies. The geographic and temporal expansion of modernist studies has thus occurred alongside, if it has not corresponded with, the turn to affect, as well as new phenomenology and new materialism, in the humanities and social sciences. On the one hand, then, a recent critical thrust in modernist studies has focused on the dispersal, difference and distance of literature; on the other, there has been a renewed interest in phenomenological presence and that which can be rendered intimately real through the arts, and literature particularly. Given this double movement, radically contrasting readings of texts have come to fruition: for example, it can be said, as Franco Moretti does, that '*Ulysses*, with its Latin title referring to a Greek hero, and written by an Irishman moving between Trieste-Zurich-Paris is the clearest sign of a literature for which national boundaries have lost all explanatory power'.[12] And elsewhere, as Oona Frawley suggests, 'Joyce's *Ulysses* … can (and has been read) as a history book, in the sense that it represents and comments on so much of the Irish past that the reader is deemed able to rely on its representation'.[13] Undoubtedly, various politics have brought about this situation: the need to dismantle Eurocentrism has resulted in the global and temporal expansion of modernist studies, and the need to speak again of the body and the extratextual world has emerged after the exploits of deconstruction and poststructural criticism. Though coincidental with the new modernist studies, the strands of this double movement evidently give rise to an aporia, thus establishing a potential paradox within this area of study: that is, the conundrum through which literary modernism can be understood as both a mode of world literature as well as a breeding ground for phenomenological presence. Positioned in terms of this paradox, Irish modernism may be read as engaging the dynamics of a specific modernity through its unique and respective modes of representation and non-representation; and similarly, it is potentially heterogeneous to a specific modernity to which it might be made equivalent.

This paradox has antecedents in the critical definition of modernist literature. As Sean Latham and Gayle Rogers have recently suggested, critics of modernism have 'had to wrestle with the questions of whether literature *represented* the alienated, massified conditions of modernity – and if so, perhaps further accentuated them – or offered a bulwark against their ill-effects by creating objects of eternal structure and order'.[14] While understandings of modernist literature as creating objects of eternal structure and order have long been on the wane in the field, a prevalent feature of the new modernist studies has concerned the connections and differences between modernist aesthetic practice and the historical realities of modernity. With a stress on context, modernism in some quarters has been stretched to denote literature *in* modernity. And so Jessica Berman, for example, in *Modernist Commitments*, a text largely symptomatic and representative of the concerns of the new modernist studies, suggests,

> Modernism ... stands for a dynamic set of relationships, practices, problematics and cultural engagements with modernity rather than a static canon of works, a given set of formal devices or a specific range of beliefs. ... Even where modernism seems to exhibit certain formal preoccupations, such as textual defamiliarization, refusal of strict verisimilitude, or play with the vagaries of space and time, it is clear that these are neither necessary nor ubiquitous conditions but rather signs or symptoms of a particular attitude toward a specific literary horizon of expectations. Nor can we pretend that such a list of preoccupations stands in for the practices, relationships or problematics that motivate the great variety of modernisms as they emerge worldwide.[15]

Correspondingly, Irish modernism is likewise defined by Castle and Bixby: 'We take it as axiomatic that Irish modernism is not simply about the arts, or about artistic innovation and experimentation but about political concerns, commercial interests and media technologies as well.'[16] A similar approach to modernism is registered by Jonathan Flatley in *Affective Mapping*, where modernism represents a 'symbolic space wherein what counts as modernity, what modernity is or should be, and for whom, is contested, debated, reevaluated, or otherwise articulated'.[17] Outlining the affective presence of modernity in modernist production, Flatley writes that 'the situation of modernism is one in which modernization is felt to be incomplete, still in progress, and thus potentially redirected'.[18] Julie Taylor has similarly echoed Flatley's hypothesis concerning the affective relationship between modernism and modernity: 'The modernist art work might be understood as a space for processing or registering new traumas and new delights; as a vehicle to jolt its reader out of quotidian modes of perception; as a mournful or melancholic response to loss or a hopeful indexing of progress.'[19] Elsewhere, the difference between modernism and modernity remains a prominent feature of discourse. Lauren Arrington, for example, has written that 'modernism is separate from modernity, and denotes an experimental style that reacts against conventional forms. If these terms are not carefully defined, then Modernism becomes a useless aesthetic category and is synonymous with the modern.'[20] And so Arrington elsewhere calls for a 'new formalism [that] may prove vital, since close readings of Irish modernism's technical innovations illuminate ... its markers of originality'.[21] Moreover, prominent critics such as Frederic Jameson, Moretti and Raymond Williams have developed influential accounts of modernism as defined by the imperial world order, economic and political structures, and, particularly, the uneven development of global capitalism. In contrast, critics such as David Damrosch, Jahan Ramazani and Gayatri Chakravorty Spivak have theorized literary production as the play of cultural differences across borders where aesthetic representation maintains a certain autonomy from the political and economic structures of a unified global capitalism. Put broadly, the convergences and divergences between modernism and modernity are integral to the new modernist studies. While cultural studies has brought about a decentring of modernist studies and loosened its bind on a set of canonical texts, the older terms through which modernism was measured – crisis of representation, fragmentation, mobilization of epistemological doubt – have not disappeared or become redundant. The field thus remains entangled in a continuous and productive process of definition, and so the indistinction between modernism and modernity remains an intricate, pertinent and productive feature of its remit.[22]

Carrying this critical irresolution in a recent definition of Irish modernism, Jean-Michel Rabaté has suggested that 'Irish modernism has always been a matter of hearing language with new inflections or seeing reality differently as much as refashioning history'.[23] Underlining its modernist features, Rabaté positions the indeterminacy of modernist art in relation to history and loosens the determinism of Irish modernism's nationalist and historical bind. Reading Irish modernism as such – as that which is both different and relative to the legibly historical – puts the apparent extratextual referent of Irish modernism, namely Irish history, beyond guarantee depending on, in Rabaté's terms, the inflection of language and the different seeing of reality: that is, terms which imply the radical alterity of modernist literature. Thus, tacit in Rabaté's account is an understanding of Irish modernist literature as potentially heterogeneous and at a distance to the concerns and facts of early-twentieth-century history.

Rabaté's account of Irish modernism in this instance raises the question of the proximity and the distance, and the affinity and the difference, of Irish modernism to Ireland's history in modernity. It allows for an understanding of Irish modernism as standing on both sides of the equation concerning modernism's relation to, and dissimilarity from, extratextual historical realities. As such, it offers a methodological possibility for theorizing this paradoxicality. Thought through the double movement evident in modernist studies currently – the turn towards the worldly and affect – Rabaté's philosopheme merits further exploration to demonstrate its wider ranging implications, as well as to probe operative conceptualizations of Irish modernism. Such is the aim and subject of this book, which seeks to think anew the vicinities of Irish modernism and thus the critical and theoretical paradigms through which the term can be conceptualized. First, then, it is necessary to take stock of recent critical discourse on Irish modernism.

Mapping Irish modernism

Rabaté's account of Irish modernism contrasts with other contemporary theorizations of the term. In the recent *Cambridge Companion to Irish Modernism*, Enda Duffy writes that 'Irish modernism and Irish postcoloniality were parallel projects'.[24] For Duffy, 'Irish modernism stands bifurcated by the historical dividing line of the Easter Rebellion and the War of Independence',[25] and can be understood as constituted by 'successive anticolonial and postcolonial modernisms'.[26] What distinguishes Irish modernism from other modernisms is the 'epistemic-changing transformation' of 'the rebellion and the achievement of independence'.[27] As Duffy suggests, 'Irish literature changed on April 21, 1916. This gave Irish modernism an intense intimacy with political revolution as its central energizing impulse.'[28] As such, for Duffy, 'the interaction of literature and politics could generate a specifically local modernism'.[29]

Duffy's conceptualization of Irish modernism in this instance is preceded and anticipated by a host of criticism which has explored the relationship between colonialism and modernism. Notably, Declan Kiberd's *Inventing Ireland* and Emer Nolan's *James Joyce and Nationalism* respectively situate the politics of modernist aesthetic practice in relation to postcolonial reading strategies. Similarly, following Jameson's 'Modernism and Imperialism', later critiques such as *Modernism and Colonialism* have explored how 'the question of innovation and formal experimentation, so often associated with modernism, is related to … colonialism',[30] 'how modernist literary practice was variously shaped by the contemporary geopolitical scene, and how the modernist revolution can be understood as a critical engagement with the British and, more broadly, European quest for Empire'.[31] A feature of such analyses, as is a pertinent facet of historicist criticism and evident in Duffy's diagnostic above, is an understanding of literature as determined or shaped by material base, thus belated and representative of historical realities after the fact. Irish modernism is correspondingly theorized as having 'colonial origins' elsewhere in *The Cambridge Companion to Irish Modernism*.[32] Indeed, Duffy's recent account of Irish modernism is not an isolated occurrence in contemporary scholarship. It operates, broadly speaking, as the dominant appreciation and conceptualization of the term. For example, Deaglán Ó Donghaile and Gerry Smyth have recently echoed this understanding when suggesting that 'the Irish chapter [of modernism] has a specific political inflection, born of its status as a long-unsettled colony'.[33] Similarly, Fionna Barber suggests that 'modernism in Ireland was bound up with major social and political factors during the first part of the twentieth century, especially the effects of independence and Partition in 1922'.[34] Or as Castle and Bixby suggest, disaffection, as a result of geopolitical realities which caused uneven modernization in Ireland, became 'the dominant affect in Irish art and culture after political independence, beginning with the founding of the Free State in 1922 and continuing through enactment of the Irish constitution in 1937'.[35] As such, the apparent cultural and historical realities of modernity can be deployed as a stable explicator of modernist literature, and modernist literature can be read in an active relationship of equivalence – parallel, intensely intimate with, centrally energized by – with Irish postcoloniality. What has largely heretofore defined Irish modernism, as a result of a critical language which implies a colonial origin, is its apparent rootedness in Irish colonial history. Irish modernism, as these examples show, has variously been defined in proximity to Irish monumental history, with its teleology running more or less on course with the development of modernity in Ireland. The recent *A Cambridge History to Irish Modernism*, for example, traces the development of Irish modernism through a pre-Revival form towards a mid-twentieth-century modernity in Ireland, thus rehearsing the metanarrative that Irish modernism follows the trajectory of national history. Ultimately, as Susan Stanford Friedman suggests, Irish modernism is a 'twentieth-century colonial modernism'.[36]

The respective concerns of the work undertaken by Kiberd,[37] Nolan[38] and others – the revision of Ireland's status in relation to British imperialism – provided an apposite foundation from which Irish modernism might emerge, thereby demonstrating and validating the affinity and the proximity of Irish modernist literature to the concerns of Irish history. Given the international success of such studies, amongst others,[39] it is unsurprising that Irish modernism would come to be defined in such close relation to a history of colonialism relative to Ireland. The presence of Ireland and its history as a determining concern in Joyce's and Elizabeth Bowen's writings, amongst the other Irish modernists, became, to a large extent, a staple of criticism, which ultimately, as Walker suggests, has 'effected a politicization of the category of modernism as it pertains to Ireland'.[40] Irish modernism, in such terms, was initiated as *Irish* modernism. Following dominant trends in Irish studies, and operating largely adjacent to the new modernist studies, recent readings and theorizations of Irish modernism remain inspired by historicist reading strategies: the postcolonial paradigm remains influential to this end, and it is complemented by the recent intersection of Irish studies with memory studies.

Imitative representation, the radically symbolic and the base of culture

As it concerns the relationship between text and extratextual history, the focus on historicist reading strategies prevalent at the intersections of area studies, memory studies and postcolonial studies, as well as literary studies more broadly, has catered for the explanation of radically symbolic literatures with historicist keys. For example, leaning towards making history present through literature, it has been suggested, as mentioned earlier, that Joyce's *Ulysses* 'can (and has been read) as a history book, in the sense that it represents and comments on so much of the Irish past that the reader is deemed able to rely on its representation'.[41] Elsewhere, Flann O'Brien's *At Swim-Two-Birds* and *The Third Policeman* have been read as representative and symptomatic of Ireland's uneven development. For example, it has been suggested that 'the context of disappointment, combined with an uneven social development in a still primarily rural Ireland, underlies the peculiar combination of the mundane and the fantastic in O'Brien's work'.[42] And in the case of Bowen's *The Last September* – a text in which, to quote Susan Osborn, 'similitude is often rejected in favour of jarring and unsettling inaccuracies and improprieties'[43] – it has been posited that history 'is most present … when it is most absent',[44] and thus the history of the War of Independence is deployed as an explicative tool to analyse the text and to reveal the 'full, hideous force of the reality behind words which float nebulously through the novel'.[45] As in these examples, an active critical grammar – 'reliably represents', 'underlies', 'is present' – has been adopted which tacitly incites a mimetic theory of literature as imitative and belated, and thus corresponding to received historiographical accounts. As in each example, the history of post-independence Ireland precedes the respective texts of *Ulysses*, *At Swim-Two-Birds*, *The Third Policeman* and *The Last September*, and enables their reading and explanation. In such terms, Ireland's historical contours can be read in these novels: literature, in turn, refigures historical realities and creates new memory narratives as a result of processes of symbolic reconfiguration, in turn reinforcing Irish history as the metanarrative of Irish modernism. Tacit in such accounts, then, is the assumption that events that occur to or within writing operate in a derivative or secondary relationship to economic and social histories.

Unacknowledged in such critiques are the narrative devices that (literary) historiography deploys to explain the past and present, and which simultaneously displace and dislocate past and present. As critiques of historicist methodologies have contended, narratives, and particularly historiographical (meta)narratives, carry an appeal for referentiality through their uses of the stratagems of writing. That is to say, the production of an origin for meaning outside and prior to language occurs as an act of symbolic behaviour. Jacques Derrida famously signals this predicament in *Of Grammatology* when writing that critical reading 'cannot legitimately transgress the text toward something other than it, toward a referent (a reality that is metaphysical, historical, psychobiographical[,] etc.) or toward a signified outside the text whose content could take place, could have taken place outside of language, that is to say, ... outside of writing in general'.[46] Writing, as chronologically and ontologically prior to that that which it is presumed to represent, can be none other than the location of culture's material base, an issue which was famously tackled by J. Hillis Miller in his 1986 Modern Language Association address. Following Derrida's method, Miller's specific target is the understanding and critical deployment of material base as a 'root, the ground of reality, something unambiguously opposed to the impalpabilities of language play or theoretical abstraction'[47] and 'as the name for the whole region of what presumably exists outside language'.[48] Countering such approaches to critical reading, Miller suggests that any material base cited as determining cultural production

> is a catachrestic trope, side by side with others, for what can never be approached, named, perceived, felt, thought, or in anyway encountered as such, though it is the hidden agent of all these phenomenal experiences. ... What materiality names can never be encountered ... because it is always mediated by language or other signs.[49]

Thus, if criticism does not distinguish 'phenomenality from the material', it fails to recognize that, as Miller says, 'political action taken in the name of an appeal to the material base is "based" on a speech act that is illocutionary, positional, performative, not constative'.⁵⁰ In such terms, narrative production and storytelling remain irreducible to another narrative or event that would supposedly harness determined or univocal meaning.

Pragmatizing the issue at hand: such practices of reading the (modernist) novel as belated, imitative, corresponding to and registering the processes of the actually existing world are now a prominent feature of the new modernist studies given the vertical and temporal expansion of the field, which has resulted in a diminishment of modernism's relation to difficulty and its status as an aesthetic category. Indeed, the expanded modernist canon rarely features works as oblique and experimental as Pound's *The Cantos* or Joyce's *Finnegans Wake*. Thus, such reading practices might generally seem appropriate if applied to what Roland Barthes describes, in 'From Work to Text', as a 'work' (though neither Derrida nor Miller would concur here). For Barthes, literatures which correspond to a 'work', or are moderately symbolic, 'close in on a specific signified and ... function as a general sign and it is normal that it should represent an institutional category of the civilization of the sign'.⁵¹ In contrast to the 'work', Barthes develops the concept of the 'text' to describe acts of literature, and beyond, which accomplish 'the very plural of meaning: an *irreducible* (and not merely an acceptable) plural'.⁵² The text is thus 'radically symbolic' and is 'approached, experienced, in reaction to the sign'; the field of the text 'is that of the signifier and the signifier must not be conceived of as "the first stage of meaning", its material vestibule, but in complete opposition to this, as its deferred action'.⁵³ Thus, a reading of radically symbolic literatures – texts that practice the 'infinite deferment of the signified' and whose 'field is the that of the signifier'⁵⁴ – as belated, or as a medium of a delimited cultural memory, proves problematic. As Barthes suggests, radically symbolic literatures, or texts, which defer meaning and which are 'structured but off centred, without closure', have long resisted explication by historicist keys and thus pose problems to reading strategies which make literature 'actualize elements which previously were not – or could not be – perceived, articulated, and remembered in the social sphere'.⁵⁵ One need only briefly recollect the indeterminate texts produced by Yeats (*The Tower*), Joyce (*Ulysses* and *Finnegans Wake*), Beckett (*The Unnamable*) and Bowen (*The Last September*, which slides between moderate and radical symbolism) to consider how Irish modernism is a canon replete with 'texts' and corresponds to the category of a radically symbolic literature. As mentioned at the outset, these texts, as they present oblique modes of representation which defer Ireland's historical contours, are perverse in relation to nationalist projects and projections. Their radical symbolism plays with the possibilities of discontinuity beyond the imagined centre of national allegory and myth, and thus Irish history remains unassembled by their narratives (this designation, as well as the distinction and overlap between radical symbolism and moderate symbolism, will be demonstrated throughout the chapters of this book). Thus, if Irish modernist fictions are made to represent Irish history in an active and positive grammatical sense, then the relatively new concept of Irish modernism becomes explicable largely with recourse to the development of the nation state. In turn, the radical aesthetics of literary modernism, which raise questions about how narrative is produced and which distance and estrange any easy association with monumental history, become muted and absorbed by various forms of methodological nationalism or internationalism.

This conundrum has been signalled by Colin Graham when he writes, in *Deconstructing Ireland*, that Ireland 'is always implied and implicated in criticism's voice rather than being given substance by any transparent relationship which criticism claims to have with its object'.[56] Ireland, as Graham suggests, is constituted through critical language as a 'transcendental signified'. Concerning the relationship between Irish modernist literature and Irish history, both the decolonized Ireland of nationalist historiography and the critically posited, transcendent Ireland (which exists beyond material history) are difficult to detect, when one considers *Finnegans Wake* or *The Unnamable*, for example, in coherent referential terms. Or, as Ania Loomba suggests, such definitions are often rehearsed but problematic within postcolonial theory, which 'has been accused of being unable to maintain any distinction between questions of representation, language and culture on the one hand, and material and economic realities on the other'.[57] And if, as Rabaté describes, 'Irish modernism has always been a matter of hearing language with new inflections or seeing reality differently as much as refashioning history',[58] the link between Irish modernist literature and modernity is perhaps not as clear as a parallelism; Irish modernism carries, and is constituted by, different and diverging concerns, the plurality of which proliferates any definite origin. Indeed, Rabaté's account is not isolated within the field. Walker has suggested, concerning Irish modernism, that 'artistic change might be driven by aesthetic ideology and conditions as well as by more overtly social or political ideology and conditions; perceived aesthetic ends might drive seemingly more social-political ends, as well as vice-versa'.[59] Moreover, David Lloyd, in a different register, has influentially combined literature and theory, particularly in *Anomalous States*, to recast the relationship between fiction and the postcolonial moment by tracing 'an alternative cultural politics in the resources of recalcitrance'.[60]

Weak Irish modernism

At stake in this critical bind, then, is the proximity of Irish modernism to Irish history and postcoloniality. Or put differently, the issue of whether Ireland's dominant historiographical narrative can be qualified, or is left unqualified, by the aesthetic strategies of modernist fictions hangs in the balance. If it is left unqualified, definitions of Irish modernism which infer that Ireland is a stable force which can be used to explain literary production – where Irish history, methodologically, is ever present to itself – require reconsideration and revision. In this sense, Irish modernism plays out the scenario of a 'weak theory' as described by Paul Saint-Amour in *Tense Future*. Works of literary criticism engaged with modernist literature more often than not undertake the task of defining what modernism means, and do so in a positivist manner. Saint-Amour writes, 'When the word "modernism" appears in the subtitle of a literary studies book, it can trigger two reasonable expectations: that all the primary texts discussed within will be understood as modernist, and that the book will offer a definitional model of modernism to which its central works positively belong.'[61] As pointed to above, contesting accounts of modernism are operative in the field – both on the side of and against a direct relationship between modernism and its contexts – and so the flexibility of modernism as a category of investigation allows for a variety of definitional endeavours. Saint-Amour finds in this 'a general weakening of the theory of modernism that structures the field of its study.'[62] Thus, its 'immanent theory of modernism has become less axiomatic, more conjectural, more conjunctural.'[63] Indeed, the weakening of definitions of modernism has been tacit in the emergence of narratives of Irish modernism. Striking against the formalist approaches of New Criticism, critics have located the Irish Revival as 'far from the opposite of modernism' and one of its 'incubatory moments',[64] thus inverting the models of Irish modernism proposed by Richard Ellmann and Hugh Kenner. The nationalist, premodern and rural leanings of the Revival have thus become amenable to the narrative of Irish modernism; moreover, the Revival has become one of its foundational and phenomenal moments, often anchoring its 'origins' and fortifying its narrative structure along statist lines. Narrating Irish modernism in terms of the Revival has also had the welcome effect of broadening its canon and scope, thus multiplying the artists and artworks that are malleable to discussion under its umbrella.

Simultaneously, because of the weakness of the field, as is evident by the installation of the Revival as one of Irish modernism's central moments by critics in the twenty-first century, (Irish) modernism remains open to a variety of narrative possibilities. The recent designation of the Revival as principle to Irish modernism remains built on literary-historical methodological strategies which appeal to the Revival's possibility as an originary, or incubatory, event. The origin, like Ellmann's and Kenner's respective cosmopolitan formalism, occurs as a critical installation after the fact and then gives structure to the field. The productive weakness of Irish modernism, which has facilitated the induction of the Revival as one of its originary moments, also renders possible its narration along other lines. Given that Irish modernism might not correspond directly to Irish political history, the weakness of the term legitimates its inability to act axiomatically and its openness to rearrangement. Indeed, feminist interventions in Irish modernist discourse – particularly the work of Anne Fogarty, Gerardine Meaney, Tina O'Toole and Paige Reynolds – have long traced different narrative lines for the term. Moreover, the new modernist studies, with its double turn beyond methodological nationalism to structures of affect and the worldly, provides impetus in this respect. Contrasting critical approaches allow for different emphases within the same field, and, in the case of Irish modernism, facilitates the vantage point through which an inherent divergence between *Irish* modernism and Irish *modernism* may be realized. In this sense, this book builds critically on Saint-Amour's sense of modernism as a weak theory. Charting a new mode of narration for Irish modernism, it focuses on the formal invigorations of the Irish modernist novel.

Yeats and Joyce, in their different ways, move further and further into oblique modes of representation after Ireland's moment of decolonization. Indeed, distant geographical allusions and historical traces in Joyce's omnicompetent *Ulysses* and *Finnegans Wake* continue to be discovered in contemporary scholarship. This resistance to imitatively representing Ireland's historical contours in this period is continued, respectively, in novelistic form by Beckett, Flann O'Brien and, as I later argue, Bowen. This book focuses on the latter writers, including Kate O'Brien and John McGahern, to continue the expansion of discourse on Irish modernism beyond Yeats and Joyce, the two writers upon whom the field has remained largely focused since its institutionalization. In saying as much, Yeats and Joyce are never far away from consideration and debate. As Beckett's fiction after his *annus mirabilis* is perhaps the most oblique of all corpuses in the Irish modernist canon when considered in relation to Ireland's monumental history, this book begins its reconsideration of the relationship between Irish literary modernism and Ireland's modernity with his novels. It then follows with analysis of Flann O'Brien's, Bowen's, Kate O'Brien's and McGahern's respective experiments with the novel in this historical period (I return to the particular structure and sequencing of this book in the final section of the introduction).

As a dynamically tested form throughout modernity in Ireland and beyond, and as a medium within which our current theoretical predicaments are often played out, the novel has its own history in the period of Irish modernism and provokes different and new possibilities for conceptualizing and narrating the term. Narrative, emerging through memory studies as a particularly mnemonic form, has led to the theorization of literature as a form of cultural memory, which in turn offers a window on extratextual realities. The most sophisticated theorization of literature as memory to date is Astrid Erll's reworking of Paul Ricoeur's tripartite model of mimesis, which rests on literature both mediating, and operating referentially in terms of, the extratextual world. Building on Ricoeur, as well as Wolfgang Iser, Erll theorizes how literature is premediated by memory cultures *and* refigures reality, and thus produces new memory narratives as a result.[65] The (Irish) modernist novel is a unique case in point in terms of such conceptualizations of literature as memory as it raises concerns with the referential capacities of literature through its aesthetic percepts (aggressive defensiveness, alienation, extreme self-consciousness, ironic detachment, the *désoeuvrement* of the literary work, the mobilization of epistemological doubt) which complicate how we locate literary production in terms of extratextual events, as well as the material and social conditions of production.[66]

Deployed, then, as a lens for rereading the literature which corresponds to the term, Rabaté's conceptualization of Irish modernism, positively weak in itself, offers potential for probing the presence of its apparent 'colonial origins' as well as tackling the issue which Loomba recognizes within postcolonial theory and how it relates to Irish modernism. For if, as Rabaté suggests, Irish modernism is as much a matter of indulging the inflections of language and engaging reality as a hermeneutic enigma, as well as refashioning history, its concerns and scope take it beyond the remit of an experimental representation of an extratextual historical process with which it can be read as a parallel project. As such, the various theoretical vicinities of literary modernism provide the stage for the organizing principles of Irish modernism to be probed. That is, the conundrum of the relation of the modernist text to the actually lived and historically represented world – which inscribes both the proximity and the distance of Irish literary modernism to Irish history – allows for Irish modernism to be narrated differently. Intervening in the context versus formalism debate which remains a feature of modernist studies, the term 'Irish modernism' is engaged here as a canon of singular and aesthetically concerned literary texts as much as a historical phenomenon to prompt a weakening of the term's current definitions and the possibility of its conceptualization and narration anew.

Modernism, distance and meso-analysis

Our cue might be taken then from Rabaté's philosopheme or, expanding on it, from recent discussion of the phenomenon of Irish modernism. Influential in this latter sense is the transnational and spatial turn in literary criticism, which also provides the opportunity to commence consideration of this book's titular term: 'distance'. Discussing the phenomenon, rather than the texts, of Irish modernism from a geopolitical, spatial and transnational perspective, critics have incited its international and unresolved dimensions. Arrington has written, 'Irish modernism is not simply *inter*national. Rather, it transcends the boundaries of the "nation," which were literally unfixed during its development';[67] Cleary similarly suggests that it is 'a decidedly transnational phenomenon' and as having 'developed in several different sites, many of them beyond Ireland'.[68] Moreover, Jameson's highly influential 'Modernism and Imperialism' has chartered a course for showing how modernist style is directly bound up with the history of imperialism. As is the case in such accounts, the historical cultures and environments in which literature 'happens' form the focus of discussion, and so Irish modernism is rendered as an international phenomenon based on imperial and transnational histories of interrelation and movement. As such, these propositions concerning the phenomenon of Irish modernism open the scope of its proximity and distance to Irish history, and thus suggest that the relationship between Irish modernist literature and the nation state is perhaps not as clear as equivalence. Irish modernism, then, belongs as much to an international as it does to a national history. In such terms – imperial, spatial, transnational – the articulation of Irish modernism's international features are based on material histories of international movement, and modernist literature can be read as tangibly revealing international networks of association and influence.

While the transnational and spatial turn interrupts the relationship between Irish modernism and the national paradigm, it maintains a direct relationship of imitation and belatedness between text and the extratextual. Thus, the referent(s) of Irish modernism shifts, whilst the guarantee of its referential capacities remain intact. Jameson, for example, proposes imperialism as a historical phenomenon which determines modernist style: 'As artistic content, it will now always have something missing about it, but in the sense of a privation that can never simply be made whole by adding back in the missing component'.[69] While Jameson convincingly demonstrates this proposition with recourse to E. M. Forster and Joyce, it remains in the balance whether all modernist production, and moreover all of Joyce, responds favourably to such determinations. In this sense, we return to debates concerning the autonomy of modernist aesthetic practice from the system of global capital. Derrida, for example, proposes that writing, that dangerous supplement, is already concerned with the other and outside through which identity is formed; as the other has already deposited its trace inside us, writing is always bound up with the difference of identity with itself and is already concerned with an absence of presence at an origin. Or as in Jacques Lacan's mirror image, writing is already constituted by a breach at the very inception of the imaginary. Consider Beckett as an example: his modernism always has something missing about it but can never be made whole by adding back in the missing component; and importantly in the case of Beckett, it is difficult to specifically identify a history of colonialism and imperialism as the cause of this lack. Famously, Beckett's writing remains distant to historical referents and resists historicist determination, even as historicist models become ever more sophisticated as they grapple with his work.

Irish modernism, then, as both a historical phenomenon and an act of narration performed by critics in the twenty-first century, poses critical problems: namely, how do we easily scale down and up, and back and forth, from the macro phenomenon (Irish modernism as defined beyond its affiliated artworks) and its potentially different micro object (the literary text) to arrive at such suppositions concerning the relationship between the modernist text and historical realities? To engage this dialectic between linguistic and spatial distance, a focus on text thus becomes necessary to fully interrogate the scalar relationship between Irish literary modernism (as a linguistic art) and national and international history. With that, such a focus requires attention to what Saint-Amour has recently dubbed 'meso-analysis', which is established in contrast to unselfconsciously working 'at the scalar interface between abstract theorising and individual case studies'.[70] This practice, Saint-Amour suggests, 'would curb habits of casually extrapolating from the evidence in one or two works to claims about a whole genre, mode or period, as if one could assume a smooth scalability from micro thru meso thru macro'.[71] As Saint-Amour continues, 'we need a better understanding of the middle scale's capacity to interrupt or efface rather than hold open; to harbour discontinuity rather than to be the quintessence of continuity'. To this end, theories of world literature, and particularly the contemporary importance of translation therein, prove apposite to this discussion of the relationship between text, the nation and beyond.

World literature: Franco Moretti and Pascale Casanova

The reemergence of world literature as a mode of critical investigation in recent years has catered for, to greater and lesser degrees, the destabilization of traditional forms of methodological nationalism as a dominating force in literary criticism. Highly influential to this end has been Moretti's distant reading, which is worth deliberating on momentarily given the titular term – distance – of this book so as to lay the convergences and divergences between the approach to world literature promoted by Moretti and the approach to Irish modernism that will become manifest here. Combining digital humanities with world-systems theories and Darwinian models of evolution, Moretti's distant reading observes the planetary development of literary forms. Particularly important to this end is his 'trees and waves' model, where national literatures correspond to trees 'which need geographical *discontinuity*' and which 'nation states cling to.'[72] For Moretti, 'waves are what markets do', and so the modern novel is a 'wave that runs into the branches of local traditions, and is always significantly transformed by them'.[73] Moretti thus develops distant reading as the mode of enquiry proper to a fuller understanding, and definition, of world literature, so much so that 'literary history', he says, 'will become "second hand": a patchwork of other people's research, *without a single direct textual reading*'.[74] Undoubtedly, Moretti's model is useful for telling us how literary forms arrive, develop and survive in certain places and at certain times. Particularly, it helps analyse how literary form, style and content is already a conglomeration of various forces merging from various distances. Like Jameson's spatial modernism, it shows how literatures are never simply national in their origin. The novel in such terms becomes an expression of already existing forces which can be identified, economically measured and cited as underpinning the play of the text. However, while Moretti's model shows how literary forms occur, and determines the broader trends of literary history, it does not deal with the question of the instability of literary language and how the distribution of the signifier in literature perhaps occludes the significance of the said economic forces which supposedly underscore the text. The autonomy of literary language from market forces is not Moretti's concern. And so he leaves suspended the problematic that literary language is also that which gives rise to, and hosts, the conceptualization of any national paradigm or understanding of world literature. Finding shelter in literature is this secret, which prevents a totalizing cause-and-effect analysis.[75]

Critically building on Moretti's interventions, the turn to translation studies in contemporary theories of world literature provides an alternative to such determined analysis. Rebecca Walkowitz's recent and successful *Born Translated*,[76] for example, shows how the role of translation in contemporary literary practice problematizes the location of literature and the relationship between literary language and the national paradigm, and provides the impetus for a wider consideration of the dilemma of translation in extant theories of world literature. Relevant here, then, is a (radical) reading of Casanova's conceptualization of world literary space in *The World Republic of Letters*, and particularly the function of translation therein. In that study, Casanova writes that 'the very long process, through which autonomy is achieved and literary capital hoarded, tends to obscure the political origins of literature; and, by causing the link between literature and nation to be forgotten, encourages a belief in the existence of a literature that is completely pure, beyond the reach of time and history'.[77] Critiquing this sense of an autotelic literature, and outlining a link between literary representation and the national paradigm, Casanova suggests that 'literary space translates political and national issues into its own terms – aesthetic, formal, narrative, poetic – and at once affirms and denies them'.[78] Thus, for Casanova, 'literature has its own ways and means of asserting a measure of independence; of constituting itself as a distinct world in opposition to the nation and nationalism, a world in which external concerns appear only in refracted form, transformed and reinterpreted in literary terms with literary instruments'.[79] For Casanova, then, the institution of European and world literature, arising as it has from economically and politically autonomous countries, 'cannot be reduced to political interests or used to suit national purposes. In these countries, the extraordinary and improbable construction of what may properly be referred to as the autonomous international space of literature is carried out'.[80] Important then, as per Casanova's account, is the means by which translation and aesthetic, formal, narrative and poetic concerns negotiate the relationship between the literary, literary space and its supposedly national origins. Through such instruments, for Casanova, literature asserts its independence, constitutes itself as distinct in relation to the nation and nationalism, and refracts and reinterprets political concerns. In this sense, Casanova outlines a model through which the relationship between literature and a national origin is structurally built on fiction's procurement of the absent presence of the extratextual historical world; and this occurs through the instruments of representation that literature has at its disposal, which, for Casanova, is namely 'translation'.

Crucial here, then, is the question of *translation* and what it signifies beyond its ordinary usage (the rendering of a text from one language to another). Literariness, as it is historically defined and located by Casanova, exceeds the politics of the nation and nationalism in the sense that it is *translated* from national conflicts, issues and politics. Thus, translation – and the proximity and distance it implies – manifests literature as a site of linguistic alterity in terms of both the place and places from which it emerges and to which it might relate. Through translation and literary technique, world literature, or world literary space, unlike its conceptualization in Moretti's model, manifests a distancing effect which disallows its assignation to strict identitarian categories or absolute points of origin. Indeed, the trace of its forgetting of its political origins, which constitutes it as distinct from national identities, suggests a supplementary character to literature in the sense that it is neither the same nor an other, echoing Derrida's important account of writing, that dangerous supplement, in *Of Grammatology*. As Derrida suggests, the dangerous supplement (or the literary translation, as we might consider here) 'is maddening because it is neither presence nor absence';[81] presence is both promised and refused by the supplement. That is to say, representation, which has the power of procuring an absent presence through its image and the proxy of the sign, is an illusion which sidetracks us and always bypasses, displaces, defers and, ultimately, supplements the presence of an origin.[82] In asserting that external concerns are transformed in literary terms with literary instruments, Casanova's translation, like Derrida's supplement, establishes the immediacy of the symbolic – with its affirmation and denial of the extratextual, and thus its absenting and deferral of an anterior presence – in determining and gauging the relationship between world literature and the national paradigm. A significant effect of which is that the structural absent presence – an important term which will feature throughout this book and which should be understood according to the logic of the supplement as outlined here – of an origin prior to writing is beyond accumulation to, or explication in terms of, a material or political context. Thus, far from severing the relevance of the national paradigm, world literary paradigms can, as Barry Sheils says, 'return us to the old questions of the nation and nationalism from a new angle; it asks us, in particular, to consider the sovereign paradox between national exceptionalism and global exemplarity',[83] and particularly the role of language therein. One way this paradox can be interrogated is through the question of translation, particularly as it is elsewhere theorized, and is a site

Translation and untranslatability

In a certain sense, the phenomenon of translation caters for the possibility of a world literary paradigm and the comparability of the world's languages. The early premonitions on the subject – coming from Johann Wolfgang von Goethe, as well as Karl Marx and Friedrich Engels – entailed a sense of translation as built in to world literature's success. In the terms outlined by Casanova above, though perhaps unconscious in her argument, translation operates in a different sense; it operates in terms of what can be rendered visible through language, thus translatability, and what cannot be translated, thus untranslatability. On the later, Barbara Cassin suggests that the translation of a concept 'creates a problem, to the extent of sometimes generating a neologism or imposing a new meaning on an old word'.[84] Thus, 'the untranslatable is rather what one keeps on (not) translating';[85] it is continuously translated and never absolutely translated.[86] In this sense, untranslatability expresses an interminable hermeneutic enigma, one which entails both the affirmation and denial of that which precedes and proceeds that which is to be translated. Martin Heidegger locates this problem in relation to national paradigms of thought in *Hölderlin's Hymn 'The Ister'*. Underlining the necessary role that translation plays for a people in relation to its 'own' literature, Heidegger writes,

> To the extent that we have the need to interpret works of poetry and of thought in our own language, it is clear that each historical language is in and of itself in need of translation, and not merely in relation to foreign languages. This indicates in turn that a historical people is not of its own accord, that is, not without its own intervention, at home in its own language.[87]

Thus for Heidegger, like Cassin, 'every translation is interpretation. And all interpreting is translating.'[88]

The critic Emily Apter, who worked on the translation of Barbara Cassin's *Vocabulaire européen des philosophies*, has deployed another and related understanding of untranslatability. For Apter, 'incommensurability and what has been called the Untranslatable are insufficiently built into the literary heuristic', and thus she invokes 'untranslatability as a deflationary gesture toward the expansionism and gargantuan scale of world-literary endeavours'.[89]

As Apter suggests, then, there is an 'x-factor of untranslatability that renders every translation an impossible world or faux regime of semantic and phonic equivalence'.[90] The untranslatable, following this logic, is an indomitable site of linguistic opacity and resists being made equivalent to something with which it might elsewhere correspond. In this sense, untranslatable texts are incomparable and irreducible, resisting the possibility of translation and the possibility of being made equivalent to, or interpreted through, the guise of something else. It is not difficult to conceive how the work of literary modernism belongs to both of these categories, where the text in question will never successfully be translated and where it will always require translation, in the hermeneutic sense, in order to be understood.

Recalling Casanova's terms, then – 'Literary space *translates* political and national issues into its own terms' (emphasis added) – the question of untranslatability is tacitly detectable and operative. In turn, it adds a further obscurity to the relation between 'world literary space' and the national tradition. Considered in terms of both definitions of the untranslatable – in Apter's sense, the literary work is untranslatable because it resists being translated, and in Cassin's sense, its continuous potentiality as a site for translation makes its destinations multiple and infinite – Casanova's 'translation', and the 'forgetting' it entails, suggests an incommensurability between literary text and national origin. As such, Casanova's world literary space, as much as it translates political and national issues into its own terms (aesthetic, formal, narrative, poetic), and at once affirms and denies them, also inscribes a relationship which is built on a near total untranslatability.

This question concerning the relationship of language to an identitarian origin is pushed further by Derrida in *Monolingualism of the Other; or, The Prosthesis of Origin*, where he suggests, concerning the monolingual speaker, that 'he is thrown into absolute translation, a translation without a pole of reference, without an originary language, and without a source language. For him, there are only target languages.'[91] Derrida's never inhabitable, natural or proper monolingualism, and its sense of translation-without-origin as the predicament and motivation of writing, thus indicates a further complexity to both Casanova's 'translation', Apter's and Cassin's respective definitions of untranslatability, and Heidegger's insistence on translation as a necessary intervention concerning being-at-home in one's own language. Joyce is famously read as giving this scenario a postcolonial dimension in Stephen Dedalus's encounter with the Dean of Studies in *A Portrait of the Artist as a Young Man*: 'His language, so familiar and so foreign, will always be for me an acquired speech.'[92]

Yet this speech is no less acquired by the Dean, as his intrigue concerning the word 'tundish' demonstrates.[93] His language, too, will always be an acquired speech. As Derrida inscribes, while cognizant of the postcolonial and ethical predicaments of this issue, the condition of total translation without origin suggests that the (untranslatable) text that translates and forgets its national origin is always-already without that origin, thus demonstrating an irreducible distance between a literature categorized in national terms and its relation to that nation's social and political history. This book is mainly directed to this sense of the term 'distance'.

The distance of Irish modernism

The questions of translatability and untranslatability as outlined here, and as they become inscribed in theories of world literature, serve to launch analysis and discussion of the critical paradigms through which Irish modernism can be considered and narrated. That is, these questions enable an articulation of the linguistic distance of Irish modernism, thus enabling another critical sense to 'distance' in modernist studies. The study of global modernism in its present mode, broadly new-Marxist or Wallersteinian in impetus, has been formed on a postulated spatial distance between centre and periphery, which is then negotiated by examination of the structures of artistic and literary institutions. Similarly in modernist studies, the relation between the local and global has been analysed in terms of the spatial criteria of the nation-state network and the capitalist world market. Irish modernism has variously benefitted from being situated in such theoretical paradigms, through which its geographical distance has been mapped. Elsewhere, Rabaté's *The Pathos of Distance* outlines another and different sense of the term 'distance' in modernist studies.[94] Prompted by modernist writers' uncomfortable awareness of a contradiction between egalitarianism and elitism, Rabaté gauges the affective distance of the moderns to modernity. And, more generally, as has been variously made evident through genetic criticism and the extensive use of the archive in modernist studies today, the Irish modernist text can be rendered evermore intimate with the actually lived world and its historical and political structures. This book thinks against the grain of the dominant trends in the field to repose the question of the instability and untranslatability of literary language alongside the critical means through which literary texts can be situated in terms of various details and events of the historical past. *The Distance of Irish Modernism* engages problems of representation and narrative in radically and moderately symbolic texts to rethink how fictions which correspond to the canon of Irish modernism can be read as similar and different to the cultural memories they supposedly transmit. It thus charts the ethical conundrum concerning the proximity and distance of literary language to the realities and historical phenomena to which it relates. Rather than displacing the importance of historicist models of criticism for literary analysis, this book engages literary language in its historical context to establish an ethics of reading concerning the ability of modernist literature, after the neutralization of modernism (now a temporal rather than an aesthetic descriptor) inspired by the new modernist studies, to act as a tranquil locus upon which to pose questions of memory and build historical and political genealogies. As the analysis here focuses on how literature functions as a form of cultural memory, problematics of aesthetics form, genre, language and structure are central to this critique.

This book builds on recent debates and scholarship on close reading and formalist analysis in and beyond modernist studies. The dominance of historicist modes of inquiry in literary criticism has prompted some critics to consider the fate of, and revivify, these seeming ghosts of modernist studies past. Particularly, recent reconsiderations of the practice and value of close reading and the rise of the new formalist studies have explored the ethical and political currency of the analysis of aesthetics and form, and how form relates to historical and political cultures. On the fate and place of close reading in modernist studies today – which at first blush seems to have declined given the wide-angled view of the new modernist studies – David James suggests that the unhelpful association of modes of close reading of aesthetics, form, genre and structure with the perceived bourgeois deviationist tendencies of New Criticism remains a straw man argument in the field, one which, as Douglas Mao has noted, helped 'perpetuate the myths of New Critical ontological naïveté and of a direct connection between the hypostatization of the text and antihistoricism'.[95] As James suggests, close reading has never left modernist studies. Rather, the new modernist studies defined itself in opposition to the close reading practices particular to New Criticism, while forms of close reading remained pertinent in the field to show the relation between aesthetic behaviour and how texts operate critically in history. As James contends, forms of close reading remain useful rather than inimical to the analysis of the relationship between experimental modes of representation and their historical contexts.[96] Similarly, critics working under the banner of the new formalist studies have rebuked the idea that formalist analysis is incompatible with, or antagonistic to, historicist analysis and have set out to highlight its constructive import in literary criticism. As Susan J. Wolfson suggests, 'the reductive critique of formalism, in publication and pedagogy, has had unfortunate results, not the least a dulling of critical instruments and a loss of sensitivity to the complexity of literary form: its various and surprising work, its complex relation to traditions, and its interaction with extra-literary culture'.[97] Building on such sentiments, the V21 Collective have stridently promoted a turn to formalism and theoretical reflection in Victorian studies to recentre 'formal analysis as the province of literary critical knowing', an undertaking pursued in riposte to a perceived default historicism operative in that field.[98] Particularly concerning modernist studies, Cara L. Lewis, echoing these propositions, suggests that a 'conflation between bad formalism and modernism … has kept the new modernist studies mostly at arm's length from the new formalist studies'.[99] In her excellent *Dynamic Form*, Lewis brings the insights of the new formalist studies to bear on the new modernist studies and in the process demonstrates, and insists on, the ethical and political import of formal analysis for modernist studies and, like James, its relevance to the analysis of the relationship between literature and history. As these accounts thus suggest, an approach to literature which is based on close readings, or which is formalist or theoretical in inspiration, is not necessarily antithetical to the contextualization and historicization of literary production. Neither is it the sequestration of the literary work away from the world, or a question of controverting history. Quite the opposite: it allows for new understandings and questionings of the methods through which we analyse and locate literature in history. Similarly, it caters for interrogating and revising suppositions which pit historicist analysis as antithetical to, or incompatible with, theoretical research.

Elaborating on the insights and sentiments of such scholarship, the methodology developed herein – a blend of close reading, formalist and narratological analysis, the application of philosophical theories of writing and literature (particularly Barthes and Derrida), and attention to historical context – responds to sedimented formal and stylistic problematics within the works of the authors under scrutiny which have prompted wide-ranging responses from different generations of critics. Beckett's style, Brian O'Nolan's pseudonyms and Flann O'Brien's metafictions, Bowen's vacillating narratives, Kate O'Brien's uncanny omniscient narratives, and McGahern's weaving of biography are examined in the subsequent chapters. This methodology establishes a flexible formalism – for form, as Lewis reminds us, is multifaceted and versatile[100] – suited to gauging the array of experiment in modernist fictions and, particularly, for showing how analysis of the aesthetic features of Irish modernist texts is crucial to a more nuanced understanding of the proximity and distance between Irish modernism and Irish history in modernity. Similarly, philosophical accounts and critical theories of writing lend to the elucidation and interrogation of the complex relationships between fictionality and referentiality and literature and history; indeed, such theories are long relevant to Irish modernist discourse given that a host of the most influential philosophers and critics of the past century who dealt with such questions borrowed their authority from the canonical Irish modernists: Adorno wrote on Beckett; Hélène Cixous, Derrida and Lacan were indebted to Joyce; and Paul de Man and Spivak worked on Yeats (not to mention the various philosophical works which inspired the respective Irish modernists). Moreover, the expansion of the (Irish) modernist canon to include a variety of different writers necessitates analysis and evaluation of modernism's forms to bridge so-called high and low modernist cultures. As such, this methodology also works towards an updated account of modernism's various formalisms and their import, rather than their elision in favour of an aesthetically neutral modernism.

Structure and chapter development

The following chapters focus on a single author and each chapter differs in terms of the range of works covered. The aesthetic problems posed to Irish modernist discourse by select writers and their corpuses sometimes play out across several texts (as is the case with the question of Beckett's style, Kate O'Brien's omniscient narratives, or McGahern's weaving of biography) and sometimes occur more particularly in one or two texts (Bowen's *The Last September*, for example, forms the cornerstone of accounts of her Irish modernism; *At Swim-Two-Birds* and *The Third Policeman* are exemplary of Flann O'Brien's modernism). The subsequent chapters respond to particular texts which are both indicative of an author's aesthetic mode or modes and which enable different understandings of the proximities and distances of their Irish modernism.

Chapters are sequenced to elucidate how each author's respective aesthetic strategies approximate and distance Irish history, and Ireland's place in modernity, as an informative presence. Building on the expanding and fluid contours of the canon of Irish modernism, and establishing different coordinates for the field, this book looks beyond Yeats and Joyce, whose respective works have served prominently in the definition of the field, to establish a new line of narration for Irish modernism. It interrogates writers who correspond to that canon, but whose position within it remains complex, contested and uneasy. Analysing a selection of Samuel Beckett, Flann O'Brien, Elizabeth Bowen, Kate O'Brien and John McGahern's novels in this order facilitates an analysis of high, radically symbolic modernisms (Beckett and Flann O'Brien), moderate modernisms (Bowen and Kate O'Brien) and the apparent turn to naturalism after modernism (McGahern). In this sense, *The Distance of Irish Modernism* borrows from Barthes's distinction between radically symbolic and moderately symbolic texts as an organizing principle. In a movement from high to low to late modernism and beyond – and the seeming approach towards an imitative representation of Ireland, and Irish history, that this movement entails – this structure facilitates a dual purpose. It foregrounds a different organization of Irish modernism, one structured on the question of language and representation, which is considered alongside context, to consider how and if Irish modernist fictions operate as a medium of cultural memory. Concurrently, in dismantling the metanarrative of Irish history, this structure works to critique the historicist conception of literature-as-memory made manifest via the meta-structure of the nation, as figured in Irish studies and literary studies more generally, where literary production maps on to the historical development of the nation state.

Chapter 1, 'Samuel Beckett and the Contexts of Modernism', re-examines the tensions of reading Beckett's continuous *désœuvrement* of the novel – particularly as it becomes manifest in *Molloy, Malone Dies* and *The Unnamable* – as representing cultural traumas in Ireland, Europe and elsewhere in the twentieth century. Interrogating the referentiality of Beckett's radically symbolic, or 'styleless', style, this chapter situates his writing in terms of prominent accounts of the development, ethics and politics of modern literature. It builds critically on the recent turn in Beckett studies to Theodor Adorno, who now figures prominently to articulate and conceptualize Beckett's relationship to historical events and traumas. Developing a contrast to such approaches, I deploy Jacques Rancière's schema for modern literature, wherein 'suspicion with respect to literature' was 'not born in the 1940s from historical trauma'.[101] Rancière's account provokes a consideration of *désœuvrement* in modern literature in aesthetic and historical terms, which opens Beckett's writing to other theoretical possibilities. Particularly, Barthes's conceptualization of writing degree zero, which offers an elucidation of the technical features of Beckett's style, indicates a writing wherein the word is always overabundant and pregnant with meaning and irreducible to a fixed signified, an account which contrasts with Adorno's conceptualization of Beckett's recoiling form as an adequate literary response to certain twentieth-century traumas. Situated in terms of these theories of writing, this chapter shows how Beckett's fictions maintain a proximity as well as an irreducible and untranslatable distance to the cultural memories to which they supposedly correspond.

Chapter 2, 'Brian, Flann, Myles and the Origins of Irish Modernism', interrogates the paradoxes inherent in reading the problem of the pseudonym in the Brian O'Nolan/Flann O'Brien/Myles na gCopaleen oeuvre, as well as Flann O'Brien's *At Swim-Two-Birds* and *The Third Policeman*, as determined by the historical condition of post-independence Ireland. This chapter situates the question of the multiple authorial names attached to this oeuvre in terms of various coordinates in modernist thought (Yeats, Friedrich Nietzsche, Walter Benjamin, Barthes) to think through, and expand beyond, postcolonial theories in the interrogation and explication of this phenomenon. Subsequently, through close readings of the respective metafictional narrative modes of the early novels, it argues that Ireland is an absent presence which lacks constitutive meaning in these texts and is thus supplemented by their fictional realities. These analyses show how the problematics posed by this corpus obscure any clear origin to O'Nolan/O'Brien/na gCopaleen's Irish modernism.

Chapter 3, 'Elizabeth Bowen's Modernist History', tackles conceptualizations of Irish modernism as centrally energized by Irish postcoloniality by demonstrating how *The Last September* – the novel often read as representing Ireland's transition through decolonization – structurally defers Irish independence. Through an analysis of its fractured narrative strategy, which slides between moderate and radical symbolisms, this chapter argues that colonial history is an absent presence which lacks constitutive meaning in Bowen's novel and thus suggests that Bowen's Irish modernism does not neatly reflect the story of Irish monumental history and remains untranslatable to determined forms of methodological nationalism wherein decolonization features as the equation of colonial emancipation with national liberation.

From Chapter 4, 'Kate O'Brien's 'Flawed' Modernism', the focus turns to moderately symbolic literatures which the new modernist canon encompasses. From this point in the book, the textual analysis undertaken becomes more formalist to examine the distinctions and overlap between modernist and realist modes. This chapter shows how a widely regarded 'flaw' in Kate O'Brien's romantic realisms and narratives of individual development productively leads to a different vantage point for understanding her modernism, which is often understood in political terms. Particularly, this chapter shows how O'Brien's omniscient narrative operations – as featured in *Mary Lavelle*, *Pray for the Wanderer* and *The Land of Spices* – perform a dislocation between form, content and setting, a circumstance which establishes an irreducible distance between the stories told and the characters and settings represented. This chapter thus develops terms for understanding O'Brien's modernism in formal as well as political terms to show how her novels manifest their literariness simultaneous to their recounting of stories of individual development and interventions in social and political issues.

Chapter 5, 'John McGahern and the Limits of Irish Modernism', considers where and when Irish modernism ends by interrogating binary oppositions which pit modernism as antithetical to realism and naturalism. This chapter shows how McGahern's representations of the past – particularly in *The Barracks*, *The Dark*, *Amongst Women* and *That They May Face the Rising Sun* – occur as a result of intricate narrative operations that obscure distinctions between autobiography, history and literature. It thus demonstrates how the structural artifices of McGahern's writing establish reality as a hermeneutic enigma, one which requires continuous interpretation and translation through a host of literary strategies, rather than a signified which can be captured in writing. As such, this chapter shows how McGahern's narrative modes establish a certain distance to the social realities from which they seemingly emerge.

Finally, the epilogue which completes this book engages an ethics of reading based on the analyses undertaken in the previous five chapters. This structure will ultimately prove itself to be a ruse, only a different means, another metanarrative and another ideology, for narrating Irish modernism. By the end, I show that such distinctions are useful for launching such studies but untenable when thought through the problematics and structures of untranslatability. At that point, the distance of Irish modernism will be no different if thought through Beckett, Bowen or McGahern.

1

Samuel Beckett and the contexts of modernism

Samuel Beckett's career is marked by a complex relation to Ireland. Whilst born in Foxrock in 1906 and educated in Portora Royal School, Enniskillen, Fermanagh, his lack of sympathy for Free State Ireland, and his long-regarded distaste for what he perceived as a disingenuous Irish cultural nationalism, finds its expression in the earliest of his published works. In 'Recent Irish Poetry' (1934), the 28-year-old Beckett castigates a perceived Irish poetic introspection and provincialism against a valorized modernist aestheticism; he attacks Austin Clarke, F. R. Higgins and James Stephens as antiquarian and second-hand Celtic Twilighters. In opposition, Beckett upholds the achievement of Brian Coffey, Denis Devlin and Thomas MacGreevy, modernist poets who demonstrate their indebtedness to the formal preoccupations of Arthur Rimbaud, T. S. Eliot, Ezra Pound and the surrealists. Elsewhere, Beckett encodes a distaste for faux cultural nationalism in his earliest fiction. In 'A Wet Night', the fourth story in *More Pricks Than Kicks* (1934), Beckett's protagonist, Belacqua, cowers at the introduction of Mr Larry O' Murcahaodha, whose singing is presented as having '[torn] a greater quantity than seemed fit of his native speech to flat tatters'; and Belacqua's response reinforces the distaste for O' Murcahaodha's song: '"I can't bear it ... Vinegar on nitre."'[1] Beckett's parodying of the signifiers of cultural nationalism is continued in *Murphy* (1938). Murphy hopes for his ashes to be flushed down the toilet in the bathroom of the Abbey Theatre; and while in the General Post Office in Dublin, Neary, 'contemplating from behind the statue of Cuchulain', and acting 'as though the holy ground meant something to him', 'seized the dying hero by the thighs and began to dash his head against his buttocks'.[2] Moreover, in a riposte to MacGreevy's acclamation of Jack B. Yeats as giving expression to the life of the people of Ireland in his painting, Beckett famously severs modernist achievement from the national context when he announces that 'the artist who stakes his being is from nowhere. And he has no brother. … Hence this unparalleled strangeness which renders irrelevant the usual tracing of a heritage, whether national or other.'[3] This latter statement provides the tone and impetus for a certain brand of Beckett criticism which reads Ireland as extraneous to the writer's achievements.

Notwithstanding his avowed distaste for Irish cultural nationalism and for delineations of an Irish art, Beckett remained demonstrably concerned with Irish phenomena throughout his life. His fiction and drama, particularly his earlier work, show preoccupations with Irish geographies and histories: Dublin's cityscape features heavily in *More Pricks Than Kicks* and *Murphy*; an allusion to Noel Lemass's memorial occurs in *Mercier et Camier* (written 1946/ published 1970); and in the third chapter of *Watt* (1953), Ernest Louit gives an account of a research trip in the West of Ireland to a committee at Trinity College Dublin. Moreover, in his letters to MacGreevy, after he had written 'Recent Irish Poetry', Beckett demonstrates an awe and fascination for Ireland's antiquities: in 1936, he describes Clonmacnoise as 'indescribably beautiful, as site & monument'.[4] Later that same year, again in correspondence with MacGreevy, he records his 'important' experience at Ardmore in Waterford.[5] And while wholesale references to Irish place names and political history diminish after his *annus mirabilis* when he decided to impoverish himself through French ('m'appauvrir d'avantage'),[6] Irish spectres continue to haunt *Molloy* (1951), *Malone Dies* (1951), *Waiting for Godot* (1952), *The Unnamable* (1953), *Texts for Nothing* (1959) and Beckett's later works. As such, it would be facile to sever the Irish context from a reading of Beckett's particular brand of modernism, despite his pronouncements against an Irish art.

Given this ambivalence and indeterminacy in relation to Ireland, then, Beckett's corpus poses methodological problems to how we read his work in relation to the history of his birthplace. Do the marginalia which appear in the texts point to a history which can be deployed to anchor and explain their play? Or are the references floating spectres, frail and lacking constitution, which dissipate beyond accumulation and equivalence to an anterior historical signified? Critics have long debated these issues in relation to Beckett's corpus. In recent years, his later prose and dramatic writings, those oblique texts which liquefy identifiable political or historical contours, have increasingly been read through ever renewed and sophisticated historicist paradigms. The results, however, remain inconclusive as Beckett's writings refuse to yield to determined modes of historicist criticism. As such, these problematics apply to the focus of this book, particularly as a reading of Beckett's oeuvre relative to Irish modernism caters for rethinking currently operative theorizations of that term: namely considerations of it as determined by and following the trajectory of the history of the nation state. If thought through Beckett's oeuvre, Irish modernism can be theorized at a proximity and a distance to its places and times, thus as both absenting and presenting an anterior signified which would constitute its referent. To demonstrate the stakes of this argument more fully, it is first necessary to take stock of recent debates in criticism concerning Beckett's relationship to Ireland, France and beyond.

Beckett and historicism

A persistent feature of scholarship on Beckett's oeuvre over the last decade has been the effort to outline its historical and political features and resonances, particularly in relation to Ireland and mid-century European traumas, namely the Second World War and the Holocaust. This critical trend occurs alongside the dominance of archival, historicist and materialist approaches in literary studies currently. And it in large part responds to what are often dubbed as existentialist, formalist, philosophical, postmodern or poststructuralist readings of Beckett's work, which, for many, in their different modes, have been perceived as denying Beckett's writing its veiled political engagements, its direct relation to Ireland, France and Europe, and even its historicity in some cases.[7] Séan Kennedy writes, 'In this dominant critical paradigm, issues of historical or political interest were often deemed irrelevant as critics grappled with Beckett's apparent desire to slough off the social and political.'[8] Or as Patrick Bixby suggests in a critique of overtly philosophical approaches of his corpus, the 'bourgeoisification of Beckett … short-circuits the political energies coursing through his writing and bypasses their connections to the equally charged environment of postcolonial Ireland'.[9] As per this historicist turn in Beckett studies, philosophically motivated approaches have occluded, as Bixby suggests, that 'Beckett's novels incorporate a great number of culturally specific elements', an effect of which is that such signifiers have been 'overlooked by an international readership unprepared to account for local details and … their satiric implications'.[10] Upset, in turn, is the early account of Beckett seen as having 'no time for the native nostalgia of the Celtic Twilight'[11] and as a 'consummate European … despite his Irish roots';[12] and similarly, as a formalist distant from distinct historical and political points of reference,[13] or a writer 'assimilated to a vague metaphysics, in a strange, solitary place, where suffering permits only a well-nigh inarticulate, shapeless language'.[14] And so new strands in Beckett criticism have emerged, some of which, as Andrew Gibson suggests, 'have taken it in a historicist and positivist direction'.[15]

James McNaughton, for example, has recently designated a 'need' for 'detailed materialist and historicist examination of Beckett's formal responses to, and engagement with … political context in his creative work'.[16] And positioned in terms of the historicist turn in modernist studies and literary studies more broadly, Beckett's writing now 'yields only grudgingly to such approaches'.[17] Deploying historicist, materialist and postcolonial frameworks, recent critics have undertaken the explication of Beckett's relationship to the political and cultural milieu through which he passed, with the explication of his relationship to Ireland and elsewhere being a pertinent feature of such criticism. Thus, the backlash against philosophical reading strategies, or modes of reading which seem to prevent a relationship between signifier and an extratextual signified, has resulted in a tide of historicist and materialist criticism which seeks, as Kennedy suggests, to 'interrogate the myriad ways in which Beckett's work speaks back to, or remembers Ireland' and beyond.[18] Methodologically speaking, a tacit principle of this critical turn has been the historicist trope of identifying the base of culture, thus, 'the specific political developments from which Beckett's writing emerges and to which it responds: the realization of Free-State Ireland, the rise of Nazi Germany, and the consequences of the war'.[19] Similarly, Theodor Adorno has emerged in recent accounts as a theoretical cornerstone for establishing Beckett's relationship to historical and political realities. For Adorno, 'the basic levels of experience that motivate art are related to those of the objective world from which they recoil. The unsolved antagonisms of reality return in artworks as immanent problems of form. This, not the insertion of objective elements, defines the relation of art to society'.[20] More particularly, Adorno's understanding that Beckett's work 'is ruled as much by an obsession with positive nothingness as by the obsession with a meaninglessness that has developed historically and is thus in a sense merited, though this meritedness in no way allows any positive meaning to be reclaimed',[21] indirectly paves the way for locating Beckett in terms of the politics of his places and times, while it also manifests the possibility for such political histories to speak through his texts.[22] As Kennedy writes in his introduction to *Beckett and Ireland*,

> a summary resistance to readings of Beckett's work as being intimately involved with Ireland – both before and after the *annus mirabilis* of 1946 – can no longer be justified: it [Ireland] is there in the earliest occasional pieces, as well as the last of the prose, and in many of the more well-known works that cemented Beckett's reputation along the way.[23]

And concerning the Second World War and the Shoah, McNaughton writes that *The Unnamable* is 'motivated by horror, an exterior that nevertheless reappears in the rhythms of an anxious heartbeat and an undeniable, extralinguistic compulsion to testify that reconstitutes certain aspects of social reality'.[24] In this critical language, then, Beckett's writing presents and reconstitutes the historical past. In turn, Beckett's corpus has been read against the backdrop of a broader 'crisis of identification among displaced Irish protestants'[25] and has been located 'within the political context of his native Ireland', through which it can be demonstrated, for example, as Bixby suggests, 'how his novels were affected by, or helped to articulate, a notion of postcolonial identity'.[26] His writing has also been read in terms of the wider context of mid-century European trauma, a circumstance which, from a historicist and materialist perspective, certainly expands the scope of what constitutes Irish modernism by making it relative to other, non-Irish, politics; and in this sense, the transnational referent outlines a mappable distance of Irish modernism.

Historicist problematics

Given his elusive prose, however, the effort to make Beckett speak of the historical and the political has not always proven an easy task. The turn to historicist and materialist paradigms in Beckett studies has produced contrasting and vexed results, particularly in terms of the theorization of the relationship between Beckett's texts and how they 'represent' Ireland and elsewhere. As Rónán McDonald suggests, 'passing comments about a supposedly Irish feature of a writer like Beckett can often seem suggestive, but they also run the risk of a very unnuanced taxonomy of national characteristics'.[27] As such, other critical efforts have been less positivist in the face of such a seductive yet untameable oeuvre. As David Lloyd writes, 'Beckett's relentless deconstruction of the very terms of representation thus presents an absolute difficulty for cultural studies of any kind. ... The very allusions and references that seem to suggest a possibility of stabilising reading ... play against one another and refuse to cohere.'[28] Steven Connor's Heidegger-inspired reading of *Molloy* suggests that 'the worlding of the world, the production of the world as such, finds a resistance and a complication in the work of Beckett', and so Connor decries 'efforts to distort Beckett back into ethnic intelligibility'.[29] As per such appraisals, the refusal of Beckett's writing to cohere around particular referents repeatedly defers the possibility of designating a context, or contexts, from which the writing emerges or to which it responds. In turn, completely different referents for the oeuvre can be designated: as Jean-Michel Rabaté suggests in *Think, Pig!*, 'in

Beckett's texts, Paris is everywhere and a nowhere, and accompanies plots as a shifting referential tissue.'[30] Emilie Morin, attuned to the multivalent referents of Beckett's work and the particular problem of Beckett's relation to Ireland, has explored his relationship to the Irish Literary Revival and how his writing can be read as both engaging and resisting Irish literary legacies. With a focus on critical theory, translation and the bilingualism of the Beckett corpus, Morin ultimately resists making deterministic equations between Beckett's work and his Irish heritage: 'The Irish trivia scattered throughout his texts are signifiers of this conundrum, their specificity proving insufficient to signify anything other than Beckett's simultaneous engagement with, and disengagement from, the historical and cultural contexts that fashioned his development as a writer.'[31] As Gibson writes, 'Ireland is intermittently a vestigial presence in Beckett's texts, but so is France, and elsewhere. ... The traces come and go, multiplying throughout the corpus.'[32] The weakness of these Irish trivia in relation to the other warring forces of signification in Beckett's texts thus allow for such different readings of the potential referents of his work. Still unsettled, then, despite the sophistication of recent historicist analyses of the corpus, and Morin's recent and influential account of Beckett's political engagements, is the relationship of Beckett's aesthetic practices to his birth country, the cultural milieu in which he lived, the politics of his times and the places through which he passed. Given this indeterminacy in the face of extratextual history, a mode of reading considerate of, and extending beyond, historicist and materialist modes seems necessary to articulate Beckett's relationship to Ireland and elsewhere.

Methodology thus becomes a crucial issue as one tackles Beckett's texts with the extratextual as a concern. A historicist or materialist reading strategy, it seems, must engage with theory so as not to reduce Beckett's 'stylelessness' to a symptom or set of symptoms. Or as Gibson suggests, 'there cannot but be a serious place for philosophy or theory in Beckett studies, because, in the long run, it is the works and not the archive that must chiefly concern us, and the works so largely subtract history and the archive from the foreground'.[33] In this sense, form and style re-emerge as primary and important sites of contention. Like any body of writing that will be read as a form of cultural memory, the texts themselves remain of primary importance. The archive, historical information and material artefacts will always be secondary to, and tools for approaching, the corpus as long as it is the text which remains synonymous with modernism and the literary. And so, as Gibson continues, 'the question for Beckett studies will eventually be when and how it can re-admit theory as the necessary complement to the materialisms, and exactly what form that theory should take when it returns'.[34] This chapter establishes a theoretical frame for situating these problematics. Building on Jacques Rancière's critique of modern literature as a sceptical art, one that turns its focus on its own condition and potentialities, it situates Beckett's writing in terms of the ethics and politics of Roland Barthes's writing degree zero, which Rabaté has recently renewed as an apposite explication of Beckett's famous styleless style. In turn, this chapter compares the stakes of Barthes's concept with Adorno's indirect and recoiling form to regauge the relationship between the formal and stylistic properties of Beckett's writing and its related historical and political realities. It commences analysis with *Mercier et Camier* and its English translation, *Mercier and Camier*, to track the aesthetic and technical particularities of Beckett's movement towards referential diminution with *Molloy*, *Malone Dies* and *The Unnamable*, texts that constitute fitting examples of Beckett's writing degree zero and which thus form the main focus of this chapter.

Stinking artifice

Mercier et Camier, written in 1946 and published in 1970, stands on the precipice of Beckett's transition to writing in French and thus serves as an exemplary case at the beginning of this investigation. While Beckett's decision to write in his adopted language is often understood as a move to write outside of the inherited styles of English, and to *écrire sans style* by impoverishing himself through French,[35] *Mercier et Camier* is rife with abstruse historical details which complicate understandings of Beckett's newly chosen literary language as a turn away from the historical and political anchors of Ireland and elsewhere. Military historical details, some long past and some more recent, identifiably pervade Beckett's text as it features allusions to wartime practices, and figures whose endeavours in war ultimately ended without success. Following his four novellas and corresponding with his work with the Red Cross in Saint-Lô in Normandy after the end of the Second World War, *Mercier et Camier* records traces of Irish and French histories of emigration, exile, foreign assistance and military involvement, as well as wartime cultures of surveillance, accounts which Elizabeth Barry and Morin have influentially and respectively elaborated.[36]

In the first chapter, for example, Mercier's and Camier's respective arrivals and departures are painstakingly recorded until they meet. And at the end of the same chapter, they relate the impression that they are being watched: 'I too have the feeling, said Mercier, we have not gone unobserved since morning. Are we by chance alone now? said Camier'[37] (*'En effet, dit Mercier, je crois que nous avons des témoins depuis ce matin. Serions-nous seuls, à présent? dit Camier*'[38]). (The French text is quoted alongside the English as I will later conduct comparative analysis.) The recording of their activities and their sense of being watched establishes a surveillance echo which resonates with aspects of Beckett's biography. It particularly connects to Beckett's wartime activity of classifying and translating particulars for the resistance cell Gloria SMH, an information network which was ultimately penetrated by the Gestapo, famed as an agency of security and surveillance in Germany and Germany-occupied Europe.[39] Similarly, it links to Beckett's early life in Dublin where the intelligence branch of the Dublin Metropolitan police collected information on Fenian activity and, after 1919, worked as an active intelligence agency against the IRA. The connection to this latter history is supported in the novel through an allusion to Lemass's memorial. Lemass, of the Dublin Brigade IRA, fought in the General Post Office in the Easter Rising in 1916 and joined the occupation of the Four Courts during Ireland's Civil War. After the end of the Civil War, Lemass was captured by Free State agents in Dublin in July 1923, and his body was subsequently found mutilated in October of the same year in the Dublin mountains. Indeterminate in *Mercier et Camier*, these details seem to point beyond the text to evoke affiliations with wartime activity both directly and indirectly related to the life and times of its author, and thus enable the relevance of biographical and historicist approaches to Beckett's corpus, as do the oblique and undetermined references to various historical figures in the text. Simultaneously, as we will see, such traces prove problematic, and beyond accumulation, to determined historicist explication because their meaning remains incomplete and undecidable in the novel.

Also in the first chapter, after Mercier and Camier take shelter from wet weather at a pagoda, the narrator describes a 'huge shining copper beech, planted several centuries earlier, rudely nailed to the bole, by a field Marshal of France peacefully named Saint-Ruth'[40] (*'Au centre, ou à peu près, s'élevait un hêtre pourpre immense et luisant, planté, à en croire l'enseigne grossièrement clouée au tronc, par un maréchal de France du nom paisible de Saint-Ruth, plusieurs siècles auparavant*'[41]). The tree and its plaque, as well as the subsequent account of Field Marshal Saint-Ruth, point to the history of St. Ruth's Bush beside Kilcommadan Hill in Galway which reputedly marks the location where Charles Chalmot de Saint-Ruhe, a French cavalry officer who served Louis XIV, died in the Battle of Aughrim while in command of James II's Jacobite army. Transplanted from rural Galway into the novel's unnamed cityscape, the tree serves the explication of Saint-Ruth's story and death in the text: 'he was struck dead by a cannon-ball, faithful to the last to the same hopeless cause, on a battlefield having little in common, from the point of view of landscape, with those on which he had won his spurs'[42] ('*qu'il fut tué – le maréchal – par un boulet de canon, toujours au service de la même cause désespérée, sur un champ de bataille n'ayant que très peu de rapport, au point de vue du paysage, avec ceux où il avait fait ses preuves*'[43]). This information, however, seems lost on Beckett's tramps as 'Mercier and Camier did not know the place'[44] ('*Mercier et Camier ne connaissaient pas cet endroit*'[45]) and seem unperturbed by the tree's meaning. While the tree opens onto a military history which historical analysis elucidates, then, its meaning remains vestigial to Beckett's tramps, as per this latter information, and thus features as an irresolute detail in their expedition.

As does another reference to this same period of history which occurs later in the first chapter as Mercier and Camier become aware of a ranger at the pagoda, an appearance which prompts the narrator's allusion to Patrick Sarsfield, a leading figure in the Jacobite army during the 1689–91 Williamite-Jacobite War in Ireland who died in the Battle of Landen in Belgium in 1693 after helping negotiate the Treaty of Limerick and entering exile in France during the Flight of the Wild Geese. In an account of the ranger, the narrator suggests he was 'inspired by the example of the great Sarsfield'[46] ('*Fort de l'exemple du grand Sarsfield*'[47]) and that 'he had risked his life without success in defence of a territory which must have left him cold and considered'[48] ('*il avait failli crever dans la défense d'un territoire qui en lui-même devait certainement le laisser indifférent*'[49]). The allusion to Sarsfield thus provides an oblique coordinate for elaborating the ranger's present state – 'Invalided out with a grudging pension'[50] ('*Invalide à quinze pour cent*'[51]) – after what appears to be his involvement in the First World War with the Irish factions of the British army. The narrator clarifies the ranger's Irishness with a link to nationalist politics at the time of the First World War by suggesting that he would 'have been wiser on his part, during the great upheaval, to devote his energies to the domestic skirmish, the Gaelic dialect, the fortification of his faith and the treasures of a folklore beyond compare'[52] ('*il lui semblait parfois qu'il aurait mieux fait, pendant la grande tourmente, de se consacrer aux escarmouches domestiques, à la langue gaélique, au raffermissement de sa foi et aux trésors d'un folklore unique au monde*'[53]). And though Mercier and Camier pay off the ranger in exchange for his disappearance, they later show awareness of his involvement in the war – 'he's a hero of the great war'[54] ('*c'est un héros de la grande guerre*'⁵⁵). Nevertheless, their understanding of the ranger's past life is cast in doubt when the narrator relates, 'Conclude nothing from those idle words, Mercier and Camier were old young'⁵⁶ (*'Ne déduisez rien de ces paroles en l'air, Mercier et Camier furent vieux jeunes*'⁵⁷). Like Saint-Ruth's tree, then, the meaning of the historical trace is negated soon after it is qualified in the text, thus rendering an instability to its overall meaning within the tramps' journey and the novel's narrative structure.

Similarly in doubt is Mercier's and Camier's knowledge of recent Irish nationalist affairs. In the seventh chapter, they encounter what appears to be Lemass's cross in the Featherbed mountains in Dublin. The narrator suggests that the cross which Mercier and Camier came upon 'was the grave of a nationalist, brought here in the night by the enemy and executed. ... His name was Masse, perhaps Massey'⁵⁸ (*'C'était la tombe d'un patriote, amené par l'ennemi à cet endroit, la nuit, et exécuté. ... Il s'appelait Masse*'⁵⁹). Though, as the narrator adds, on top of its own confusion as to the intended name for the memorial (which is expanded in the English text), 'All that, and no doubt much more, Mercier and perhaps Camier, had once known, and all forgotten'⁶⁰ (*'Tout cela, ils l'avaient su, Mercier et Camier, et sans doute bien d'autres choses encore, mais ils avaient tout oublié*'⁶¹). Again, then, the meaning and relevance of the historical trace is undermined as it is related in the text, thus making its significance irresolute to both the characters and the narrative operation, as well as a historicist critique that would mine such details in the explication of the text in terms of extratextual historical contexts.

In turn, such allusions and figures, of which Mercier and Camier do not provide a complete understanding, and which do not coalesce in the text, provide historical resonances and spectral coordinates for Beckett's involvement in the Second World War, disenfranchised military deaths for the French in Ireland, the Irish in France, Republican and Free State activity in the Irish Civil War, and the Irish in the First World War. The traces of surveillance activity in the first chapter establish links, perhaps unconscious, to the ghosts of Beckett's youth in Dublin or recent past in Paris; after Gloria SMH was compromised, Beckett's close friend Afred Péron was captured by the Gestapo in August 1942 and subsequently perished shortly after his release from the Mauthausen concentration camp in 1945. And the failed involvement of Irish and French peoples in military and nationalist causes – both recent and long past – provides complex and oblique historical traces through which Beckett might be read as interrogating his own predicament as an Irish aid to the Red Cross in Saint-Lô in the aftermath of the Second World War in 1946. As per such details, then, with *Mercier et Camier*, as with *More Pricks Than Kicks* and *Murphy*, Beckett, despite his turn to French, is ostensibly working in the shadow of political histories, as well as a Joycean encyclopaedism, as he does not manifest the same referential impoverishment in his adopted writerly language that he would later demonstrate in *Molloy, Malone Dies, Waiting for Godot, The Unnamable* and his later texts. Concurrently, the qualification and negation of such historical details in *Mercier et Camier* – which signals a development towards a technique of countering an utterance as it is asserted that would later become typical of Beckett's style – prevents these allusions from becoming definitive anchors which allow for a deterministic biographical or historicist reading of the text. Beckett's extratextual allusions in *Mercier et Camier*, then, are simultaneously approximated and distanced by the aesthetic strategy instituted in the novel, which straddles Joyce's omnicompetence and Beckett's later style, and which, more particularly, builds on the scepticism of Gustav Flaubert's *Bouvard et Pécuchet* (1881),[62] a narrative schema relevant to elucidating how these traces are structured in the text.

While establishing such biographical and historical resonances, the text calls attention to the stink of artifice – 'what stink of artifice'[63] (*'que cela pue l'artifice'*[64]) – through which it does so, in turn pointing its readers in the direction of, and demonstrating its indebtedness to, *Bouvard et Pécuchet*, the novel from which Beckett's text derives some of its central impetuses. Not only does *Mercier et Camier* rework Flaubert's eponymous couple, but it also demonstrates its affinities with, and expands, Flaubert's scepticism concerning the totalizing endeavours of realist narrative schemas. *Bouvard et Pécuchet*, like Beckett's novel, features a series of episodes in which the characters achieve very little, and so their psychological development, and narrative progress, remains deliberately unachieved in the text. In the episodes which comprise *Bouvard et Pécuchet*, Flaubert's pseudocouple attempt to master a new area of knowledge, yet the results are always far from positive as they misconstrue and misappropriate the knowledge they apprehend. Each episode ends in failure and each subsequent episode constitutes a new and dislocated beginning. Building on Flaubert, Beckett's tramps are even more aimless and feckless than the French writer's would-be academics. In search of the elusive thing they should be doing ('Did what they were looking for exist?', 'What were they looking for?', 'There was no hurry'[65]), Mercier and Camier leave the city, return to it and leave it again; they arrange meetings that fail to take place; and they contemplate, and engage in arguments about, leaving one another, yet fail to do so. Moreover, in *Mercier et Camier*, the chapter summaries which occur after every second episode serve as a further and obvious debunking of the artifice – namely narrative sequencing and plotting – through which a sense of development and progression is achieved in realist narrative. Even more explicit than Flaubert, Beckett's recapitulations of episodes in which very little happens and no major progress is achieved establishes a direct satire of conventional plot-driven narratives that evince a sense of progress through time. In this broader sense, *Mercier et Camier* is actively participating in a history of modern literature where, as Rancière (whom I return to in more detail below) suggests, literature, with Flaubert, Joyce and Proust, becomes an 'ambiguous stage on which two anti-genres, the novel and the essay, double, oppose or intertwine with one another'.[66] And in Beckett's case, this ambiguous stage serves to establish a particular response to literary history, as well as an ambivalent and complicated account of his relation to Ireland and France.[67] As a result of the episodic structure of the book, the historical and political references which feature in the text resist cohering around a narrative centre, and so their significance is curtailed as Beckett borrows from Flaubert's satiric schema. The various historical and political references, in such terms, are absorbed by Beckett's sceptical project which, as it builds on Flaubert, shrouds, if not sacrifices, the potency of these allusions and their direct relation to the life and times of the author, in the process establishing an irreducible distance between the textual operation and extratextual contexts which might be located as dictating its cause of play.

Mercier and Camier and Rancière's modern literature

In addition to what is already a sparse and oblique novel, the English translation, *Mercier and Camier* (1974), subjects the referential detail of the French text to a process of diminution (an aesthetic feature that would become increasingly apparent in Beckett's style throughout the 1950s and 1960s), a feat which poses further problems to biographical and historicist readings of the work. An example of this process which occurs with the translation of the French text into English is particularly evident at the beginning of the fourth chapter. The opening paragraph in both texts, which is reproduced line by line from the French to the English versions, is typical of Beckett's oblique landscape descriptions which remain irreducible to any particular geographical landscape: 'The field lay spread before them. In it nothing grew, that is nothing of use to man. Nor was it clear at first sight what interest it could have for animals. Birds may have found the odd worm there.'[68] Following this, in both the French and the English texts, Camier is presented as reading his notebook. In the French text, various details of what Camier has recorded therein are presented, such as

> *20.10. Joly, Lise, 14, quitte dom. 14 à 8 comme d'hab. pr. éc. Cartable, tête nue, jambes id., sandales, sans mant., robe bleue. Mince, blonde, jol., conf. Pas vue en classe. Phot. réc. Parents purée. 25. Att. hausse.*[69]

Curtailing such encyclopaedic traces in *Mercier and Camier*, Beckett cuts these notebook entries entirely from the English text. Subsequently in both texts, Camier tears the leaves that he has just read from his notebook. Thereafter, the beginning of a dialogue which appears in the French text, and which relates how Camier feels after tearing these leaves from his notebook, is diminished in the English text: '*Voilà, dit-il, je me sens plus léger. ... Je me sens plus léger, dit Camier. Les photos, je les garde pour l'instant. Il tâta sa poche.*'[70] The dialogue between the two in the English text includes just one mention of 'I feel lighter now' and the reference to keeping the photos is omitted. The effect of these omissions – the content of Camier's notebook, the repetition of how he feels and his keeping of the photos – results in a more impoverished and oblique presentation of Camier's personae and thus a broader stripping away of the various details which comprise the characters' psychologies.[71]

And such textual deduction also pertains to the historical and political echoes of *Mercier et Camier*. Though it maintains its references to Field Marshal Saint-Ruth and Patrick Sarsfield, specific historical resonances – such as a reference to the Old Military Road in the Dublin mountains (*C'est l'ancien chemin des Armées*, in the French text[72]), which provide a location for Lemass's memorial – are omitted in *Mercier and Camier*. On this specific detail, the French text reads: *Un chemin encore carrossable traverse la haute lande. C'est l'ancien chemin des armées. Il coupe à travers de vastes tourbières, à cinq cents mètres d'altitude, mille si vous aimez mieux.*[73] The English translation, however, omits the second sentence and thus the historical allusion: 'A road still carriageable climbs over the high moorland. It cuts across vast turfbogs, a thousand feet above sea-level, two thousand if you prefer.'[74] With the exclusion of this translation, then, Beckett resists including a place name that would convincingly locate his tramps in the Dublin mountains. Similarly, regarding Mercier and Camier's suspicion of being surveyed in the first chapter, the active '*je crois que nous avons des témoins, depuis ce matin*'[75] (which literally translates to 'I believe we have witnesses') is reduced to 'I too have the feeling ... that we have not gone unobserved since morning'.[76] The passive formulation in the English text renders a paranoia to Mercier's statement and diminishes the sense that they are actually under observation. In this instance, then, the French text is more direct while the English text is more opaque, the resulting effect being a diminution of the potency of the potential echo with surveillance cultures in Paris in the 1940s and Dublin in the 1920s. Moreover, in the seventh chapter, the incomplete rendition of Lemass's name in the French text is expanded in the English text to 'Masse, perhaps Massey', an inclusion which has the effect of obscuring the reference further as it establishes doubt in the accuracy of the narrator's recall, as well as the possibility that the name might be otherwise rendered.[77] Inversely, a reference to a 'slow and easy'[78] (a shorthand name for the Dublin and South Eastern Railway which operated between Dublin City Centre and Foxrock between 1846 and 1925) is incorporated to replace '*un omnibus*'.[79] However, the semantic opacity of 'slow and easy', which maintains Beckett's movement towards a zero degree of writing, in an unlocalizable geographical terrain defers Dublin as the novel's setting. Indeed, critics have long debated where *Mercier et Camier/Mercier and Camier* is set, but they have failed to conclude, despite the illusions to features of Ireland's landscape, whether France, Ireland or elsewhere constitutes its location.

Beckett's foray, then, into formal poverty and aesthetic dryness throughout the 1950s and 1960s prompts a further diminution and suppression of fixed referential detail in *Mercier and Camier*. Regarding this general turn to aesthetic scepticism in modern literature, Rancière suggests,

> Suspicion with respect to literature and the withdrawal before a more fundamental 'unworking' [*désœuvrement*] were not born in the 1940s from historical trauma or the political demystification of the function of discourse. They belong to the system of reasons that make 'literature', since the Romantic revolution, the name given to the productions of the art of writing.[80]

The implications of Rancière's argument concerning modern writing establish a problematic concerning the motives behind Beckett's, or any twentieth-century writer's, aesthetic scepticism and its growth or development across a corpus. Rancière offers an account of the writer torn between the history of their world and the history of writing: after Flaubert, 'neither its object or its intention have ever served as a guarantee'; and because literature has the 'misfortune of speaking only in words, it thus has to make the work both the realisation and the refutation of its intention'.[81] In a further remark which seems readily applicable to Beckett's writerly trajectory, Rancière suggests that 'the weakness of the means at its disposal ... is what taught literature to tame the myths and suspicions that separated it from itself to invent the fictions and metaphors of a sceptical art in the strict sense of the term'.[82] Indeed, '*désœuvrement*', a term developed by

Maurice Blanchot to suggest the undoing of the literary work, and which Beckett used as early as 1935 in correspondence with MacGreevy,[83] appositely describes the state of inertia to which Beckett would subject the novel and, particularly, its attendant logic of representation. From *Mercier et Camier* to *Mercier and Camier*, this realization and refutation of intention, while already evident in the 1946 French text, becomes more apparent with the English version of the novel (1974), a transition which, as we consider the overall trajectory of Beckett's career, becomes manifest through the problem and opportunity of style and translation and which extends beyond the twenty-eight-year period bookended by *Mercier et Camier* and *Mericer and Camier*. As such, this line of increased linguistic scepticism from Flaubert to Joyce and *Mercier et Camier* to *Mercier and Camier* elucidates a different motivation to Beckett's aesthetic development, one which complicates understandings of Beckett's style as a direct response to, arising from and maintaining the presence of the difficulties and traumas of his life and times. As the translation of *Mercier and Camier* demonstrates, Beckett's aesthetic of diminution is an ongoing process throughout his career, one which lends to considering Beckett, after Flaubert, within a lineage of literary history and aesthetic (under)development that is concerned with turning literature towards (telling the story of) the conditions of its own making; and crucially, the development of this history occurs at a distance from the political domain of the life and times of the author. In such terms, then, Beckett's stylistic development is already engaged in literary and representational terms, and it is not necessarily determined by, though it is responsive and incorporates allusions to, histories of European and postcolonial trauma.

Thus, as Pascale Casanova suggests, Beckett is usefully understood in relation to the various literary traditions in which he can be elucidated as participating.[84] The approach instituted in these pages, however, diverges from Casanova's on the issue of how literature 'translates' national and political affairs into aesthetic terms. Casanova reads Beckett's work as revealing its and his place in 'Irish literary space' and 'world literary space' more generally.[85] As the examples of *Mercier et Camier*/*Mercier and Camier* demonstrate, Beckett's historical and political resonances refrain from cohering around any fixed centre or origin. The method advanced here suggests that despite Beckett's obvious allusions to and engagements with the historical and literary world, his work develops an irreducible distance to, and thus an untranslatability in terms of, determined points of origin which might be located as anchoring and determining the play of the texts. And indeed, Beckett intensifies this aesthetic effect in his subsequent search for an absence of style.

Barthes's writing degree zero and Beckett's inert modernism

Beckett's 'styleless' aesthetic of referential diminution becomes fully apparent following *Mercier et Camier* and his *annus mirabilis* with *Molloy, Malone Dies, The Unnamable* and *Waiting for Godot*, texts in which he developed his famed subversion of the narrative and formal structures that had constituted and signalled the accomplishment of fictional and theatrical genres. On this aesthetic shift, Rabaté suggests that Barthes's writing degree zero 'offers the best gloss on Beckett's attempt to write without a style'.[86] Inspired by the neutral mode occasioned by the *Nouveau Roman* and its relationship to the history of French literature, Barthes's concept offers a model for accumulating the technical features and the ethics of Beckett's aesthetic scepticism within Rancière's schema of modern literature which makes 'the work both the realisation and the refutation of its intention'.[87] For Barthes, the word in writing degree zero 'is encyclopaedic, it contains simultaneously all acceptations from which a relational discourse might have required it to choose'.[88] 'It therefore achieves a state,' as Barthes continues, 'which is possible only in the dictionary or in poetry ... and is reduced to a sort of zero degree, pregnant with all past and future specifications.'[89] As such, 'each poetic word is thus an unexpected object, a Pandora's box from which fly out all the potentialities of language'.[90] Crucially then, 'this Hunger of the Word ... initiates a discourse full of gaps and lights, filled with absences and over-nourishing signs, without foresight or stability of intention, and thereby so opposed to the social function of language that merely to have recourse to a discontinuous speech is to open the door to all that stands above nature'.[91] It entails the search for a 'colourless writing, freed from all bondage to a pre-ordained state of writing'.[92] In the sense implied here, Barthes's writing degree zero involves producing a language which is, aporetically, preceded and proceeded by continuous translation. Beckett's styleless writing – achieved through epistemic qualification and negation, rhetorical paradoxes and the imbrication of problematics of translation into the form and content of the novel – contributes to this process by producing discourses of discontinuity and gaps without stability of intention.

A fitting example of this aesthetic endeavour occurs early in *Molloy*. Beckett's eponymous tramp suggests all at once to confound the location of character, plot and setting, and thus undoing the general tenets of the novel: 'I speak in the present tense, it is so easy to speak in the present tense, when speaking in the past ... I went on my way, that way of which I knew nothing.'[93] Added to this confusion of location and temporality, Beckett's concurrent unworking of subjectivity disrupts the possibility of a self-fulfilling protagonist as Molloy remains unidentifiable to himself: 'Yes, it sometimes happens and will sometimes happen again that I forget who I am and strut before my eyes, like a stranger.'[94] Pertinently, Beckett applies this same strategy to Molloy's geography. Consider the following passage where Molloy describes his region and its characteristic meteorological phenomena:

> Yes, the great cloud was ravelling, discovering here and there a pale and dying sky, and the sun, already down, was manifest in the livid tongues of fire darting towards the zenith, falling and darting again, ever more pale and languid, and doomed no sooner lit to be extinguished. This phenomenon, if I remember rightly, was characteristic of my region. Things are perhaps different today. Though I fail to see, never having left my region, what right I have to speak of its characteristics. No, I never escaped, and even the limits of my region were unknown to me. But I felt they were far away. But this feeling was based on nothing serious, it was a simple feeling. For if my region had ended no further than my feet could carry me, surely I would have felt it changing slowly. For regions do not suddenly end, as far as I know, but gradually merge into one another. And I never noticed anything of the kind, but however far I went, and in no matter what direction, it was always the same sky, always the same earth, precisely, day after day and night after night. On the other hand, if it is true that regions gradually merge into one another, and this remains to be proved, then I may well have left mine many times, thinking I was still within it. But I prefer to abide by my simple feeling and its voice that said, Molloy, your region is vast, you have never left it and you never shall. And wheresoever you wander, within its distant limits, things will always be the same, precisely.[95]

Exemplary of Beckett's referential diminution and writing degree zero, the account presents aporia after aporia, achieved through rhetorical strategies of assertion, alteration, irony, nullification and reinstatement, to create a discourse without stability of intention. The aphasic Molloy describes the meteorological characteristics of his region, though he suggests things might be different today. He effaces his right to speak of his region, though, paradoxically, he has never left it. He suggests he has not escaped his region, yet he does not know its limits; he feels they are far away. He is sceptical of the logic of borders as his perceptions always reveal the same meteorological conditions; notwithstanding, he does not disavow the logic of borders as he maintains the possibility that he might have left his region many times. He concludes, subsequent to these deliberations, that a change in region will not affect his fortune: 'Things will always be the same, precisely.'⁹⁶ The axiom of this 'precisely', however, is undermined by the qualifications and disqualifications of the previous sentences which interrupt precise designation concerning region and weather, thus rendering its usage at best ironic, as does the strange word order of the sentence in which it appears. And while Molloy's world in this instance seems atemporal and unreal – neither the geographical or meteorological conditions change – he simultaneously produces language in this supposed vacuum, which would also suggest that his world is not as unreal as he relates, and so Beckett's fictional world straddles a real/false dichotomy.

Pursuing the location of Molloy's region in a historical reality, Bixby reads this passage through a postcolonial perspective and finds that 'Molloy dismantles a series of important representational strategies implemented in the production of maps' which have analogous links to the ways in which colonial power asserts itself. Bixby suggests that 'on an island partitioned between north and south, United Kingdom and Irish Republic, his [Molloy's] inability to identify variations in local geography gives the lie to geographical distinctions and border demarcations that link regions with particular communities, social activities, and economic formations'.⁹⁷ Bixby thus deploys Irish postcolonial history as a lever to ground Beckett's prose to show 'how the legacies of colonialism and nationalism shape the landscapes of his mature fiction'.⁹⁸ Indeed, Molloy's region potentially bears a historical similarity to, and is thus associable with, a partitioned Irish landscape. Molloy's admission that 'da, in my part of the world, means father' would strengthen this link.⁹⁹ As would his suggestion which seems to imply the conservative sexual politics that became manifest in post-independence Ireland: 'It is true they were extraordinarily reserved, in my part of the world, about everything concerned with sexual matters.'¹⁰⁰ In making this delineation, however, Bixby's analysis risks deciding what remains undecidable in the text. In ascribing Molloy's confusion to external affairs dictated by national and imperial history, this critique insists on the novel as belated representation and overlooks Beckett's particular unravelling of the subject upon which the usual coherence of the novel is built. Indeed, a pertinent feature of Beckett's texts with and after *Molloy* is a plural first-person narrative voice containing multiple speakers whose accounts overlap and disperse beyond the possibility of centralized accumulation. In the case of *Molloy*, the self-estrangement particular to Beckett's character – Molloy's aimless search for his dead mother from whose room he reports; his dispossession in language; the multiple figures he encounters within himself; his doubling by Moran who similarly fails in his quest in the second half of the novel – already undermines the possibility of a simple designation of his cultural or national belonging. Thwarting affiliations, Beckett's text disbands with a coherent account of the subject's psychological state, discernible objects and a broader portrayal of an existing state of affairs – the main anchors which dictate the genre of the novel – in favour of a discontinuous, formless and fragmentary account which is replete with absence and lacunae, one which is predicated on not saying and not representing, and which interrupts any logic of subjective or external continuity or progress. While the account of Molloy's region invites a critical intervention to make it mean more than it relates, then, Beckett's ongoing *désœuvrement* of the novel makes the account recalcitrant, and overabundant, to explication in terms of any determinate referent, or in terms of the historicist and materialist analysis that has become so prominent in Joyce studies, and Irish and modernist studies more broadly. Rendered through a strategy of epistemic qualification and negation, a series of aporias and thus a writing degree zero, Molloy's region maintains an irreducible distance to any implied cultural predicament which it might be said to represent[101] and thus plays out the paradox outlined in the introduction to this book: namely, that Irish modernism can be read as both similar and irreducibly different to the cultural memories it supposedly transmits.

Continuing to defy the tenets of identity, totality and unity particular to the conventional novel, such aesthetic distancing through a procedure of qualification and negation is also evident in an often-quoted excerpt from *Malone Meurt/Malone Dies*, wherein Beckett's narrator seems to incite a slogan of Irish republican nationalism:

> *Oui, c'est ce que j'aime en moi, enfin une des choses que j'aime, le don de pouvoir dire* Up the Republic! *Par example, ou* Chérie! *Sans avoir à me demander si je n'aurais pas mieux fait de me taire ou de dire autre chose.*[102]

> Yes, that's what I like about me, at least one of the things, that I can say, Up the Republic!, for example, or, Sweetheart!, for example, without having to wonder if I should not rather have cut my tongue out, or said something else.[103]

Beckett's use of 'Up the Republic' in *Malone Meurt/Malone Dies* finds a precedent in Nancy Cunard's rallying of various modernist authors to contribute to the pamphlet *Authors Take Sides on the Spanish War*.[104] On Cunard's invitation to contribute to the pamphlet, Beckett provided a short response: ¡UPTHEREPUBLIC! By 1937, then, Beckett has already dislocated this stock phrase of Irish nationalism from the context of anti-imperialist sentiment and relocated it, following the rules of Spanish punctuation, to the context of Spain's Civil War. Beckett next locates it in the French text of *Malone Meurt*, where its relevance to Irish republicanism remains obscure. *Malone Dies* restores the slogan to an English language context, yet the morphology which the slogan has undergone throughout Beckett's career – from its usage relative to the Spanish Civil War to its occurrence in the French language text *Malone Meurt* – disrupts any easy equation of the term in the English text with Irish republicanism. Though the appearance of this nationalist slogan has enticed critics to read Beckett in a postcolonial or Irish context,[105] it seems overly positivist to suggest that it recalls Beckett's 'other republic'[106] or, because of its semantic opacity in the context of Beckett's novel, the trials of Irish history, particularly given Beckett's limp nationalism, long played out in his correspondence with MacGreevy. Moreover, Malone prefaces the usage of the term by signalling his total dislocation in language: 'But I tell myself so many things, what truth is there in all this babble? I don't know. I simply believe I can say nothing that is not true, I mean that has not happened, it's not the same thing but no matter.'[107] The slogan's appearance, then, already comes with the forewarning of its empty recitation. The safety of language as babble provides Malone the ability to say 'Up the Republic' or 'Sweetheart' in a joking manner, and so he can avoid any concern of committing treason or saying the wrong thing. In turn, Malone does not have to cut his tongue out because he does not have to abide by the located convictions of such terms. Having already lost his way in language, he can iterate slogans without the consequence of reproducing intentional meaning, and thus in a manner of discontinuity rather than a continuity of form and structure prevalent to the governing dynamics of the realist novel. In an embrace of formlessness and plurality, then, Malone's usage of 'Up the Republic' maintains an irreducible distance to an Irish nationalist history which might be implied as underpinning its signification. Though it maintains an affinity to, and remains legible in terms of, Irish history and the history of the Civil War in Spain, it refrains from disclosing such histories as anchors which support and confer meaning on the usage of the term.[108] In Barthes's terms, then, the 'absences and over-nourishing signs'[109] of writing degree zero prevent any deterministic reading of Malone's 'Up the Republic!', or Molloy's 'region' or 'da', or 'my part of the world', as the origin of the word becomes interminably obscured in this neutral writing which empties the sign of singular meaning.

Translation and writing degree zero

Along with Beckett's particular undoing of the generic and conventional features of the novel through an aesthetic process of qualification and disqualification, each text's coexistence in two languages spurs major complication to referential readings of his fiction, as this example from *Malone Dies/Malone Meurt* suggests (a problematic which, because most texts have been translated, or their translation overseen, by Beckett, critics can tacitly disengage as vital). For as Beckett's texts are manifest within more than one linguistic economy, the meaning of each is always elsewhere translated and different. Thus, where the apparent Irish content of *Malone Dies* seems to allow for the text to be read in terms of specific criteria, its translation, *Malone Meurt*, can problematize the stability of that mode of reading: 'Up the Republic' is at an even greater remove from Irish politics in the French text than it is in the English text. As such, Beckett's fictions always defer self-present meaning as they are elsewhere rendered in another language. In *Malone Meurt*, Malone can say 'Up the Republic' without having to wonder if he should have kept his mouth shut ('*de me taire*'). In *Malone Dies*, Malone's reaction is more violent; he can use the slogan without wondering if he should have cut his tongue out. In such terms, then, translation breeds a dual problematic: Beckett's self-translations, as Sinéad Mooney, Morin and Connor have respectively demonstrated,[110] confound the idea of the original text, as well as disfiguring its structure. Simultaneously, as the above-quoted passages also signal, translation informs Beckett's writing degree zero and his impoverished aesthetic of referential diminution, and prompts a further recognition of the mobilization of epistemological doubt therein.[111]

As is evident on closer inspection of both excerpts quoted from *Molloy* and *Malone Dies/Malone Meurt*, the effects of translation are detectably at play. Regarding *Molloy*, Molloy's appreciation of his region is based upon another voice, though supposedly his: 'But I prefer to abide by my simple feeling and its voice that said, Molloy, your region is vast, you have never left it and you never shall. And wheresoever you wander, within its distant limits, things will always be the same, precisely.'[112] The use of the second-person pronoun thus suggests that Molloy, at minimum, is a split subject – a feature recurrent in the novel: 'Inside me too someone was laughing'[113] – and translating information from an unidentified elsewhere as a result. In turn, this account may or may not be Molloy's and creates the potentiality that it is a citation, and thus refuses, echoing Rebecca Walkowitz's deliberations on the born-translated novel, to 'match language to geography'.[114] Similarly, the appearance of 'Up the Republic!' in *Malone Meurt* suggests that a translation has occurred for these words to appear in Malone's account, yet the origin of that translation remains unrevealed, and, again pre-empting Walkowitz, 'block[s] readers from being "native readers"'.[115] As both examples demonstrate, Beckett's fictions incorporate translation as part of their aesthetic and formal procedures as a means of dismantling the coherence of the subject. In this sense, the equation of Molloy or Malone as speaking subjects with any antecedent and extratextual history or politics diminishes the manner in which the texts imbricate the enigma of translation into their form. And these procedures later come to the fore in *The Unnamable*: the narrator, like Malone, seeks 'a voice of my own, in all this babble',[116] prompting it in turn to 'say what I hear, I hear what I say, I don't know, one or the other, or both',[117] thus underlining the narrator's predicament of the first-person 'I' and the potential multivalent sources of its discourse.

Simultaneous, inherent and an important precedent to Beckett's styleless aesthetic and *désœuvrement* of the novel, then, is the question of translation that traverses his career and corpus. In Paris, Beckett worked with Péron on the translation of Joyce's 'Anna Livia Plurabelle' from *Work in Progress* (later *Finnegans Wake*) into French (1930). He later conducted nineteen translations for Nancy Cunard's *Negro* anthology (1934), as well as the translation of thirty-five Mexican poets, amounting to more than one hundred poems, for UNESCO's *Anthology of Mexican Poetry* (1950); and he undertook various translations for Eugene Jolas's *transition* and later Georges Duthuit's *Transition*. Notable in relation to this latter feat is his translations of Guillaume Apollinaire, Rimbaud and surrealist poetry, namely works by Andre Bréton, René Char and Paul Eluard.[118] One effect, then, of inciting this history of translation work is to elucidate Beckett within various literary lineages: a cosmopolitan literary history based in Paris, a history of polyglot modernism, Francophone literary history and a political history of literature in relation to race. In this sense, Beckett is rendered present to different communities and political concerns (which are beyond the direct concern of Irish modernism): namely, the anti-fascism of the surrealists and the anti-racist concerns of Cunard's anthology. Another effect of invoking this concern with translation is to position Beckett's writing degree zero and stylistic choices in terms of the absence, ghosting and spectrality that translation entails.

The 'pure sounds, free of all meaning'[119] that Molloy hears connote the continuous translatability of all language and its being without origin, its untranslatability in the sense of its incomparability, its materiality and its being nourished by absence: 'Sounds unencumbered with precise meaning were registered perhaps better by me than by most.'[120] Molloy's 'sense of identity', as is suggested earlier in the novel, is 'wrapped in a namelessness often hard to penetrate';[121] thus, 'there could be no things but nameless things, no names but thingless names'.[122] And this condition affects Molloy's ability to communicate successfully: 'This is perhaps one of the reasons I was so untalkative, I mean this trouble I had in understanding not only what others said to me, but also what I said to them. It is true that in the end, by dint of patience, we made ourselves understood, but understood with regard to what, I ask of you, and to what purpose?'[123] And so language, in its inability to be translated into meaning, becomes a site of dislocation: 'And to the noises of nature too, and of the works of men, I reacted I think in my own way and without desire of enlightenment.'[124] The condition of translation haunting Beckett's work – the substitutability of all language which inhibits one's ability to coherently locate identity – is continued in *Malone Dies*: 'But I tell myself so many things, what truth is there in all this babble?',[125] and pushed further in *The Unnamable* to completely distort the origins of the subject: 'Having nothing to say, no words but the words of others, I have to speak';[126] 'these voices are not mine, nor these thoughts, but the voices and thoughts of the devils who beset me.'[127] However measurable the direct effect which the surrealism or the *Negro* anthology translations had on Beckett's work, then, the way in which the residues of translation and its attendant problematics are activated and incorporated in his later writing mark the relationship between authorship, language and narrative as a hermeneutic enigma. Thought in these terms, translation, as it contributes to his unworking of the conventions of the novel, provides a predecessor and alibi for, and complements the other technical features of, Beckett's writing degree zero, that 'transparent form of speech' which 'achieves a style of absence'[128] and establishes a new literary ethics.

Ethics, politics, referentiality: Adorno, Barthes, Blanchot

Crucial to Barthes's writing degree zero, and its applicability to Beckett's distant and inert modernism, as Rabaté points out, is that the loss in stylistics prompted by this style of writing results in an ethical gain, a detail which is particularly significant to our overarching concern with Beckett's investment in an aesthetic of referential diminution and how we read the vestigial historical traces recorded in his works. In opposition to Jean-Paul Sartre's committed literature which directly engages with historical and political issues, writing degree zero opens literature, as Barthes suggests, to a 'new humanism' where 'literature is openly reduced to the problematics of language' and where 'poetic freedom takes its place within a verbal condition whose limits are those of a society and not those of a convention'.[129] As Barthes mentions with reference to Louis Ferdinand

Celine, 'the adoption of a real language is for the writer the most human act'.[130] This establishes a new morality of authorship in contrast to Sartre's committed literature where the writer insinuates and persuades a particular aim.[131]

Writing degree zero, then, offers another nuance, or an alternative lens, to late modernism, within which Beckett has often been categorized, to situate the ethics of his style. As a late modernist, Beckett can be made relative to a modernist project of working through literary forms and political experiences, while forging a riposte to the ambitions of the high modernist aesthetic, laying bare its ruins and transcending its limits.[132] Simultaneously, late modernism keeps with the European avant-garde by bringing together signifiers from an array of contexts, and so Beckett's late modernism would partake in a 'critical art constituted by constant transformation and paradox'.[133] Additional when considered in terms of writing degree zero, then, is a specific account of the ethics of Beckett's style; the sense of a critical art achieved through processes of juxtaposition, as in a late modernist account, reveals little of the relation of Becket's writing to questions of ethics and politics. Barthes's writing degree zero, with its insistence on the difference of the word with itself, and through which the meaning of the word remains absent and abundant, provides further detail to the ethics of Beckett's endeavour. Namely, Beckett's rhetorical paradoxes – achieved through qualification, negation, variation, irony, repetition and translation – destabilize a fixed and localizable aim and position in language, and thus amount to a renunciation of knowing for a style and ethics of unknowing. As when Molloy ponders his mother's death: 'The truth is I don't know much. For example my mother's death. Was she already dead when I came? Or did she only die later? I mean enough to bury. I don't know. Perhaps they haven't buried her yet.'[134] *The Unnamable* similarly performs this process as content: 'How proceed? By aporia pure and simple? Or by affirmations and negations invalidated as uttered.'[135] And like 'region', 'da' or 'my part of the world' in *Molloy*, or 'Up The Republic' in *Malone Dies*, Beckett's obtuse language resists confidently asserting a signified which can be brought to bear on the signifier. While these terms signify, they deny the speaker or reader any fixed location in language, and so Beckett's inert modernism refrains from weighing in with an identifiable politics on a particular referential subject. Indeed, Beckett's motivations for investing in a form of writing degree zero, or a neutral writing, after the Second World War diverges with other contemporary considerations of the relationship between Beckett's writing and politics, particularly Adorno's understanding of modern art as recoiling from the objective world while relating the unsolved antagonisms of reality as a problem of form.

Rabaté's renewal of Barthes's writing degree zero as the best gloss on Beckett's attempts to write without style is accompanied by the argument that such writing 'has very little to do with a committed literature explicitly discussing the events of the times'.[136] To this latter point, it must be added that Barthes's target for dispute concerning a committed literature is Sartre and not Adorno. Notwithstanding, Beckett's writing remains straddled upon both sides of an equation that is repeatedly tacit in literary criticism concerning modernist literary language: politically committed (in Adorno's indirect recoil rather than Sartre's engaged writing) in one sense, and ethically neutral in another (Barthes's writing degree zero). Again, the question of method is crucial to these conclusions: notably, Adorno's model deploys historicist and materialist analysis to arrive at its conclusions; Barthes infers a philosophy of writing to explicate the ethics of writing degree zero. Barthes's concept, however, does not emerge from a vacuum as an ahistorical and autonomous concept of writing. As Barthes outlines, its legacy can be traced to the French Revolution, and so a presence of French literary history and its political engagements is tacit within its development. In this sense, writing degree zero elucidates Beckett as present to a French literary lineage originating with the French Revolution, which, for Barthes, had the strange effect of leaving classical language intact until its ultimate depreciation with the writing degree zero of Camus and Celine and, we might add, Beckett's Irish modernism. This in itself presents unique opportunities to Irish modernism when Beckett is taken as a means of renegotiating Barthes's concept. It similarly poses problems to Casanova's point that Beckett 'can be understood only in terms of Irish literary space'.[137] If Beckett belongs and partakes as much in a French literary history as an Irish heritage, then conceptualizations of Irish modernism must encompass these respective histories within its scope, thus pushing Irish modernism beyond a transnational phenomenon with Ireland as its centre. And similarly, if writing degree zero is 'the anticipation of a homogenous social state',[138] and acts as the only form of writerly response that could entail a new humanism in the mid-century after its various historical traumas (the Second World War, the Shoah, the Algerian war, the Irish Civil War and Soviet communism, to mention a few that affected Beckett's life), it would seem to correspond to a form of political engagement, despite its having little to do with a committed literature explicitly discussing the events of the times.

While Camus and Celine are important predecessors to Barthes's concept, the solution to the current paradox is perhaps Blanchot, who acts as a lynchpin for both Barthes and Beckett in the exploration of this new style. Blanchot's 'neutral' style (*le neutre*), which is picked up by Barthes in *Writing Degree Zero*, asserts the radical alterity of language, its difference with itself and its resistance to becoming self-identical. As Blanchot suggests in *The Infinite Conversation*, 'the unknown is always thought in the neuter. Thought of the neuter, or the neutral, is a threat and a scandal for thought'.[139] The neuter, as Blanchot continues, 'is that which cannot be assigned to any genre whatsoever: the non-general, the non-generic, as well as the non-particular. It refuses to belong to the category of subject as much as it does to that of object'.[140] Moreover, as Blanchot writes, 'this does not simply mean that it is still undetermined and as though hesitating between the two, but rather that the neuter supposes another relation depending neither on objective conditions nor on subjective dispositions'.[141] In this sense, the neuter suspends the possibility of self-identity, while also making identity that which is born through the difference of language with itself. Ultimately, as Rabaté suggests, the neuter promotes 'a debunking of the belated political rectitude of many writers who were caught posturing in distasteful pseduo-heroics'.[142]

Important to outline here, then, is Beckett's link to Blanchot, as well as Duthuit. Through Blanchot – whom he translated and read – Beckett's diminutive and inert modernism can be theorized as engaging a critique of the disclosure of self-identity and its reading in literary language. Duthuit's negation of Sartre's critique of 'engaged writing' in *Transition* similarly provides an alibi for Beckett's rejection of committed writing and his move towards writing degree zero and its accompanying critique of a committed self-present language. Crucially, then, Beckett's aesthetic of diminution and inertia, when understood in terms of writing degree zero, operates at a greater remove, at a greater mobilization of epistemological doubt, than Adorno's recoiling and indirect form. The latter, through a negation of historical trauma, ultimately reveals the forces of history as present. As Daniel Katz writes of Adorno's critique, Beckett's 'not-saying implies a pointing not only to the place where the image does *not* appear, but to the ban which prohibits it'.[143] Pushed to a radical limit, Barthes's 'absences and over-nourishing signs' that operate 'without foresight or stability of intention', when also thought through Blanchot's neuter which affirms the difference of language with itself, signifies a writing which is fundamentally supplementary in character. That is, as Derrida suggests of the supplement, a writing which makes 'visible a distancing which is neither the same nor an other'.[144] This differs from Adorno's account that 'the unsolved antagonisms of reality return in artworks as immanent problems of form. This, not the insertion of objective elements, defines the relation of art to society.'[145] Writing degree zero, the Pandora's box of language, entails an unknown element to the word, one which ethically obscures the unsolved antagonisms of reality that might, or might not be, in Adorno's terms, the problem of form. The morality of form as per Barthes's writing degree zero and Beckett's aesthetic scepticism, when considered after Blanchot and Derrida, becomes translation without a pole of reference.[146] This, in turn, does not scupper the distinction being carried here between Adorno's art and Barthes's writing degree zero. Rather, it pushes Barthes's concept to a more radical distinction, one where the ethical dimensions of its form can be made more specific to the question of Beckett's diminutive aesthetic, its in-built translation effects and its relationship to the extra-linguistic.

The Unnamable's referents

The Unnamable constitutes the apotheosis of Beckett's *désœuvrement* of the novel as he empties the form of all its generic conventions; it also represents the instance in the Beckett canon where our current critical bind becomes most fully apparent and difficult because of the mode of representation instituted in the text. 'Where now? Who now? When now?':[147] the famous questions with which the novel opens do not refer to a subject who would pose them; and the coherence of the subject who might pose them is suspended in the lines that follow: 'Unquestioning. I, say I. Unbelieving. Questions, hypotheses, call them that. Keep going, going on, call that going, call that on.'[148] To this predicament of 'going on', the narrator quickly follows with the postulation of an aporetic impasse which logic and reason will not aid in superseding: 'What am I to do, what shall I do, what should I do, in my situation, how proceed? By aporia pure and simple? Or by affirmations and negations invalidated as uttered, or sooner or later?'[149] Disoriented, 'ephectic' and unknowing,[150] the narrator similarly suffers from linguistic estrangement throughout the novel: it speaks 'their language', which 'they have crammed me full of to prevent me from saying who I am'.[151] And in this state, the narrator will 'speak of things of which I cannot speak', is 'obliged to speak' and 'shall never be silent'.[152] From the beginning and throughout, then, the narrative strategy of *The Unnamable* carries the weight of Adorno's recoiling form, Barthes's style of absence and Blanchot's neuter; and so the novel lends itself to a variety of potential referents and reading strategies.

The limits of expression demonstrated in the text have prominently provoked critics to read *The Unnamable* as a form of Holocaust testimony, wherein the narrative both defers, and is immensely affected by, the Shoah. As Adorno suggests of Beckett's post-war works, of which *The Unnamable* is the most prominent example:

> Beckett has given us the only fitting reaction to the situation of the concentration camps – a situation he never calls by name, as if it were subject to an image ban. What is, he says, is like a concentration camp. At one time he speaks of a lifelong death penalty. The only dawning hope is that there will be nothing any more. This, too, he rejects.[153]

Situated relative to the Second World War, *The Unnamable* becomes intrinsically bound up with a history which it defers because its deficient words (the narrator's 'nameless images' and 'imageless names' which prompt representative difficulty) and recoiling form ('if in my situation one may speak of facts, not only that I shall have to speak of things of which I cannot speak'[154]) constitute an ethical link between language, history and Holocaust testimony. In such terms, the deflection of the capacities of even basic representation ('But an instant, an hour, and so on – how can they be represented? A life, how could that be made clear to me, here, in the dark, I call that the dark, perhaps it's azure, blank words, but I use them'[155]) operate at a remove from history to negotiate its trauma and ineffability. Refraining from allegorical representation, and respecting Adorno's image ban, Beckettian testimony is thus constituted by a language without origin, already in complete translation, which consequently lends itself to being read in terms of specific historical circumstances; circumstances which, as it is well known, directly affected Beckett's life. Concurrently, its traces of potential Holocaust signifiers and allusions to prisons and slaughterhouses – 'How are you? Underneath me! We're piled up in heaps';[156] 'upon us all the silence will fall again, and settle, like dust of sand, on the arena, after the massacres'[157] – are suggestive, as critics have written, of the Shoah as the text's potential signified. For example, McNaughton writes that *The Unnamable* 'tries to draw the curtain on objective historical horror that the narrator nevertheless deeply fears and borrows from'.[158] And Alysia E. Garrison suggests that '*The Unnamable* testifies not only to transhistorical trauma, but also to historical trauma'[159] and that 'we should look closely at the utterances and images in *The Unnamable* to read the historical half-life faintly present, from which the text (de)generated'.[160]

Elsewhere, critics have extended the potential referents of the novel beyond the Shoah. Dispossession and the relation to the other are prominent tropes in postcolonial theory and criticism, particularly in relation to Ireland's colonial history; and so this context remains applicable to Beckett's novel.[161] Stephen Spender famously wrote in his 1958 review of the novel that Beckett's theme with *The Unnamable* is the 'very Irish one in this century: the identity of opposites'.[162] More particularly, Mark Quigley has read the novel as elucidating the fate of the colonial subject whose representation is 'caught up in hegemony's negotiations of power' and within which 'traces of the colonizer linger most deeply'.[163] Jude R. Meche reads Beckett's characters as entangled in a pursuit of identity 'that cannot be confirmed without the verification of an opposing other', a conflict played out in the novel through Mahood and his caretaker Marguerite which 'resembles the postcolonial model of the conflict between colonizer and colonized'.[164] And Declan Kiberd has designated the voice in Beckett's writing after *Murphy* as 'unambiguously Irish'.[165] Opening the novel to other referents, Mark Nixon reads the narrator's 'I was never elsewhere, here is my only elsewhere'[166] as preceded and linked to Beckett's feeling of disorientation expressed in a two-and-a-half-line poem preserved in one of Beckett's 1937 German diaries: 'Always elsewhere/In body also/The dew falls and the rain from.'[167] As such, 'Beckett's feelings of disorientation, compounded by the realisation that Germany was yet another "elsewhere" rather than a potential source of creative and personal stability',[168] marks for Nixon a moment of recognition on the path to *The Unnamable*.

Moreover, as the example of memory studies reminds us to supplement chronological historiography with a more fluid, less rigid approach that investigates what is and is not remembered from the past, we can posit other, and less monumental, events which may have affected the novel's style and form. A provocative and polemical example concerns Beckett's relationships with Georges Pelorson and Francis Stuart, who, during the War, worked for the Vichy administration and the Abwehr in Berlin, respectively.[169] Pelorson, an acquaintance of Beckett's since his studies at the *École Normale Supérieure*, operated as a collaborationist during the war years. In 1947, Pelorson (who took the name Georges Belmont after the war) was sentenced to fifteen years of forced labour for his wartime activities. Notwithstanding, Beckett continued his relationships with Pelorson – he helped Pelorson to find a publisher for his writings – and Stuart in friendly terms after the war. Simultaneous to his friendships with Pelorson and Stuart, Beckett is undoubtedly mourning the loss of his long-time friend, Péron, who perished after leaving Mauthausen in 1945. And in this same period in which he remains on good terms with Pelorson and Stuart, Beckett is writing *L'Innomable/The Unnamable*, which occupied him from 1951 until its English translation was complete in 1958, a period of writing which, as James Knowlson has indicated, is notably permeated by the pathos by Péron's fate. As suggested, *The Unnamable* has been read as performing a unique form of ethical testimony to the atrocities of the camps and other atrocities during and after the Second World War; its translatorial effects and over-nourishing signs comprising a rare literary mode, as Adorno and other critics have recognized, that is just and proper in the face of such an inestimable historical event. Thought through his relationships with Pelorson and Stuart, however, these translatorial effects and over-nourishing signs might also comprise the evasive and shameful means of dealing with his activity of expressing sympathy with former collaborationists in the aftermath of the war. This, in turn, adds another layer, less heroic (to repeat Adorno's term) and more bathetic, to the ethics of Beckett's testimony and his investment in a writing degree zero with its attendant distaste for pseudo-heroics. Such strange potentialities occur as a residue of the distance of Beckett's modernism to a host of possible contexts.

The Unnamable thus remains enigmatic in terms of a host of referents as its narrative strategy of qualification and disqualification abrogates each and any force which might be cited as an origin to the narrator's identity: 'Someone speaks, someone hears, no need to go any further, it is not he, it's I, or another, or others, what does it matter, the case is clear, it is not he, he who I know I am, that's all I know, who I cannot say I am.'[170] Moreover, the other which visits the narrator remains irreducible to any fixed identity or any localizable origin: 'The other advances full upon me. He emerges as from heavy hangings, advances a few steps, then backs away. He is stooping and seems to be dragging invisible burdens.'[171] And even with the hint that 'Bally' was the site where 'the inestimable gift of life had been rammed down my gullet',[172] *The Unnamable*, like *Molloy* and *Malone Dies*, defers Ireland and elsewhere as an informative presence which would anchor the prose, thus rendering an undecidability to Beckett's status as a postcolonial or a Holocaust writer. *The Unnamable*, then, operates in terms of Adorno's recoiling form and simultaneously corresponds to Barthes's writing degree zero because its style, which is nourished by absence, remains beyond accumulation to a specific and determined reading strategy. Untranslatable, the text resists being totally translated into another context while it cannot stop being translated into other contexts. In such terms, Beckett's aesthetic of diminution, heightened in *The Unnamable*, manifests a distance which is neither the same nor an other: it supplements a variety of available referents. With the origin of its linguistic play always obscured, Barthes's account of writing degree zero acts poignantly alongside Adorno's recoiling form to outline Beckett's ethical testimony in relation to the historically traumatic: Beckett's unnamable and over-nourishing signs – from elsewhere translated, operating through assertion and negation, bearing the difference of the sign with itself – affirm and defer a literary engagement with questions of identity, trauma and the unrepresentable.[173]

Irish modernism adrift

Beckett then becomes a fitting exemplar of, and helps us see, the radical potentialities of an Irish modernism which allows for its texts to be read as both relative and different to the historical realities they supposedly represent. Situated in terms of Rancière's schema for a sceptical modern literature, and in the contrast between Barthes's writing degree zero and Adorno's recoiling form, the over-nourishing signs which constitute Beckett's prose host and disallow a variety of potential referents and set Irish modernism adrift from its place, time and any anterior signified(s) which would act as its anchoring referent(s). While the various historical allusions and contexts of Beckett's writing establish the possibility of reading particular histories in(to) his texts, his particular brand of inert modernism (which for the most part only increases in obliquity after *The Unnamable*) refrains from gathering these allusions as stable signifiers that refer beyond the respective narrative operations to extratextual entities, events or realities whose presence would then be reconstituted in and/or by the works. Beckett's writing degree zero, with its focus on absence, lacunae and negation, defers the possibility of generating self-present meanings that would lead to the disclosure of historical referents. For this reason, Beckett's writing remains interminably open and resistant to contextual explication, and thus beyond accumulation to a historicist discourse that would complete and qualify the structural gaps of modernist literatures with historical details, or scale smoothly between the literary text and a macro historical metanarrative. The relationship between Beckett's Irish modernism and the geopolitical histories of modernity, in such terms, is untranslatable and always open to conjecture. As a result, Beckett's supposed referents are destinations that happen only after the fact of linguistic play taking place. This is not to deny the various important and real histories that precede the texts, but rather to suggest that these histories, because of the radical symbolism instituted through Beckett's aesthetic of diminution, can only arrive after the fact through the critical act, a circumstance which opens the narrative of Irish modernism and the Irish modernist text to radically different histories and ever new contingencies. In turn, the aesthetic scepticism and referential obliquity of (Beckett's) modernism, when thought in terms of philosophies of literature and historical context, dramatically alters how we narrate Irish modernism. For if Irish modernism is defined by its colonial origins, or the metanarrative of Ireland's history in modernity, then the scope of the field becomes delimited to specific questions and politics, as well as particular modes of reading. Missed, in turn, as a result of the opportunities occasioned by Beckett's textual properties and the particular ethics of his aesthetic modes, are the different histories and contexts that could comprise its make-up and which the irreducible distance of his modernism allows us to suppose.

2

Brian, Flann, Myles and the origins of Irish modernism

The writings of Brian O'Nolan/Flann O'Brien/Myles na gCopaleen have rarely found a home within various historical formulations of Irish modernism. The Yeats–Joyce–Beckett trinity continues to operate to its neglect. The 1930s Irish modernists – the assemblage of Samuel Beckett, Brian Coffey, Denis Devlin, Thomas MacGreevy and George Reavey – struck a different temperamental chord to na gCopaleen's *Cruiskeen Lawn* and O'Brien's *At Swim-Two-Birds*, *The Third Policeman* and other novels. And the different accounts of Irish modernism presented in recent collections (*The Cambridge Companion to Irish Modernism*, *A History of Irish Modernism*) mention O'Nolan/O'Brien/na gCopaleen only in passing. One such reason for these omissions, as Rónán McDonald and Julian Murphet suggest, is that 'Flann O'Brien has always been difficult to categorise'.[1] For McDonald and Murphet, however, the new modernist studies, with its expansion of the scope and content of modernism, offers a corrective to these omissions, as well as a place for the O'Nolan/O'Brien/na gCopaleen corpus relative to the achievements of those other Irish modernists, particularly along postcolonial and statist lines. This chapter reads the issue of categorizing this oeuvre as a productive problem for conceptualizing Irish modernism. Simultaneously, it builds critically on the opportunity that the new modernist studies provides for incorporating this corpus into modernist and Irish modernist discussion. Specifically, it assesses the malleability of the various pseudonymic and metafictional strategies particular to this writing to received and rehearsed definitions of Irish modernism. In turn, it interrogates the impact of the radical symbolism of this corpus on how, where and by what conceptual justification we locate cultural memory in relation to modernist literary practice. It first addresses the critical coordinates of these issues.

Locating Brian, Flann and Myles

Preceding and coinciding with McDonald and Murphet's claim, there has been a critical upsurge on this body of writing since the turn of the century. Despite being kept at bay during various institutionalizations of Irish modernism, the writings of O'Nolan/O'Brien/na gCopaleen have increasingly been cited as poignant commentaries which hit to the core of and exposed many cultural and political contradictions prevalent in the period of post-independence Ireland. Terence Brown writes that *An Béal Bocht* 'comprehensively satirised the literary exploitation of the western island, in a hilarious send up of reminiscence'.[2] Joe Cleary includes O'Brien in a group of writers whose satirical works 'excoriated the gap between idealised images of Ireland cultivated by official state culture and the mundane realities of the new society'.[3] The historian Diarmaid Ferriter, on numerous occasions in *The Transformation of Ireland 1900–2000*, incorporates O'Brien as a commentator on contemporary Irish politics.[4] In recognizing the cultural significance of this body of writing, particularly as a vehicle of expression of, and response to, the dynamics of modernity in Ireland, such critics, amongst others, have facilitated a historicist inflected rediscovery of the O'Nolan/O'Brien/na gCopaleen oeuvre over the past two decades.

In these texts and elsewhere, 'Flann O'Brien', though often inaccurately deployed, has generally operated as an umbrella term to simplify and reduce problems of appellation when discussing this work. In response, more recent criticism has confronted the problem of authorship which it poses. With such a multiplicity of authorial titles and voices to contend with, there has emerged a need to account for the movement of names between the works to which they are respectively related: *At Swim-Two-Birds*, *The Third Policeman*, *An Béal Bocht*, *The Poor Mouth*, *The Hard Life*, *The Dalkey Archive*, *Cruiskeen Lawn* (a newspaper column in the *Irish Times* which featured from 1940 to 1966) and so forth. Broadly speaking, critics have responded by ascribing particular writings to a particular pseudonym (*At Swim-Two-Birds* and *The Third Policeman* were authored by Flann O'Brien; *Cruiskeen Lawn* was authored by Myles na Gopaleen and Myles na gCopaleen; *An Béal Bocht* was authored by Myles na gCopaleen, and its translation, *The Poor Mouth*, was published as authored by Flann O'Brien); and more often than not, the pseudonyms are linked to Brian O'Nolan/Brian Ó Nualláin. This procedure, however, is not without its attendant problems as the figure of Brian O'Nolan has enticed different appraisals and remains a critical enigma. McDonald, in a discussion of O'Nolan's 'worldview', writes that 'the formal audacity of O'Brien's novels contrasts with the orthodox values of Myles na Gopaleen's journalism'.[5] Joseph Brooker has written that O'Nolan deliberately performs in a different voice when writing as na gCopaleen for the *Irish Times* and that this voice was abnegated in the novels.[6] Carol Taaffe suggests that 'the distinction between Myles and Flann is extremely precarious' and that O'Nolan 'did not really hide himself behind these various masks'.[7] Maebh Long, in removing the focus on O'Nolan's agency, suggests that criticism must act with a certain impersonal distance because of the 'marked differences between the character … that is Myles na gCopaleen and the author Flann O'Brien, and that O'Nolan cannot be naively conflated with his authorial personae'.[8] To this problem of agency, Jennika Baines adds dilemmas of stature and temporality: 'During O'Nolan's lifetime, the persona of Myles na gCopaleen was much more widely known than that of Flann O'Brien'.[9] Confounding the issue further, Richard Kearney has suggested that 'Brian O'Nolan vehemently denied any knowledge of his pseudonymous creations'.[10] And Paul Fagan imbricates the role of the reader in this problem: 'O'Nolan's project of representing and exploring a series of selves … is bound up with his resistance to the authority and ethicality of the reader's impossible epistemological vantage point in the literary event'.[11] Moreover, O'Nolan's close friends partook in these pseudonymous projects: Niall Sheridan edited *At Swim-Two Birds*; O'Nolan, Sheridan and Niall Montgomery conducted collaborative letter writing escapades to the *Irish Times*; and Sheridan and Montgomery, on occasion, wrote the *Cruiskeen Lawn* column. On this latter point, as Long suggests, na gCopaleen, irrespective of the writer, became 'the means through which an idea, pun, invention, argument, theory is voiced' and provided 'whatever backdrop that theme requires'.[12] Notwithstanding, 'Brian O'Nolan' increasingly serves in criticism today, if not somewhat reductively, as the authorial agent when referencing this oeuvre, thereby enabling a unified means for analysing the various writings by the various pseudonyms which are linked to O'Nolan, as well as facilitating the possibility of their comparison within a holistic structure.

Offering a theorization of the issue of the pseudonyms, McDonald and Murphet have recently pointed out that 'this flight from the inherited straitjacket of a named, self-consistent subjectivity' can be conceived in both national and modernist terms,[13] thus as belonging to 'an Irish tradition of self-concealment and self-invention' and a modernist 'dismantlement of any unitary core of artistic responsibility'.[14] As Brian O'Nolan/Brian Ó Nualláin grew up in an Irish-language speaking family, the postcolonial spectre of a lost Gaelic culture and language has long served as a historical pretext to anchor the conundrum of identity specific to this bilingual modernist corpus which moves between a hybrid of Irish and English language pen names. And with the expansion of the new modernist studies, as McDonald and Murphet suggest, these national and modernist tendencies need not be understood as antithetical but as compatible under a broader definition of modernism, and particularly as relative to Irish modernism: 'Critical attention has shifted from the apparent collision between Irish culture and international modernism to their previously obscure collusions.'[15] Elsewhere, Ronan Crowley has tacitly substantiated McDonald and Murphet's claim that O'Nolan's play with pseudonymity has 'precursors in an Irish tradition of self-concealment or self-invention';[16] deftly demonstrated, Crowley manifests O'Nolan's use of pseudonyms as related to authorial practice particular to the Irish Revival, which, as pointed to in the introduction of this book, has become one of Irish modernism's key moments. In such terms, the pseudonym as a modernist problematic becomes explicable in terms of the cultural dynamics of post-independence Ireland.

This treatment of the pseudonyms and their relation to O'Nolan, a problem of narrative itself, is also often deployed when reading the O'Nolan/O'Brien/na gCopaleen corpus (a designation which I keep here to maintain the enigma of authorship which is posed by this body of work). The various works which constitute that canon are increasingly rendered in both national and new modernist terms, and are often related to Ireland's postcolonial status and the uneven development of modernity. Problems of indeterminacy, resistance and representation inherent to the oeuvre have thus been tackled in recent criticism. Thierry Robin argues that the fiction performs 'a transgressive stance towards history',[17] and McDonald and Murphet suggest that it 'registers the recalcitrance and resistance of a world that defies pat representation'.[18] As in the second instance, there is the suggestion of a reality perceived as resistant and then captured in the act of writing. Given the prevalence of cultural and materialist analysis in literary studies currently, as we have seen in Beckett studies, the narratives of *At Swim-Two-Birds* and *The Third Policeman* have been read as representative and symptomatic of Ireland's uneven development. For example, it has been suggested that 'lurking in the background of [*At Swim-Two-Birds* and *The Third Policeman*] is the cataclysmic joke of an impending war from which Ireland stands aside, whose imminence is having a direct effect on the Irish present, and whose outcome will have an incalculable effect on the Irish future'.[19] Directly concerning *At Swim-Two-Birds*, it has been proposed that 'the cultural confusion of 1930s Dublin underscores the crowded passages of *At Swim-Two-Birds*'.[20] And elsewhere, 'the context of disappointment, combined with an uneven social development in a still primarily rural Ireland, underlies the peculiar combination of the mundane and the fantastic in O'Brien's work.[21] As in these examples, an active critical grammar – 'in the background is', 'underscores', 'underlies' – has been adopted which incites a mimetic theory of literature as belated, thus imitating the extratextual world after the fact. Given such equation of modernist literary practice with national paradigms, these indeterminate texts, like the pseudonymous play, are located in relation to a specific signified. In each example, the historical realities of post-independence Ireland precede the respective texts of *At Swim-Two-Birds* and *The Third Policeman* and enable their reading and explanation. In such terms, Ireland's historical contours can be read in these novels in a manner akin to currently operative theorizations of literature as a form of cultural memory, namely that literature is preceded by a memory culture and that it creates new memory narratives as a result of processes of symbolic reconfiguration.[22] Because of a critical grammar which suggests imitation and referentiality, then, this literature becomes explicable with recourse to the development of the post-independence Irish state.

Irish postmodernism

Consequently, the question of postmodernism has been suppressed in relation to this corpus in recent years. With the rise of the new modernist studies and its recent global, transnational and spatial turn – and particularly its emphasis on how the registration of political or economic unevenness presupposes forms of direct referentiality – postmodernism has been absorbed under the banner of a longer modernist *durée*, and its distinguishing criteria – distrust of grand narratives and so-called scientific facts, language games, metafiction, parody and pastiche – have become displaced from critical fashion. Notwithstanding its terminology becoming outmoded, the critical language of postmodernism remains a latent feature of broader modernist debate and discussion. Critics such as Marjorie Perloff and, more recently, Adam Meehan have demonstrated that 'conceptions of subjectivity commonly attributed to postmodern theory had already been articulated in modernist fiction before 1945', in turn unsettling the constructed barriers which distinguish modernism from postmodernism.[23] Postmodernism, in such terms, becomes subsumed in modernist discourse rather than elsewhere to its remit. Recognizing it as already inherent to modernism thus allows for a reconsideration of a host of 'postmodern' problematics alongside some of the tendencies of the new modernist studies. The O'Nolan/O'Brien/

na gCopaleen oeuvre stands as an apposite case in point in this respect given its play with ambiguity, fragmentation and metalepsis. For example, O'Brien's *At Swim-Two-Birds* and *The Third Policeman*, unlike na gCopaleen's newspaper column, are not explicit explorations or referential representations of the subject of post-independence Ireland. Though parts of the oeuvre assume more direct concern with Ireland (particularly *Cruiskeen Lawn*), the early novels are, as Long writes, marked by 'the joy of giddy whirling through the paradoxes of logic and language'.[24] Similarly, despite the welcome opportunities for comparative analysis established by a centralized 'O'Nolan studies', O'Nolan, as demonstrated by the above and differing critical appraisals concerning the relation between the pseudonyms and the man, proves a slippery centre through which to harness this corpus. The various pseudonyms – Flann O'Brien, Myles na gCopaleen, Myles na Gopaleen, George Knowall, Brother Barnabas, An Broc, John James Doe and Count O'Blather, amongst many others suspected – proliferate beyond, rather than cohere around, one individual and an identity crisis determined by the trauma of Ireland's postcolonial linguistic heritage.

Presenting unique problems to the critical practice of equating, and scaling up, the literary object to the general example, this oeuvre presents a particular opportunity for a reconsideration of operative definitions of Irish modernism, which are often based as much on artist's biographies, national politics and transnational movements as they are on aesthetic conundrums and artistic works. Sclerotic in relation to any fixed referent, the O'Nolan/O'Brien/na gCopaleen corpus, as a new site of interest in Irish modernist studies and new modernist studies, is a very indeterminate and contradictory assemblage from which to scale up or draw any conclusions. This chapter responds to the paradoxical play of the pseudonyms and the radical symbolism of O'Brien's early novels to establish a more nuanced reading of the relationship between this corpus and Ireland, doing so through the weak conceptual parameters of Irish modernism, dislocating in the process some of the key tenets of that term. Like the enigmatic relationship between the pseudonyms and O'Nolan, the articulation of a correlation between the explicitly artificial narrative procedures of the fiction and an extratextual signified requires a theoretical frame which caters for referential excess and indeterminacy as well as a material link. In terms of the relation between this corpus and Irish modernism, then, attention is required to what Paul Saint-Amour has dubbed 'meso-analysis', which, as outlined in the introduction, is established in contrast to unselfconsciously working 'at the scalar interface between abstract theorising and individual case studies'.[25]

In this spirit of meso analysis, this chapter re-engages the question of the pseudonyms to interrogate the suggestion that O'Nolan 'did not really hide himself behind these various masks ... and that the illusion was fairly transparent'.[26] Establishing an overlap between modernist and postmodernist thought concerning the 'postmodern' criteria through which authorship becomes a mode of displacement and fragmentation,[27] it explores how correlates in modernist literature and criticism impact theorizations of the issue of O'Nolan's masks, in turn complicating the possibility of a critical homology between Irish modernism and the life and times of O'Nolan. Similarly, it interrogates *At Swim-Two-Birds* and *The Third Policeman* concerning their relationship to Ireland, particularly as it is deployed as a critical tool which precedes, and is thus explicative of, the texts, as well as an object whose history the texts would thus demonstrate through their participation in Irish modernism. Like the relationship between the pseudonyms and O'Nolan, it is argued that the relationship between these fictions and Ireland is incomplete, that they overtly demonstrate an inability to (fully) represent the contours of that historical phenomenon, and that Ireland is an absent presence in, and thus supplemented by, *At Swim-Two-Birds* and *The Third Policeman*. Particularly, this chapter suggests that both novels present narrative strategies which effect a resistance to the imitative representation of the state of the nation by means of an erasure of memory which is the product of metafictional procedures. In this sense, post-independence Ireland is not necessarily a resistant reality which is registered and hence remembered through, and thus stabilizes, the narrative modes of *At Swim-Two-Birds* and *The Third Policeman*. Rather, the destruction of memory, as it is performed differently in both novels, ensures that Ireland looms in and over these novels as both a real and unreal spectre, a trace that is the mark of the absence of its own self-presence, and lacking constitutive meaning therein. Thus, where definitions of Irish modernism have often been concerned with its origins and metanarratives, this chapter demonstrates that those naming devices are difficult to coherently identify in one of its now key moments, always obscuring its origins and remaining unidentifiable by a singular name.

The ambiguity of the mask

Criticism on the O'Nolan/O'Brien/na gCopaleen corpus has already seen the delivery of some timely interventions on the issue of the pseudonyms. Adrian Oțoiu has specified in detail the particularity of each of the pseudonyms and how they differentiate. The premises put forward here rest on Oțoiu's groundwork, particularly his insistence that there are 'significant differences among these names'.[28] Oțoiu suggests, 'Some are meant for usage in the public sphere (distinct from the cultural one); some are mere fictional façades, with no trace of a purported identity behind them; some point to complex identities, either competing that of the flesh-and-blood author, or inhabiting the fictional space.'[29] Similarly, Long has recently provided a fresh account of how the O'Nolan/O'Brien/na gCopaleen corpus does not always correspond to the individual body of the man who, for various reasons, needed to claim the identity of those pseudonyms. Indicating that the inspiration for *The Third Policeman* might not have been 'original' but born from the direct plagiarism of a short story by his friend, Niall Sheridan, Long's findings complicate understandings of the novel as a work authored individually by O'Nolan,[30] thus adding to the growing appreciation that *At Swim-Two-Birds* and *Cruiskeen Lawn* were respectively authored by collaborations led by O'Nolan. Reflected in these accounts is the crisis of authorial intention inherent to (post)modernist literature and thought, which, in the following, is elaborated upon with reference to Walter Benjamin's, Friedrich Nietzsche's, W. B. Yeats's and Roland Barthes's respective meditations on artistic destruction, concealment, mask wearing and authorship. These coordinates serve to establish conceptual parameters beyond nationalist models to engage the complexity of the relationship between the masks and their origins. They similarly serve to instigate reflection on where analysis of Irish modernism begins.

In his *Irish Times* obituary for O'Nolan, Montgomery gives an account of the writer which resonates with Benjamin's description of 'the destructive character', a concept which is related here to elaborate the stakes of Montgomery's tribute to O'Nolan and his pseudonymous activity. From the outset, the terms of Benjamin's destructive character – that anonymous persona intent on the destruction of bourgeois values and liberation from subjectification and which 'knows only one watchword: make room; only one activity: clearing away'[31] – are tacit in Montgomery's account which outlines the anarchic and insurrectionary impulses that constituted much of the O'Nolan/O'Brien/na gCopaleen corpus. Casting O'Nolan in the plural, Montgomery writes that 'he descended, like a shower of paratroopers, deploying a myriad of pseudonymous personalities in the interests of pure destruction'.[32] And through this multiplicity of paratroopers and pseudonyms, as Montgomery continues, 'most dazzling was his consistent presentation of uncommon ideas as common sense: the delirium on which he imposed order was very real to him – he hypnotised a generation into believing that it was Ireland'.³³ As he dons the pseudonym in the interest of pure destruction and establishing the uncommon as common, O'Nolan resembles Benjamin's destructive character who 'rejuvenates in clearing away the traces of our own age' and 'cheers because everything cleared away means to the destroyer a complete reduction, indeed eradication, of his own condition'.³⁴ Thus, O'Nolan's Ireland, to recast it in Benjamin's words, 'is simplified when tested for its worthiness of destruction'.³⁵ And for Montgomery, as for Benjamin, such disruption and destruction is dependent on, and attained by, the erasure of the subject, which in the case of O'Nolan is readily achieved through the array of pseudonyms. As the empty persona allows for an ever greater reach of subversion, O'Nolan's destructive pursuits and plural and vacuous identities are co-dependent. It is, then, not difficult to see the importance of the many masks to an understanding of the anarchic and insurrectionist energies of the O'Nolan/O'Brien/na gCopaleen corpus. As Benjamin suggests of its necessary lack of identity, the destructive character, in its endeavours to distort received cultural wisdoms and to reduce 'what exists ... to rubble', 'sees nothing permanent' and 'tolerates misunderstanding'; and 'for this very reason, he sees ways everywhere. ... [H]e always positions himself at a crossroads'.³⁶ Indeed, the narrator of *The Third Policeman* echoes this position in a seeming metacommentary on the pseudonym: 'Do you recall that you told me I was not here at all because I had no name and that my personality was invisible to the law?'³⁷ Thought in these terms – disbanding with fixity, permanence and being understood – the pseudonym enables the various and wide targets of the O'Nolan/O'Brien/na gCopaleen corpus: from the convention of the novel to the multiple disappointments and hypocrisies of Free State culture and beyond. And as Benjamin elaborates in one of his more famous concepts, 'the technique of reproduction detaches the reproduced object from the domain of tradition. By making many reproductions it substitutes a plurality of copies for a unique existence'.³⁸ This process results, for Benjamin, 'in a tremendous shattering of tradition which is the obverse of the contemporary crisis and renewal of mankind'.³⁹ In such terms, the destructive character, as well as the reproduction of the author that occurs with the mask, delights in the obfuscation of authenticity, intention and originality so as to facilitate a destruction and shattering of tradition. Thus, O'Nolan's pseudonymous play, when thought through Montgomery's and Benjamin's accounts regarding the specific relationship between the pseudonyms and such anarchic literary efforts, derives less from an identity crisis caused by his culture than it does from a strategic effort to rattle the very roots of that culture.

Preceding and anticipating Benjamin, Nietzsche and Yeats respectively meditate on the fate of such mask wearers through their conceptualizations of the relationship between the mask and the individual. In *Beyond Good and Evil*, Nietzsche ponders what remains of the individual after the mask has been donned. In a much quoted aphorism on the concealment of goodness and shame, he writes, 'Everything profound loves the mask; the profoundest things of all hate even image and parable.'[40] With this, Nietzsche discusses the agency involved in the cultivation of a mask by the individual who has something either good or shameful to conceal: 'There are occurrences of so delicate a description that one does well to bury them.'[41] The necessity of such creations lie in the understanding that, for Nietzsche, both histories of benevolence and shame need to be cultivated and protected so as to remain instructive and continuously productive. Moving beyond the control and ownership of the mask by its cultivator, Nietzsche introduces the idea that the mask is also cultivated from without and is a creation which proliferates in spite of the individual. He writes,

> Such a hidden man, who instinctively uses speech for silence and concealment and is inexhaustible in evading communication, wants a mask of him to roam the heads and hearts of his friends in his stead, and he makes sure that it does so; and supposing he does not want it, he will come to see that a mask is there in spite of that – and that that is a good thing. Every profound spirit needs a mask: more, around every profound spirit a mask is continually growing, thanks to the constantly false, that is to say shallow interpretation of every word he gives, every step he takes, every sign of life he gives.[42]

Even if the profound individual or thing does not want to cultivate or wear a mask, or if the individual who has cultivated a mask and at a later point would like to discard it, it is not always possible to do so. Profundity, or the profound thing, necessarily entails the constitution of a mask, thus creating the enigma of the profound thing's origin and putting the good and shame which precedes it beyond representation. The mask, then, is not just a product of the person, but a product of the work they produce; and like the work produced, the meaning of the mask proliferates beyond the control of the individual who produces the work. As such, a potential danger of the mask is that the wearer becomes permanently lost behind its visage as it multiplies in meaning, a dilemma which Yeats addresses in his work.

In a manner reminiscent of Benjamin and Nietzsche, Yeats probes the enigma of the mask in his autobiographical writings. He writes that all happiness depends on having the energy to assume the mask of some other self; that all joyous or creative life is a rebirth as something not oneself, something which has no memory and is created in a moment and perpetually renewed. We put on a grotesque or solemn painted face to hide us from the terrors of judgement, invent an imaginative Saturnalia where one forgets reality, a game like that of a child, where one loses the infinite pain of self-realisation.[43]

Donning the mask, then, the writer undergoes a transformation, or a 'rebirth', 'as something not oneself', and so the mask wearer escapes subjectification.[44] And crucially, as a result of this process, the mask takes precedence over, and obscures, the subject, a circumstance which Yeats outlines in his poem 'The Mask': 'It was the mask engaged your mind/And after set your heart to beat/ Not what's behind.'[45] Thus, the mask roams and entices the interest of the public sphere, and not the individual behind it. Like Benjamin and Nietzsche, then, Yeats posits an insurmountable and irreducible distance between the mask and the biography of its wearer because the mask has no memory and is perpetually renewed from moment to moment both by its readers and the work of its fabricator(s). Criticism on Yeats's work has remained alive to this facet of his poetic practice; moving away from a binary approach to Yeats's life and corpus – exemplified in the man and the mask methodology deployed by Louis MacNeice and Richard Ellmann[46] – recent work has affirmed multiplicities and variations, as well as inconsistencies, of identity stemming from the mask.[47]

After Yeats – if not on a par with him – the other prominent man-of-many-masks in the canon of Irish literary modernism is O'Nolan. A fundamental difference between these two mask cultivators, beyond their identitarian dissimilarities, is that the latter's critics are immediately and always faced with the question of his pseudonyms given that he steadfastly published under these names and others. Yeats's readers can always treat the poet's masks as an eccentricity of a writer who can be understood as having heavily indulged in the spinning and weaving of autobiography. The same is not the case for O'Nolan, though that is not to say that critics have discovered anything less about his life. In doing so, criticism has often set aside the logic of the mask – the tool in Montgomery and Benjamin's respective terms which caters for destruction, and that in Nietzsche's and Yeats's terms which serves to destroy personal memory so as to make literature happen – to go from the mask to the life, and thus generate the biography and historical circumstances to explain the literature. As a result, and as is a standard feature of historicist criticism, the life and times of O'Nolan are often used as critical tools to explicate various aspects of the output attached to his name. As per such criticism, it can be suggested that 'it was also during his UCD days that O'Nolan first began experimenting with pseudonymous alter egos, most famously as Brother Barnabas in the student publication *Comhthrom Féinne*'.[48] Though a truism, such trends have led to the suggestion that the image of O'Nolan as a 'diffident individual skirting behind the masks of Flann, Myles and their various associates' is 'more a creation of his readers than his work', and that 'it is … questionable how important these individual identities are in themselves'.[49] This lack of engagement with the complexity of O'Nolan's many masks is symptomatic of some criticism of the O'Nolan/O'Brien/na gCopaleen corpus today. As in the above example, a tendency has developed to limit the play of the masks and pseudonyms so as to understand O'Nolan's life.

Pseudonym as text

There are two obvious reasons for this trend in O'Nolan/O'Brien/na gCopaleen criticism. The first: the problem of pseudonymity, and the significance of each pseudonym and how they differ and function in relation to Brian O'Nolan's biography and persona is very difficult to unravel. It is thus unsurprising that criticism has sought a homogenizing, or a one-caters-for-all, approach. The second reason, and which is important and particular here: the influence of new historicist and cultural materialist methodologies are evident in this phenomenon. Broadly speaking, both modes, which were respectively developed by Stephen Greenblatt and Raymond Williams, read texts as cultural documents which reveal the distribution of ideology and power in the respective period under analysis.[50] In recent years, the broadscale focus on ideology and power has dwindled in literary criticism, but the reading strategies of these approaches have remained, they have a stronghold in literary criticism currently and are often deployed to piece together the life and times of the writer under investigation. The influence of this is clear in the wealth of criticism that has emerged on the O'Nolan/O'Brien/na gCopaleen corpus in recent years. A feature, on occasion, of such criticism, however, is that it very often works against the mask and pseudonymity to reveal Brian O'Nolan as the authorial agent. For example, regarding the pseudonyms, it has recently been suggested that 'the ambiguity was created by the author himself, to be sure, and he was almost delighted that many failed to recognize him as the man behind Myles or Flann. But once we are certain that the author is dead – and we are – there is no point in keeping up this distinction.'[51] As such, the recommendation comes that 'it is time for literary criticism to make a step further and speak of Brian O'Nolan, the author'.[52] Though only recently prescribed, the sentiments of this dictum have tacitly been operative for some time. The results, however, of the annulation of the significance and difference of the individual pseudonyms, have in some cases led to the situation in which O'Brien, having been made equal to na gCopaleen and O'Nolan, has been cited as a novelist, a journalist and an almost political correspondent by critics slightly less accustomed to the histrionics and hoax-playing of pseudonymous writers of fiction. It has thus been suggested that 'the chronicles are part and parcel of Flann O'Brien's literary imagination and cannot be separated from his so-called major work ... the very structure and themes of *Cruiskeen Lawn* cannot be ignored as they are integral to Flann O'Brien's satirical genius'.[53] Elsewhere, 'Flann O'Brien estimated there were 1,200 licensed dance halls in the 26 counties, accounting for perhaps 5,000 dances annually, but he suggested there were another 5,000 unlicensed'; and that 'Flann O'Brien suggested an Irish bank, in the sense of a banking concern dedicated to furthering the interest of Ireland, did not exist'.[54] What is particularly destabilizing for historical verisimilitude in making na gCopaleen and O'Brien equal to O'Nolan is that the journalism cited might not even be verifiable.

The suggestion, then, that O'Nolan's reticent image is 'more a creation of his readers than his work'[55] underscores what Nietzsche describes as the potentiality of the mask to proliferate through the work of the reader: to quote Nietzsche again, 'around every profound spirit a mask is continually growing, thanks to the constantly false, that is to say shallow interpretation of every word he gives'.[56] Leaving Nietzsche's ill-fated designation of literary criticism aside for the moment, the idea that O'Nolan is a 'diffident individual skirting behind his masks',[57] rather than diminishing its significance, reinforces the logic of the mask as it occurs in both Nietzsche's and Yeats's terms: as Nietzsche suggests, 'such a hidden man, who instinctively uses speech for silence and concealment ... is inexhaustible in evading communication';[58] or as Yeats writes, 'it was the mask engaged your mind, And after set your heart to beat, Not what's behind'.[59] In this sense, it is, to rephrase Taaffe, unquestionable how important these individual identities or masks are in themselves. Rather than revealing O'Nolan as hidden behind them, the various masks and pseudonyms which are attached to his name function differently to displace any holistic identity which can be attributed to it whilst also confounding the use of his biography as an equalizing critical tool.

As such, the understanding of the problem of the pseudonym as (post) modernist and textual is significant to this issue, and contextualizing the question of the mask within that theoretical landscape provides an alternative framework for its conceptualization, as the examples of Benjamin, Nietzsche and Yeats demonstrate. Similarly, the fragmentary and radically symbolic forms which are a respective feature of O'Brien's novels and some of na gCopaleens's journalism establish these texts as hermeneutic enigmas which resist easy classification and identification with a stable author figure. For this reason, the extent of Montgomery's and Sheridan's contribution to this corpus is beyond precise accumulation because, as well as not knowing with precision the full scope of their involvement,[60] the radical symbolism of the writing destroys the trace of the author. To quote Long again: na gCopaleen becomes 'the means through which an idea, pun, invention, argument, theory is voiced' and provided 'whatever backdrop that theme requires'.[61] Barthes, particularly attuned to this dilemma concerning the relationship between the writer and the radically symbolic text, theorizes this predicament in 'From Work to Text'. He writes that the text

> can be read without the guarantee of its father, the restitution of the inter-text paradoxically abolishing any legacy. It is not that the Author may not 'come back' in the Text, in his text, but he then does so as a 'guest'. If he is a novelist, he is inscribed in the novel like one of his characters, figured in the carpet; no longer privileged, paternal, aletheological, his inscription is ludic. He becomes, as it were, a paper-author: his life is no longer the origin of his fictions but a fiction contributing to his work; there is a reversion of the work on to the life (and no longer the contrary).[62]

Indeed, *At Swim-Two-Birds* anticipates Barthes's meditation as two of its narrators become involved in the stories they are telling: Dermot Trellis famously features in his characters' story, and the student narrator saves Trellis from death by reconciling with his uncle. If Barthes's logic of the text is accepted, then, the author proceeds the text as much as they precede it. In such terms, the identity of the mask and the pseudonym is as much constituted by the text as by the writer who attaches the pseudonym to the text. As each new critical reading then proliferates the meaning of the text, the identity of the pseudonym is invested with further and different meaning. In these terms, as Barthes suggests, the word 'bio-graphy re-acquires a strong etymological sense' given that the act of writing becomes the act of creating a life as text; thus, the works of Marcel Proust or Jean Genet respectively allow their lives to be read as text, where text, as Barthes describes, is 'structured, but off-centered and without closure'.[63] Rather than O'Nolan lurking in the shadows or hiding behind these pseudonyms, then, it is the pseudonyms which continually give O'Nolan his posthumous identity, in turn making the name 'Brian O'Nolan' another mask, the final pseudonym, which is constituted and developed by this corpus. And this intricacy, at least in the case of this body of work, returns the question of the foundations and origins of Irish modernism to the specific dynamics of the text alongside, if not in place of, the location and time of the author's life. Probing this problematic further, the remainder of this chapter analyses how the modernism of O'Brien's *At Swim-Two-Birds* and *The Third Policeman* relates to the historical condition of post-independence Ireland.

Dissimilar and interrelated fragments

Like the pseudonyms, the narrative of *At Swim-Two-Birds* similarly resists easy classification and gives rise to dilemmas of cause and effect, and affinity and difference, concerning localizable historical origins through which its narrative structure might be explained. In her commentary on *At Swim-Two-Birds*, Taaffe writes that the narrator's biographical reminiscences 'clearly expose the contrast between Joyce's Dublin and post-independence Ireland … [they give] the impression that an unrelenting cynicism is the prevailing feature of intellectual life in 1930s Ireland'.[64] This 'framing narrative' – which Taaffe later suggests 'firmly roots this work in progress in 1930s UCD'[65] – is itself, as Long points out, a narrative fragment 'which stems from the narrator's autobiographical frame-tale'.[66] Both related to and separate from post-independence Ireland, it functions first and foremost as a structural device in the literary system and narrative fabric of *At Swim-Two-Birds* to commence the novel and introduce its three separate openings as says the narrator, 'One beginning and one ending for a book was a thing I did not agree with.'[67] The narrator introduces The Pooka MacPhellimey, Mr John Furriskey and Finn Mac Cool. The Pooka MacPhellimey is a ghost, 'a member of the devil class'.[68] Mr John Furriskey 'entered the world with a memory but without a personal experience to account for it', and Finn Mac Cool 'was a legendary hero of old Ireland'.[69] The narrator presents three characters who lack common relation and, though they take part in the same novel, are kept isolated from each other as it embarks. The narrator forewarns of this strategy: 'A good book may have three openings entirely dissimilar and inter-related only in the prescience of the author.'[70] The separation of narrative lines which are 'dissimilar and inter-related' and later conjugated outlines the artificiality and contrived nature of the narrative strategy. As it descends into non-reality, *At Swim-Two-Birds* performs fantasy and delusion by means of its fabricated and fragmented narrative structure and demolishes what was previously known as the novel to perform the idea that 'a satisfactory novel should be a self-evident sham'.[71] In her analysis of the novel, Long interrogates its fragmentary form and suggests that 'the sense of failing to achieve quite what has been promised, as what is promised can (perhaps) never physically exist, is precisely the right mode in which to represent Ireland of the 1930s'.[72] The following elaborates on this analysis of the text as an 'impossible project'[73] to interrogate the extent to which *At Swim-Two-Birds* can be read as actively representing 1930s Ireland and, particularly, the completeness and equivalence of that representation.

As the novel proceeds, it builds upon the process of fragmentation established at the outset: biographical reminiscences are presented between extracts from the narrator's novel and other extraneous fragments. Like Furriskey, it seems as if the narrator was born a novelist/student without a past in modern Dublin. There are no memories of parents, siblings or childhood. Moreover, the narrator's uncle, with whom he lives, is presented without any reference to wife, children or sibling(s). The situation of their living together is dissimilar (unalike, contrasting to 'normal' familial relationships) and interrelated (they live together). The narrator's domestic life thus resembles the relationship between the characters who partake in his novel. This dissimilarity and interrelatedness stems from the fact that nearly everything that happens in *At Swim-Two-Birds* is made relative to the writing of the narrator's novel. Most of the biographical reminiscences make overt reference to it and historical time is subordinated to its writing. The past, with the exception of Irish mythology, a narrative in itself, remains absent. As in the case of Furriskey, who was equipped with a memory but cannot provide a narrative of the past, memory as a faculty of recollection is rendered obsolete. In turn, the characters of the narrator's novel are dissimilar not because they are different but because, as the respective cases of The Pooka and Furriskey attest, there is no verifiable past to recount; and the other characters will not listen to Finn. The history of the Irish devil class is unknown, Furriskey was born at twenty-five and Finn will appear anachronistic to every other character. Yet, the characters are interrelated because they share (they are written into) the space of the narrator's novel. Similarly, the narrator and his uncle do not allude to there being any other family members who would lend to a discernible genealogy which they share. This raises the possibility that 'uncle' may be an empty signifier, used for the sake of convenience. The writing of the novel within the novel thus operates as an open structure to which the various fragments of *At Swim-Two-Birds* correspond. This structure, based on a procedure of conjugating dissimilar and interrelated fragments, is created by means of a performance which is also an erasure of memory – or like Benjamin's destructive character, it 'rejuvenates in clearing away the traces of our own age; it cheers because everything cleared away means to the destroyer a complete reduction, indeed eradication, of his own condition'.[74] The absence of recollection by the characters (with the exception of Finn) creates dissimilarity between them; they have nothing in common because there is no past which they remember and share. Yet it is also the absence of memory that creates the situation by which their relations can be labelled 'inter-related' as opposed to familial, genealogical or historical. The conjugation of narratives creates the situation in which memory cannot exist because, if it did, it would destroy the order that the characters occupy. Rather, they are allowed 'a private life, self-determination and a decent standard of living'.[75] As a result, narratives of the past are deployed only in instances concerning Finn. Yet, given that the narrator performs an 'incursion' into Irish mythology,[76] it is unclear how the importation of Finn into his novel should be understood when that story has, admittedly, been blitzed. As in this instance, a narrative of the past, when recollected by the narrator, is supplemented when written. The mythological past is not remembered or represented by the narrator but, instead, reimagined for the new purposes of the narrator's novel. As such, the narrator exploits mythology by supplementing that 'past', and thus, as Derrida writes of the supplement, 'makes an image ... by the anterior default of a presence'.[77] *At Swim-Two-Birds*, in these terms, draws attention to the overt manipulation of memory that occurs in the creation of narrative and has the cynical effect of demonstrating that satire is perhaps the finality of every narrativization of memory.[78]

As various characters are imported from different circumstances, the narrative demonstrates an inability to maintain a harmony between that which it conjugates. Such is the case when Finn relates the story of Mad King Sweeney. His recounting of this poem is the only instance in *At Swim-Two-Birds* when a recitation of past events is undertaken at length. But it falls on deaf ears despite being presented in earnest by Finn. Dismissive of Finn's poem, Shanahan introduces Jem Casey, a poet and 'a poor ignorant labouring man',[79] and Furriskey shows great interest in Shanahan's assertions of the quality and vitality of Jem Casey's poetry. When Shanahan remarks that Furriskey and Lamont should 'take that stuff your man was giving us a while ago ... without heed', Furriskey undertakes Finn's momentary defence before agreeing that it is 'a big mistake' to focus too heavily on such material.[80] The memory of the mythological past is thus renounced by Furriskey, Lamont and Shanahan. As they recount 'A Pint of Plain is Your Only Man', Finn falls asleep; and when provoked by Furriskey to respond to the poem, Finn relapses into telling the tale of Sweeney. The failure of forced cohabitation and conjugation, as manifested in this scene, becomes evident as the two groups lose interest in one another. Shanahan, Lamont and Furriskey choose to negate a supposedly shared cultural memory and silence the pertinence of the mythological past and thereby exclude Finn from their group. The situation by which their relations can only be labelled 'inter-related' is maintained. Thus, the narrator extends the gesture of reconciling past and present to demonstrate the processes of narrative conjugation that are necessary to achieve that effect. At the formal level, the narrator succeeds in amalgamating two of the narrative strands with which the novel embarks; but the conjugation is unsuccessful because the narrative strands fail to reconcile as they are amalgamated. A contradiction is thus produced by forcing a collection of entities which have nothing in common into cohabitation. In these terms, that which is ostensibly 'Irish' in the text is radically unrooted, even if the action occurs in contemporary Dublin.

The narrator, albeit, has another reason for including Finn in his novel. Finn is hired by Trellis to act as a guardian for Peggy, and so Finn loses his previous status as a legendary hero to serve in a new role as a guardian of 'domestic servants'.[81] Thus, an import from Irish mythology has been remembered in such a way as to give credence to his position in the contemporary situation in the Red Swan Hotel. Paul Ricoeur, in *Memory, History, Forgetting*, writes that

> forced memorisation is … enlisted in the service of the remembrance of those events belonging to the common history that are held to be remarkable, even founding, with respect to common identity. The circumscription of the narrative is thus placed in the service of the circumscription of the identity defining the community.[82]

In these terms, the narrator of *At Swim-Two-Birds* is performing the malaise of forced memorization. Finn is a culturally remarkable character and thus the narrator has decided to resurrect him from memory and have him hired by Trellis as a guardian of modern morality. The results, however, are disastrous. Finn is unable to adapt and is consequently unable to perform the task for which he has been hired. Furriskey and Peggy 'took a little house in Dolphin's Barn and opened a sweety shop and lived there happily for about twenty hours out of twenty-four'.[83] Finn's heroic stature and narratives of the past have no effect on the other characters and he becomes ineffective and completely out of place. As M. Keith Booker writes, '*At Swim* demonstrates a disjuncture between modern Irish culture and the culture of the medieval past'.[84] The idea of Ireland which 'should' bind their amalgamation is absent and thus the conjugation of these narrative lines does not succeed. Finn's inclusion proves to be deliberately redundant in that it allows the narrator to render the forced memorization of mythology as meaningless. Myth, then, fails as a method, as T. S. Eliot writes, 'of controlling, of ordering, of giving shape and significance to the immense panorama of futility and anarchy of contemporary history'.[85] Rather, in *At Swim-Two Birds*, myth features in the form of radically redundant narrative fragments.

Writing without origin

When Declan Kiberd suggests that the project of the narrator of *At Swim-Two-Birds* 'might be read as an attempt to restore a lost unity or at least to glue all the shattered pieces together as best as he can',[86] he both underscores the procedure established by the narrator – the constitution of his novel on a foundation of dissimilarity and inter-relatedness – and incites the possibility that an origin precedes its narrative play. *At Swim-Two-Birds* will not restore a lost unity, however, because there is no common origin through which that unity can be established. The novel can be read as the narrator's attempt 'to glue all the shattered pieces together as best as he can'[87] in the sense that these stories are set beside each other on the premise that they are individual fragments; but these stories which 'are constantly embarked upon, only to be interrupted by others before they can reach their appointed conclusion',[88] will not reach any conclusion because they have no shared memorial origin. This is made manifest throughout the novel by means of the irreconcilability of the narrative lines with which it embarks. Furriskey, Finn and The Pooka are all set alongside each other but will remain an isolated or incomplete part of something they cannot decipher because of their forced conjugation and lack of shared memory. Correspondingly, the incidental allusions to American fiction, medieval French, Russian literature and psychoanalysis are provided without belonging to a determined world system. As are the various found texts which appear in the novel: a letter from a horseracing tipster, the Conspectus of the Arts and Sciences, the epigraph from Euripedes. Not to mention the references to mythology and generic forms that feature through medieval Irish poetry, Irish mythology, fairy tale and the devil story. The ability to hold transitory information is a fundamental function of narratives that mimetically represent historical phenomena. *At Swim-Two-Birds*, however, is rife with memory deficit and proceeds nonetheless, lending a schizophrenia to its narrative form. The disappearance or the loss of a part of the narrator's manuscript does not hinder his project. He continues inspired by his loss.

At Swim-Two-Birds can thus be likened to the schizophrenic in the sense that, as Gilles Deleuze and Félix Guattari describe, the schizophrenic encodes information in memory but continuously produces narratives fragments which are accompanied by gaps.[89] The narrative creates gaps in its interrelation of dissimilar entities without explanation. The consequences of hybrid conjugation, however, are fatal. The birth of Orlick Trellis leads to the extermination of the content of Trellis's novel which exterminates the content of Trellis himself and, in turn, exterminates the narrator's novel. The narrative strata become so overfolded that the product performs upon itself because it is a sham; but this performance is an epistemological process as it produces realities which depend on the decisions made when writing; as Long suggests,

> the trope of a writing that produces not product but immediate effect is taken to greater extreme in the torture of Trellis, where persecution and writing about persecution becoming identical; writing is the production not of text but of manifest effects, and as such writing has immediate physical and ontological implications.[90]

The alternative realities thus possible are infinite; each narrative fragment can be rewritten and realigned. Indeed, as O'Nolan suggests in a letter to Patience Ross in September 1938 concerning an early manuscript of the novel, of which parts O'Nolan deems are 'terrible', 'the diseased bits can be cut out and replaced – possibly by a few pages from the Berlin Telephone Directory of which I have a copy, 1919 edition'.[91] Material can thus be translated from anywhere and made relevant to the novel's structure (dissimilar and interrelated), which in turn becomes a global network of affiliation; one, as Rebecca Walkowitz writes of the born-translated novel, 'which is less exclusive and less bounded than the nation's "community of fate"', as well as a possessive collectivism through which art and the nation would become intertwined.[92] Rather, as per Emily Apter's concept of 'deowned literature', 'translation, seen as authorised plagiarism, emerges as a form of creative property that belongs fully to no one'.[93] By means of its polyvocal introduction, its constant reorganization of form, its translation of various materials and its tendency towards hybrid conjugation, *At Swim-Two-Birds* writes, rather than represents, the absolution of fragmented universes, the mapping of divergences and the exploding into fragments of something that is innocent (the novel).[94] In doing so, it resists rendering the form of a holistic or shattered structure which might be anterior to it.

This understanding of the instability caused by the various fragments of *At Swim-Two-Birds* is at odds with the view that, by the same narrative process, it provides 'a moving shot of Irish culture at a significant point of transition',[95] or the idea that 'taken in isolation, many of these fragmentary mini-narratives provide brief archaeologies of the overdetermined culture of postcolonial Ireland'.[96] The 'Ireland' that is cited in these examples precedes and underpins the text, and acts as a critical tool which explicates its form. In this sense, 'Ireland' is written into the text as formative by the critical voice, and thus the text is made to represent post-independence Ireland after the fact. As this reading has aimed to demonstrate, however, everything that is 'Irish' in the text has no memorial origin (the fragments are 'dissimilar and interrelated') which ties it to Ireland. Ireland, rather, is an absent presence in the novel, not verifiably determining its cause of play. In these terms, the text supplements Ireland and Irish identity in the sense that, as Derrida writes of the supplement, 'it is not simply added to the positivity of a presence ... its place is assigned in the structure by the mark of an emptiness'.[97] Thus, as Jean-Michel Rabaté suggests that 'Irish modernism absorbed quickly various influences without unifying them',[98] *At Swim-Two-Birds* amalgamates Irish marginalia and trivia without belatedly representing, in a narrative of completion, the historical condition of post-independence Ireland.

Metaleptic play

A similar resistance to the representation of localizable extratextual origins is performed in *The Third Policeman*. Principally, the artificial process of narrative conjugation which the novel institutes is quite straightforward and is observable at the topographical level of the text. Put simply, it consists of the narrator making de Selby's philosophy the perspective from which he tells his story. The artificiality of that process becomes manifest through the footnoting of the main narrative, which is contextualized by another (invented) narrative. The effect of this second narrative, presented in the footnotes, has been questioned by critics. A general trend in criticism of *The Third Policeman* has been the consideration of it as a recreation of Faustian tragedy, wherein 'the narrator is a debased Faust, and Divney a debauched Mephistopheles'.[99] From this perspective, everything that happens to the narrator in the novel is retribution for the crime he commits, a feature of which, as Ondřej Pilný suggests, is that 'virtually all commentators on *The Third Policeman* have noted that a substantial part of the narrator's punishment consists in the fact that de Selby's bizarre theories are actually valid in The Parish and the doomed protagonist has to face their consequences'.¹⁰⁰ Criticism on the novel has also been concerned to locate its roots in the historical situation of post-independence Ireland. It has been suggested that the 'ludic spirals of this version of hell signal not the absurdity of "life" but the opacity of a system that is never less or more than concrete or immanent with the political, historical, economic and social registers that, though parodied, are always present';¹⁰¹ the Irish Free State has been implied as formative to this end. Taaffe searches for an Ireland in the text and, though reticent, pronounces its presence. She writes that 'if its landscape is recognisably Irish, it is also a parody of Irishness' and that 'its strange country may not be quite identifiable as Ireland, but is not quite familiar enough to be anything else'.¹⁰² Elsewhere, John Attridge has described the reality of *The Third Policeman* as a 'defamiliarised Ireland'.¹⁰³ And Michael Rubenstein has read the novel 'as an imaginative mapping of the nation-state' where 'the hell of *The Third Policeman* is the landscape of the national imaginary incorporated into the state's modern grid, resulting in sublime horror and comic farce'.¹⁰⁴ A different reading of *The Third Policeman* is put forward in the following, one that suggests the narrator effects a deliberate plan of escape, an escape from memory, and that the results are disastrous but intentional. Thus, instead of the narrator inhabiting a reality in which he is repeatedly punished, it is demonstrated here that the narrator pursues pleasure (the pleasure of focalizing reality through de Selby) through an active strategy that involves removing both memory of the past, his community and the outside world as actors in his life. In line with this understanding of the novel, the following argues that the historical condition of post-independence Ireland lacks constitutive meaning in, and does not verifiably determine, *The Third Policeman*'s narrative procedure.

The novel opens with the unnamed narrator giving the story of his life thus far: he is bereaved of both parents and lives on a plot of land which is tended by John Divney, a man employed by the narrator and paid by his accountants. Also mentioned is the narrator's love of de Selby, a philosopher or savant for whom the narrator 'committed [his] greatest sin'.¹⁰⁵ The narrator recounts the development of his and John Divney's plot to kill Old Mathers and rob his 'black cash-box'.¹⁰⁶ It is odd that the narrator gets involved in the plan to kill Old Mathers; he is financially secure, he has an inheritance and a house. At the beginning of the novel he says that 'I knew that if my name was to be remembered it would be remembered with de Selby's'.¹⁰⁷ Thus, the killing of Old Mathers has nothing to do with his destiny. What has become compromised, however, is the narrator's control over his home: 'After it was useless trying to tell [John Divney] it was

I who owned everything. I began to tell myself that even if I did own everything, it was he owned me.'[108] In turn, the narrator recognises the black cash box as an opportunity for change; 'if marriage meant that he himself would leave I think I would be very glad of it.'[109] For John Divney to leave, however, the latter would have to become financially independent; and if he did leave, the narrator could devote himself to de Selby. The narrator thus embroils himself in the murder of Old Mathers to remove John Divney from his life and to dedicate himself to the study of de Selby; it was for de Selby that the narrator 'committed [his] greatest sin'.[110]

Once the totality of the crime is achieved, the narrator undergoes a euphoria which is a focalization of reality from the perspective of de Selby's philosophy. Chapter one ends with the narrator on his way to collect the black cash box, and chapter two opens with the announcement that 'de Selby has some interesting things to say on the subject of houses'.[111] In chapter one, de Selby's thought is not presented, only the titles of his books, the names of his most prominent commentators and the narrator's obsession with the savant. In chapter two, after the crime, the narrative is presented with heavy reference to de Selby. Like Deleuze and Guattari's drugged and masochist bodies which seek to create a plane of consistency of desire,[112] the narrator, by means of committing the crime, creates the situation in which de Selby becomes integral to how he experiences and presents reality. As McDonald writes, 'it is the impulse to enter a sphere of philosophical abstraction, represented by de Selby, that leads the narrator to murderous disavowal of community obligation and local life'.[113] At the formal level, this is achieved by the footnoting of the narrative with extracts from, and commentaries on, de Selby's philosophy. From chapter two, then, the environment has changed, and the narrator acknowledges it as such. No longer on a mission, he is on a 'visit',[114] and his reality bears a likeness to a host of de Selby's warped observations about the universe ('a journey is a hallucination';[115] 'the usual processes of living [are] illusory'[116]):

> The outside light of morning had faded away to almost nothingness. I glanced out of the window and gave a start. Coming into the room I had noticed that the window was to the east and that the sun was rising in that quarter and firing the heavy clouds with light. Now it was setting with the last glimmers of feeble red in exactly the same place.[117]

The twenty-seven footnotes that occur after chapter two, as Keith Hopper writes, 'serve to lend credence to the ontological status of the imaginary de Selby'.[118] The effect, as Robert Lumsden suggests, is that 'the spirit of de Selby's footnotes has leaked into the text proper'.[119] Or as Hopper writes, 'de Selby's eccentric theories help shape the fabric of the narrator's hell'.[120]

This procedure of narrative conjugation – the narrator's thoughts with de Selby's philosophy, and thus the translation of de Selby's philosophy into a mode of existence – manifests the narrator's disconnection from John Divney and his unidentified community: 'There was nothing familiar about the good-looking countryside which stretched away from me at every view. I was now but two days from home ... and yet I seemed to have reached regions which I had never seen before and of which I had never heard.'[121] The outcome is the absolute deterritorialization of the narrator. All memory of his previous life is relinquished in the constitution of a new reality in which he has no identity:[122] 'I did not know my name, did not remember who I was. I was not certain where I had come from or what my business was in that room. I found I was sure of nothing save for my search of the black box. ... I had no name.'[123] Under the watch of John Divney, his work on de Selby was extrinsic and corresponding to a pleasure that could face interference. To create an uninterrupted relationship with de Selby – or, in Deleuze and Guattari's terms, to create a plane of consistency of desire[124] – the narrator necessarily involves himself in the murder to free desire from organization. Without identity ('I am not tied down for life to one word like most people';[125] and as Sergeant Pluck suggests, 'You can do what you like and the law cannot touch you'[126]) the narrator unties 'the pseudobond between desire and pleasure as an extrinsic measure'.[127] In doing so, the narrator creates and experiences the absolute singularity of focalizing reality from de Selby's perspective, through which he undergoes a becoming-de Selby. A becoming for Deleuze and Guattari 'constitutes a zone of proximity and indiscernibility, a no-man's land, a nonlocalisable relation sweeping up the two distant or contiguous points, carrying one into the proximity of the other'.[128] In this instance, the two contiguous points are the narrator and de Selby. In chapter one, they were in contact but separate. From chapter two onwards, the narrator becomes free from of all points (John Divney, his home, his community, Ireland), and they are thus uninformative of his subsequent experience: 'My surroundings had a strangeness of a peculiar kind, entirely separate from the mere strangeness of a country where one has never been before. Everything seemed almost too pleasant, too perfect, too finely made. Each thing the eye could see was unmistakable and unambiguous, incapable of merging with any other thing or being confused with it.'[129] As Terence Brown suggests, 'the narrator steps into a fantastical zone where Nature's laws of time and space no longer seem to apply, [this] is in fact the reality he now occupies and what we have taken for normality is unreal, phantasmal'.¹³⁰ The narrator has thus brought himself into proximity with de Selby by destroying the memory of the past, a feat which resonates with Deleuze and Guattari's proposition that 'becoming is an antimemory'.¹³¹ In the same way that 'pleasures, even the most artificial, are reterritorialisations' which interrupt the continuous flow of desire, 'memories always have a reterritorialisation function'.¹³² Memory, in such terms, is a preventative measure which would inhibit the narrator's internal focalization of de Selby. In this sense, the destruction of his past is essential for the narrator to achieve his objective of becoming lost in a process of total translation where little is identifiable ('It was a queer country we were in'¹³³), or understandable ('This is not today, this is yesterday'¹³⁴), and where the atomic theory is at work and bicycles develop human potentialities ('Michael Gilhaney', said the Sergeant, 'is an example of a man that is nearly banjaxed from the principle of the Atomic Theory. Would it astonish you to hear that he is nearly half a bicycle?'¹³⁵). Despite such anomalies, the narrator proceeds with his search: 'I decided without any hesitation that it was a waste of my time trying to understand the half of what he said.'¹³⁶ He succumbs to the strange talk of the policemen: 'The scene was real and incontrovertible and at variance with the talk of the Sergeant, but I knew that the Sergeant was talking the truth and if it was a question of taking my choice, it was possible that I would have to forego the reality of all the simple things my eyes were looking at.'¹³⁷ And the narrator uses de Selby's philosophy as a solution in these circumstances: 'I would have given much for a glimpse of a signpost showing the way along the "barrell" of the sausage after I had been some two minutes back in the white day-room with Sergeant Pluck.'¹³⁸ Ultimately, as the narrator's soul, Joe, suggests, 'Anything can be said in this place and it will be true and it will have to be believed.'¹³⁹ The narrator heeds this axiom as he proceeds with Sergeant Pluck on the road to eternity for which 'there is no signpost'.¹⁴⁰ The road leads them into a 'well-lit airy hall which was completely circular and filled with indescribable articles very like machinery',¹⁴¹ a place which, as Sergeant MacCruiskeen explains, 'has no size at all … because there is no difference anywhere in it and we have no conception of the extent of its unchanging coequality'.¹⁴² And significantly, in a metaleptic transgression of the boundaries between the novel's supposed narrative levels, de Selby's world-shaped sausage theory in which there is only one direction ('if one leaves any point on the globe, moving and continuing to move in any "direction", one ultimately reaches the point of departure again'¹⁴³) dictates its reality: MacCruiskeen thus suggests to the narrator, 'If you want to take another walk ahead to reach the same place here without coming back you can walk on till you reach the next doorway and you are welcome. But it will do you no good and even if we stay here behind you it is probable that you will find us there to meet you.'[144] The narrator, in such terms, has established the unfortunate, but desired, situation in which reality is focalized from de Selby's perspective.

Through this strategy, then, the novel bypasses and defers the historical condition of post-independence Ireland as an informative presence, despite the prevalence of Irish trivia (county councils, national schools and Mullingar, amongst other vestigial traces) in the text. Rather, that which the text manifests – the absolute deterritorialization which the narrator undergoes in the pursuit of experiencing reality through de Selby – ensures the reality produced will always be a supplementary reality. In the logic of the dangerous supplement, the narrative procedure of *The Third Policeman* deliberately and ironically manifests that it is 'exterior, outside of the positivity to which it is super-added, alien to that which, in order to be replaced by it, must be other than it'.[145] And like *At Swim-Two-Birds*, the narrative process of rendering memory extraneous interrupts the possibility of reading *The Third Policeman* as constituting an imitative mimesis of an extratextual signified. In turn, the novel remains to be read in relation to, and as different from, Ireland as a specific historical entity; untranslatable into a definitive context, it both resists and demands constant interpretation and translation. Its sclerotic disidentification of a determined historical anchor beyond itself caters for its varied reading as a Faustian tragedy, hell itself if read as the narrator's afterlife, a defamiliarized Ireland, and a focalization of reality through de Selby's philosophy. The conjugation of narratives (the first narrative with de Selby's philosophy), draws attention to the procedures of metalepsis that are at play and thus manifest the metaleptic process through which the story-world of the novel is created. In a manner similar to the earlier novel, it makes manifest its fictional status as an artefact and differently undermines the mimetic capabilities of the novel.

Irish modernism with(out) Ireland

By presenting fictional realities which perform the hybrid conjugation of fictional realities, *At Swim-Two-Birds* and *The Third Policeman* can be read as responding to literatures and ideologies – supplements in themselves – which resurrect cultural memory and prescribe it to a readership and population as applicable to national identity. In this sense, these novels, through parody and satire of culturally informative texts, seek to affect a recognition of literature as literature, prevent its consumption as reality and showcase the dangers of taking fiction as the law. What can thus be inferred is that these novels are active historical agents that are responsive to the literary culture from which they emerge as they seek to purge their society of falsely created memorial crutches – mythology, representations of rural poverty – by means of narrative performances which produce schizophrenic realities that are translations of literary realities. In turn, the consideration of these novels in relation to Irish culture will always be well founded. However, the critical tendency to consider these novels in an active relation of representation to post-independence Ireland has the effect of suggesting that the political condition of the nation from which these novels emerge is transmitted by these texts in a form of experimental equivalence. In challenging the representational claims of imitative and referential forms of writing, these novels are, in Barthes's terms, 'structured but off-centred, without closure'[146] and thus defer the possibility of belatedly representing a signified. Both texts supplement Ireland, 'making visible a distancing which is neither the same nor an other',[147] and thus Ireland disappears as a fixed entity as their respective narrative strategies are instituted In this sense, both novels are differentiated from much of the rest of the O'Nolan, O'Brien/na gCopaleeen oeuvre, particularly na gCopaleeen's *Cruiskeen Lawn* given its often moderately symbolic character. In such terms, the early novels resist being explained by O'Nolan, na gCopaleen or O'Brien's other writings as they differentiate themselves from the types of modernist modes that are instituted in the latter texts.

Genre is thus a crucial tool which sustains the possibility of reading a resistance to the imitative representation of the state of the nation in these texts. Its compression for the service of reading the historical period of post-independence Ireland can only strip these novels' formal singularities of their potency and produce a flat and standardized understanding of what constitutes (Irish) modernist literature. The radically symbolic narrative textures of *At Swim-Two-Birds* and *The Third Policeman* are integral to understanding the respective performances of literary destruction that they manifest, and their similarity and difference to, and affirmation and denial of, Ireland Concurrently, the same can be said for the problem of authorship posed by this body of work. The role of authorship as an historically stabilizing or determining factor in historicist approaches has the effect of reducing the indeterminacy and resistance created by the shifting pseudonyms of Flann O'Brien/Myles na gCopaleen, amongst the many others, to one proper name. As Derrida suggests, the proper name has 'no meaning, no conceptualisable and common meaning; they only have a referent';[148] 'when one claims to compare proper names and individuals, …

the comparison intends to compare the comparable with the comparable, the comparable with itself'.[149] Without discussing the implications of the hollowness of the proper name, an immediate problem in this case is that each pseudonym has more than one potential referent: in every case O'Nolan will serve as a referent, but so will the individual and unique parts of the oeuvre that the respective pseudonym corresponds to, thereby dividing the oeuvre from itself. As the recent publication of *The Short Fiction of Flann O'Brien* attests, criticism is still dealing with this problem. A story by John Shamus O'Donnell is included by the editors as 'an invitation to Flanneurs' to further investigate its likely authenticity as a work attributable to Flann O'Brien'.[150] Whatever the result of those investigations, a resistance to the representation of stable historical entities is still very much at play, all the while expanding the theoretical potential, and problematizing the origins, of Irish modernism.

3

Elizabeth Bowen's modernist history

Elizabeth Bowen holds a complex position within the canon of Irish modernism,[1] a feat largely stemming from her various affiliations and a wide critical reception. As Seán Ó Faoláin has written, Bowen declared herself as 'born and reared in Ireland, living in England, and writing in the full European tradition';[2] and because her writing conjugates and hybridizes genres – it blends modernist tendencies with bildungsroman, gothic, realism, romance and social comedy, amongst other forms – she has been regarded as an Anglo-Irish gothic writer, a British wartime writer, a modernist writer, a social realist writer and a Unionist writer.[3] In turn, Bowen has occupied a position in the margins of high and Irish modernism: not quite Irish, not quite English, not quite European; and not quite a modernist or realist either: Virginia Woolf's unclassifiable (non-)Irish other for some.[4] Bowen has thus always been elsewhere to narrow definitions of modernism, as well as the Yeats–Joyce–Beckett formulation and the 1930s assemblage of Irish modernism, making her a plural and enigmatic figure who evades simple categorization.

Similarly, Bowen's writing complicates what we identify as women's writing and its concerns; indeed, Bowen once stated that 'I am not, and never shall be, a feminist.'[5] Following Ezra Pound's terms for hard modernism,[6] which should not be identified with the gender of the author, Bowen's novels are the opposite of wobbly or hesitant; their narrative structures and operations are extremely deliberate, leaving little to chance. Simultaneously complicating their 'hardness', psychological ambivalence (the characters of *The Last September*, for example, remain ambivalent to the history that seems to be assailing their country) and stylistic ambiguity (the blending of realist and modernist forms) are pertinent features of Bowen's textual remit. Thus, as well as complicating expectations concerning national belonging and equivocating different definitions of modernism, her writing straddles what can be expected of hard and soft and masculine and feminine textualities, and thus modernist women's writing;

the valencies of Bowen's texts erode the possibility of specific ideological categorization or origination, the complications always multiplying in the face of delimitation.

While recent developments in the new modernist studies have secured Bowen's position in a broader modernist canon, her position in Irish modernist discourse remains irresolute. Feminist revisions of the modernist canon (particularly analysis of the formal autonomy of a host of supposedly middlebrow writings)[7] and the substantiation of late modernism (a mode of modernism concerned with formal self-consciousness while suspicious of, and critically revising, the central tenets of high modernism)[8] have been influential to Bowen's incorporation and centralization in modernist discussions over the last two decades. Particularly, her wartime novels have been critically feted as sites of interrogation for the cultural implications of the Blitz. Irish modernism, on the other hand, has, broadly speaking, emerged as a historicist and postcolonial discourse, largely concerned with the conditions of textual production. As such, Joe Cleary sees Bowen as belonging 'as much to the story of English as to Irish modernism'.[9] Indeed, only two of her ten novels – *The Last September* (1929) and *A World of Love* (1954) – are concerned with Irish matter. Contrastingly, Lauren Arrington suggests that 'Irish modernism accommodates writers who lived and wrote in and about Ireland, as well as those who were Irish by birth but who lived and worked outside of the country'.[10] As per the latter terms, Bowen is easily categorized, as is the case for Arrington, as an Irish modernist. Despite such grounds for inclusion, Bowen continues to remain absent, or glossed only in passing, in some of the major institutional responses to Irish modernism: *The Cambridge Companion to Irish Modernism* (2014) and *A History of Irish Modernism* (2018). Educated and living in England from 1906, Bowen was detached from the concerns of the Irish Literary Revival which, as of recently, is a key narrative fulcrum for Irish modernism. As Maud Ellmann writes, 'it [the Revival] completely passed her by, although her family lived for seven winters in spitting distance of the Abbey Theatre'.[11] Notwithstanding this detachment, Bowen, in 1942, declared herself as an 'Irish novelist':

> I regard myself as an Irish novelist. As long as I can remember, I've been extremely conscious of being Irish – even when I was writing about very un-Irish things such as suburban life in Paris or the seaside in England. All my life I've been going backwards and forwards between Ireland and England and the Continent but that has never robbed me of the strong feeling of my nationality. I must say it's a highly disturbing emotion. It's not – I must emphasise – sentimentality.[12]

Indeed, despite her self-definition as an Irish novelist, the disturbing emotion and lack of sentimentality concerning her writerly nationality, which reverberates in her writing, maintains rather than solves the enigma of Bowen's relation to Ireland. As does her position as a 'kind of spy', as Roy Foster puts it, during the Second World War when she provided information on the question of Irish neutrality to the British Ministry of Information, a feat which subsequently had her name recorded under erasure in Brendan Clifford and Jack Lane's *The North Cork Anthology* (1993).[13] Given such irresolutions, then, her work remains suspended in the liminal position of always becoming Irish modernist writing; it functions both within and beyond that canon. As such, to understand Bowen's writing as Irish modernism is to also tacitly imply that it maintains different and diverging concerns, the plurality of which proliferates the meaning of Irish modernism, as well as any definite origin which could be deployed as a critical tool to explain her texts.

A particular case in point concerning definitional praxis of Irish modernism is Bowen's *The Last September*, a text which seems to signal, while maintaining a distance to, Irish postcoloniality. When described as 'set in "the troubled times" – that is, the guerrilla conflict between the Irish, in arms for freedom and the British troops still garrisoning the land',[14] as well as a 'serene evocation of the final days of colonialist Ireland'[15] – *The Last September* would seem the Irish modernist novel *par excellence* which lends itself to a parallel reading with Irish postcoloniality. However, the mimetic mode which *The Last September* manifests can also be read, particularly in terms of its penetration of gendered social spheres, as obfuscating the War of Independence, destabilizing any fixed connections with the signifier 'The Troubles', deferring the postcolonial state which independence apparently brings, and putting in abeyance the historical understanding that Irish independence was won. Indeed, the novel presents a Big House environment so focused on its own turnings that the movements of history are not revealed in self-knowing form:[16] the 1916 Easter Rising, the War of Independence and the Irish Civil War, those events that exist as subject to Irish cultural and political remembrance, as well as the First World War, lack self-present meaning in the text.[17] Instead, in relating an ascendency story, it adds to the lineage of the Anglo-Irish Big House tradition, and the manner in which that tradition is recorded is perplexing. To read Bowen is for many an experience of immediate discomfort and labour. Her novels are so overwritten that it seems they are trying to protect themselves from their readers. Specifically regarding *The Last September*, the clunkiness and difficulty of the prose automatically creates a barrier between text and reader, and the narrative operation makes it difficult to discern who is speaking. As Bowen writes to Jonathan Cape in 1948, 'I'd rather keep the jars, "jingles" and awkwardnesses – e.g. "seemed unseemly", "felt to falter". They do to my mind express something. In some cases I *want* the rhythm to jerk or jar – to an extent, even, which may displease the reader.'[18] Naturally, such formal and stylistic features have drawn very different responses from critics concerning *The Last September's* relation to extratextual historical realities. Consider the following prominent and influential readings of the novel in recent years.

Susan Osborn suggests that our attempts to confine the world of *The Last September* to 'natural' and 'realistic' shapes will constantly be interrupted by what she suggests is the 'monstrosity' of the text itself.[19] Through a very close reading of the novel's mimetic mode, Osborn suggests that 'the mental image or meaning created by the words cannot always be judged similar, analogous, or even identical to what we know about the world from sense data directly … or from the words'.[20] Andrew Bennett and Nicholas Royle enable a greater parallelism between Bowen's novel and Irish postcoloniality, though they refrain from positing a homology or pointing to a particular historical reality which might be said to underpin the novel's play. They suggest that people, rather than being characterized, are 'being thought' in Bowen's writing,[21] which they note 'relates to the question of political and national boundaries':[22] 'The dissolution of the boundaries of the self is mapped onto the problematic construction of political boundaries in the Ireland of 1920.'[23] Jed Esty locates the antidevelopment plot of the novel in terms of the uneven development that is a manifest feature of both personal and political life in colonial contact zones, and thus reads Lois Farquar, *The Last September's* main protagonist, as a 'frozen adolescent figure whose own uneven development seems to correspond to the temporal oddities of the surrounding colonial history.'[24] Particularly for Esty, 'the language of the book encodes the broken and jagged time of a dying colonial modernity into the trope of adolescence, destabilizing the allegory of individual and social progress endemic to the classic bildungsroman'.[25] And Neil Corcoran sees Bowen's style as both a response to and a transformation of aspects of nineteenth-century realism and high modernism. To this end, Corcoran sees Bowen as a writer who has 'arrestingly strange, but intelligible things to say about Ireland and Anglo-Irishness, and that these have not been exhaustively described or interpreted'.[26] As such, Corcoran sees Bowen as a 'writer deeply engaged with some of the most urgent matters of both personal and public history in her time' and 'as a writer whose books, bending back, say much more complicated things about these histories'.[27] As it concerns *The Last September* and colonial history, Corcoran interestingly notes that the latter 'is most present ... when it is most absent'[28] and thus deploys it as a critical and explicative tool to analyse the text and to reveal the 'full, hideous force of the reality behind the words which float nebulously through the novel'.[29]

As these divergent critical appraisals show, *The Last September* stands as an exemplary case concerning definitions of Irish modernism – from Pound's comments on Joyce's modernism having nothing to do with Ireland to the more recent formulation of Irish modernism reflecting, and functioning as a parallelism, to Irish postcoloniality – because its abstruse mode of representation maintains a close yet complex relationship to the War of Independence as its historical signified.[30] Maintained in Bowen's novel is a focus on the daunting seriousness of literature as it manifests a very particular narrative strategy – sliding between the moderately and radically symbolic – which obfuscates any simple identification with ideology or politics. In turn, the relationship between (Bowen's) Irish modernism and historical revolution is perhaps divergent and not as clear as a parallelism. In response to this issue, this chapter argues, through analysis of the narrative operation of *The Last September*, that a particular feature of Bowen's Irish modernist writing is the substantiation of both a proximity and a distance, and thus a resistance to the ascription of meaning to that which, critically speaking, is often made to define the text and which it is made to remember: Irish independence.[31]

More specifically, this chapter builds on the above-mentioned critical appraisals to advance a different reading of *The Last September*, one which demonstrates how it has 'strange but intelligible things to say about Ireland and Anglo-Irishness',[32] and how the absent presence of colonial history is crucial to reading a deferral of that history in the novel. In large part, the defence built by Bowen's writing, operating, as Corcoran suggests, between nineteenth-century realism and high modernism, protects the vulnerability and uncertainty of the subject matter presented. As Ellmann notes, Bowen 'differs from the modernists in that she resurrects the omniscient narrator of the classical realist tradition. In most of her novels, she tacitly rejects the notion that the novelist should show, not tell'.[33] Such incorporations – omniscience and telling – are not simply reproduced in realist fashion in *The Last September*, however, but are recalibrated and warped as part of Bowen's oblique and obscure modernist representation which occludes simple access to a specific referent. Pertinently, in melding the Anglo-Irish example with world systems theory approaches, Matt Eatough chooses *Bowen's Court* for his analysis of Bowen's, and the Ascendency's, position in the relationship between metropolitan and colonial literatures and socioeconomic modernization and literary forms. Eatough justifies this choice by suggesting that '*Bowen's Court* has become a touchstone for scholars contesting or hoping to establish her Irish literary heritage'.[34] This is so because, as Eatough writes, 'Bowen's court departs in important ways from Bowen's experimental fiction, eschewing the convoluted syntax and elliptical narrative of the latter in favour of a realistic, linear depiction of Big House life'.[35] While a world-systems theory analysis of *The Last September* of course remains possible, its elliptical narrative and convoluted syntax, rendered through omniscience and telling, prove problematic to referential reading strategies. As it plays with and distorts realist modes of representation, particularly the tenets of omniscient narration, the novel's narrative performance has the effect of obscuring the cultural and historical reality of The Troubles, the War of Independence, and thus produces a continuous deferral of nationhood. Giving consolidated meaning to what Ireland might be, it is argued here, is a project which this novel refuses to undertake. Rather, it conjures in signification, a marriage of the readable with the impenetrable to both suggest and defer a historical reality. In such terms, it problematizes how and where we locate the metanarrative of Irish independence in relation to this novel and thus the relation between the macro narrative of Irish modernism and its constituent micro units. As this analysis goes against the grain of what has broadly been the dominant critical appraisal of Bowen's novel – that it maps onto Ireland's moment of decolonization – it undertakes a close-reading of several key passages in the text that manifest a jarring proximity and distance with the contours of Ireland's War of Independence. To demonstrate how the narrative operation of *The Last September* defers the historical event of Irish independence, it is first necessary to outline a theorization of its narrative form.

Omniscient narration

Omniscience is a controversial and contested term in modern narrative theory, particularly on the grounds that it invokes an impossible and godlike narratorial capacity. Critics such as Jonathan Culler and Nicholas Royle have productively debunked the term, denoted its obsolescence in critical vocabulary and called for specific textual engagements with the variety of narrative phenomena that become subsumed under the appearance of its operation.[36] The term is invoked here as Bowen's novel pre-empts and plays with such concerns regarding omniscience, and thus its associated terminology lends itself to an analysis of her novel's narrative operation. *The Last September* appears to feature an omniscient narrator, or what more specifically can be described as an extra- and heterodiegetic narrative device (terms of classical narratology which Culler maintains in his analysis of omniscience). Indeed, as, Culler notes, 'the best case [that] could be made for [omniscience] are those nineteenth-century novels from George Eliot to Anthony Trollope with extradiegetic-heterodiegetic narrators who present themselves as histors'.[37] As Bowen straddles the realist/modernist dichotomy, omniscience and what it connotes remain relevant to an analysis of how Bowen's modernism wrestles with realist narrative conventions. Provisionally, then, Shlomith Rimmon-Kenan's and Gérard Genette's respective sketches of omniscient narration are pertinent.

In *Narrative Fiction*, Shlomith Rimmon-Kenan offers a specific conceptualization of these terms. 'A narrator who is, as it were, "above" or superior to the story he narrates is "extradiegetic", like the level of which he is apart.'[38] And 'a narrator who does not participate in the story is called "heterodiegetic".'[39] The narrative device of *The Last September* is both seemingly above the story narrated and absent in the action. As Rimmon-Kenan suggests, it is the understanding of the extradiegetic and heterodiegetic narrator 'being absent from the story and their higher narrational authority in relation to it that confers on such narrators the quality which has often been called "omniscience"'.[40] Omniscience, though, for Rimmon-Kenan, 'is perhaps an exaggerated term, especially for modern extradiegetic narrators'.[41] Nonetheless, she maintains the utility of the term:

> The characteristics connoted by it are still relevant, namely: familiarity ... with the characters' innermost thoughts and feelings; knowledge of past, present and future; presence in location where characters are supposed to be unaccompanied ...; and knowledge of what happens in several places at the same time.[42]

In *Narrative Discourse*, Genette provides different and related specifications of the term. Genette writes that omniscient narration is a product of English-language criticism and notes that Pouillon calls it 'vision from behind' and that Todorov 'symbolises it by the formula *Narrator > Character* (where the narrator knows more than the character, or more exactly *says* more than any of the characters knows)'.[43] Genette, then, 'to avoid the too specifically visual connotations of the terms *vision, field* and *point of view*', deploys the term *focalisation* which corresponds to Cleanth Brooks and Robert Penn Warren's term 'focus of narration'.[44] Genette, in turn, 'will rechristen the first type (in general represented by the classical narrative) [what I am here analysing as omniscient narration] as *nonfocalised* narrative, or narrative with *zero focalisation*'.[45] But, as Genette later writes, 'the division between variable focalisation and nonfocalisation is sometimes very difficult to establish, for the nonfocalised narrative can sometimes be analysed as a narrative that is multifocalised *ad libitum*, in accordance with the principle "he who can do most can do least"'.[46] And as Rimmon-Kenan suggests, even 'the notion of "showing" is more problematic than it seems'.[47]

Problems of showing and focalization aside for the moment, the terms extradiegetic and heterodiegetic – and the fact that they connote a *non-human narrative device*, as Seymour Chatman suggests,[48] which is both absent from the story and a higher authority in relation to it – as well as nonfocalized narrative – 'where the narrator says more than any of the characters knows'[49] – suffice to commence an analysis of how Bowen's narrative poses problems to reading strategies which would analyse the novel as demonstrating colonial origins and as operating as a parallelism to Irish independence. Simultaneously, Bowen's narrative operation will ultimately pose problems to these accounts of omniscient narration, as well as some of the terms proposed by Culler and Royle, thus leading our analysis again towards post-classical narratology. To arrive in this terrain, this chapter demonstrates how Bowen's narrative operation dismantles the authority of omniscient narration to refer holistically to an all-encompassing and knowable history that would underpin signification, in turn adding further nuance to Bowen's modernist realism and establishing the irreducibility and singularity of her Irish modernism.

Fracture and deferral as the narrative of *The Last September*

The narrative of *The Last September* opens with an introduction to Danielstown, the Montmorencys, the Naylors, Laurence and Lois. The names of the characters are loosely presented and so one must work hard to decipher who is speaking in the opening passages of dialogue, the very first of which begins as free indirect discourse before topographically becoming dialogue on the page. It commences with the voice of Mrs Montmorency and reads as follows:

> 'And this is the niece!' she exclaimed with delight. 'Aren't we dusty!' she added, as Lois said nothing. 'Aren't we too terribly dusty!' And a tired look came down at the back of her eyes at the thought of how dusty she was.
>
> 'She's left school now,' said Sir Richard proudly.

'I don't think I should have known you,' said Mr Montmorency, who had not seen Lois since she was ten and evidently preferred children.

'Oh, *I* think she's the image of Laura – '

'– But we have tea waiting. Are you really sure, now, you've had tea?'

'Danielstown's looking lovely, lovely. One sees more from the upper avenue – didn't you clear some trees?'

'The wind had three of the ashes – you came quite safe? No trouble? Nobody at the cross-roads? Nobody stopped you?'

'And are you sure now about tea?' continued Lady Naylor.

'After all that – look, it's coming up now. No, Francie, don't be ridiculous; come in now, both of you.'[50]

This dialogue is relatively straightforward until the sentence which reads 'Oh *I* think she's the image of Laura –'.[51] It is both difficult to identify who says this sentence and to determine who Laura might be. Regarding the latter, it is later revealed that Laura is Lois's deceased mother. Concerning the speaker, it is impossible to say; it could be either Mrs Montmorency or Sir Richard. Similarly, the sentence which follows – '– But we have tea waiting. Are you really sure, now, you've had tea?'[52] – provokes momentary disorientation until a little later, because of the repetition of the offer, it can belatedly be ascribed to Lady Naylor. The two speech passages in between, after close and focused (re)reading, can be ascribed to Mr Montmorency and Sir Richard, respectively, and then the dialogue ends in a manner as perplexing as it begins. Concerning the last two sentences, it is very difficult to say who is speaking, to discern what they are directed to look at that is coming up, and to know who Francie might be. Again, with focused rereading and the benefit of information that the narrative device will later provide, it can be determined that Sir Richard is supposedly speaking and that Francie is Mrs Montmorency; but to the demand or suggestion 'look, it's coming up now',[53] it is difficult to define to what Sir Richard is referring. In the passage of narrative commentary which follows this dialogue, it is related that 'the car with the luggage turned and went around the back, deeply scoring the gravel'.[54] Sir Richard perhaps directs their attention towards this car, but nothing confirms this interpretation. The description of the car does not necessarily connect it to Sir Richard's direction, and no confirmation is later given by a character or the narrative device. An indeterminate gap in signification is thus opened between what Sir Richard says in dialogue and what is later related in narrative commentary. Moments like this are not isolated occurrences in Bowen's writing; they are a characteristic feature of it. Particularly concerning *The Last*

September, gaps in signification between character and narrative device are an important and specific feature of the narrative operation, especially in relation to The Troubles, the War of Independence (two terms which do not feature in the text), the event which apparently forms its fabric and which a host of criticism has read the novel as actively representing.[55]

In the third chapter, the narrative focus remains with the same characters and a war which is affecting the community is alluded to for the first time. Mrs Montmorency is presented as making an initial reference to it: 'Listen, Richard … are you sure we will not be shot at if we sit out late on the steps?'[56] Responding ironically, Sir Richard says, 'We never have yet, not even with soldiers here and Lois dancing up and down the avenue. … Do you think maybe we ought to put sandbags behind the shutters when we shut up at nights?'[57] The arrival of Lady Naylor with Laurence momentarily interrupts the discussion of the ongoing violence as the party relocate to the dining room. At dinner, the subject of the implied violence returns; the narrative device relates that 'Lady Naylor spoke of the way things were',[58] a sentence shrouded with ambiguity and secrecy concerning its referent. One might belatedly suspect that Lady Naylor was explaining the situation regarding the war, yet her statement is never clarified. The dialogue which follows begins with Mr Montmorency asking Laurence, 'What do *you* think of things?'[59] To which Laurence responds, 'Things? Over here?'[60] Laurence's uncertainty casts irresolution over the possibility that Lady Naylor was speaking of a war. Presented as both a highly aloof and a highly intelligent character, it is difficult to say whether Laurence is ignoring the conversation as he is ambivalently observing the table or whether Lady Naylor was speaking in so vague a manner that Laurence is indecisive as to the referent of the conversation. Laurence responds to Mr Montmorency by saying, 'Seem to be closing in … rolling up rather.'[61] The short conversation between the two men is then extinguished by Lady Naylor; after an unexplained glance at the parlour-maid, she says, 'Now you mustn't make Laurence exaggerate. All young men from Oxford exaggerate.'[62] To which Laurence responds, 'If you have noticed it … it is probably so.'[63] Again, Laurence's words promote confusion; they might be a performance of his own potential for exaggeration or refer to the fact that things are 'closing in' or 'rolling up'.[64] Either way, no clarity is provided concerning the implied war. The narrative operates in a manner which cryptically hints to it, but the overt presentation of the fact is deferred by the way the narrative device introduces the subject – 'Lady Naylor spoke of the way things were'[65] – and the invalidating manner in which the characters thereafter comment on the implied subject matter. In the manner of a radically symbolic literature, then, Bowen's novel defers, and is dilatory in relation to, a specific signified.

The narrative focus then switches to Lois. Directly following Laurence's nonchalant response, in an effort to make things more real, Lois asks Mr Montmorency, 'If you are interested, would you care to come and dig for guns in the plantation? Or if I dig, will you come as a witness?'[66] Lois has heard that there are 'guns buried in the lower plantation' and that Michael Keelan 'swears he was going through there, late, and saw men digging'.[67] Sir Richard, however, discredits what Lois has heard: 'Ah, that's nonsense now! ... I will not have the men talking, and at all accounts I won't have them listened to.'[68] Lois nonetheless persists and suggests, in order to know, 'that one ought to dig',[69] a comment which simultaneously functions as a metacommentary on the relationship between the ambiguity of the novel and the necessary performance of symptomatic reading to uncover, or dig for, what might or might not be found within its narrative fabric. In such terms, Bowen's text is self-reflexively concerned with how meaning is uncovered within its narrative operation and thus invites investigative digging while occluding direct access to a historical referent through the various narrative strategies – absence, ellipsis, omission, secrecy – which pervade the telling of this story. The conversation (and the invitation for symptomatic digging) continues with Sir Richard again challenging Lois before he introduces the subject of the army, but in no clear fashion as to why they are present: 'This country ... is altogether too full of soldiers, with nothing to do but dance and poke old women out of their beds to look for guns. It's unsettling the people naturally.'[70] The conversation remains with the plight of the army until Laurence says, 'It would be the greatest pity if we were to become a republic and all these lovely troops were taken away.'[71] This is the first mention of a republic, but for where and who remains under-defined. Lois, in reaction, calls Laurence a 'fool',[72] yet the nature of this reproach is also unclear because Lois's supposed love interest, Gerald Lesworth, has already been introduced in the narrative: is Laurence a fool for suggesting that it would be a pity for the country to become a republic or for suggesting that it would be a pity for the soldiers to leave, or both? Lady Naylor concludes this nebulous conversation concerning the implied war and the army by saying, 'From all the talk, you might think anything was going to happen, but we never listen. I have made it a rule not to talk, either.'[73] The conversation thereafter veers to other concerns and leaves the subject of the war suspended.

In chapter five, at the tea and tennis party, a different perspective is related on the implied war; Gerald and the Hartigan sisters are focalized in discussion.

After they tell him a story concerning their sister in London, a short dialogue is related in which Gerald suggests that he might be leaving soon:

> 'Well, we shall all be leaving you soon, I dare say; all we jolly old army of occupation.'
> 'Oh, one wouldn't like to call you that,' said Miss Hartigan, deprecatingly.
> ' – As soon as we've lost this jolly old war.'
> 'Oh, but one wouldn't call it a *war*.'
> 'If anyone would, we could clean these beggars out in a week.'
> 'We think it would be a great pity to have a war,' said the Hartigans firmly. 'There's been enough unpleasantness already, hasn't there? … And it would be a shame for you all to go,' added Doreen warmly.[74]

The narrative device, through free indirect narration, intervenes at this point on behalf of the Hartigan sisters to say that they 'only hoped he would not be shot on the way home; though they couldn't help thinking how, if he should be, they would both feel so interesting afterwards'.[75] This interjection is odd given that one, or both, of the Hartigans suggests that it is unsuitable to consider Gerald a member of an army of occupation and that one would not call what is happening a war. If Gerald is not a member of an occupying army and if a war is not ongoing, then there would be no reason to worry about him getting shot. The problem of ascertaining what the Hartigans believe is complicated by the fact that Norah and Doreen Hartigan are presented as almost synonymous in dialogue and by the narrative device. It is thus difficult to separate their respective opinions, to discern what their shared opinion is and to analyse the reliability of the narrative device concerning the presentation of their opinions. Even if both Hartigan sisters are concealing what they 'really' think of Gerald in dialogue, or if their responses to Gerald are heavily ironic, there is a discord between what one or both say in conversation and how they are presented in narrative commentary after the fact. This fracture in signification occurs because the accounts rendered at different narrative levels (through character dialogue at the diegetic level, and through the narrative device at the extradiegetic level) do not accord. The presence and meaning of the war, as a result, is invalidated as it is related in this scene. The narrative device creates the tantalizing possibility of their awareness of the war but not without contradicting what they say in dialogue. Thus, the reality of the war remains deferred because the content recorded in dialogue does not conform to the information presented by the narrative device.

In chapter six, with a change in narrative focus, the subject of a war is more directly alluded to in conversation. Mrs Vermont, the husband of a subaltern officer, addresses the current cultural predicament:

> All this is terrible for you all, isn't it? I do think you're so sporting the way you just stay where you are and keep going on. Who would ever have thought the Irish would turn out to be so disloyal – I mean, of course, the lower classes![76]

Mrs Carey, another attendee at the tea and tennis party, soon after responds, 'Well, I hope you are pleased with us now you have just come.'[77] To which Mrs Vermont responds, 'We came to take care of all of you ... and, of course, we are ever so glad to be able to do it.'[78] The characters continue to circumvent the implied cultural event until the narrative device offers the following explanation:

> Five days ago an R.I.C barracks at Ballydrum had been attacked and burnt out long after defence. Two of the defenders were burnt inside it, the others shot coming out. The wires were cut, the roads blocked; there had been no one to send for help, so there was no help for them. It was this they had had all been discussing, at tea, between tennis: 'the horrible thing'.[79]

As is evident from this passage, it is the burning of a barracks, and not necessarily The Troubles, which is the subject of conversation. The narrative device, in a manner similar to Mrs Vermont and Mrs Carey, when presenting its version of the burning of the barracks, minimizes the description of the event and restrains the potentiality of its proliferation. The narrative operation thus resists inferring that this event is intrinsic to a wider war and so forestalls the connection of the micro example to a macro metanarrative, which the novel refrains from providing (indeed, the location of Danielstown is not registered in the novel). As in this instance, like those previously identified, the narrative device provides certain information on an issue while the characters provide different and scant information on the same issue, thus establishing a fractured account of the event. The reader is thus left to amass and assemble the different versions that are related. As the narrative commentary proceeds, it supplies the apparent opinion about the troops and denotes a total lack of identity therein, in the process complicating their relation to ongoing events:

> No one could quite understand why Captain Vermont and the subalterns did not seem more appalled and interested. It was not apparent how the subject rasped on their sensibilities. These things happened, were deplored and accepted, and still no one seemed to look on David or Gerald, Smith, Carmichael, or Mrs Vermont's Timmie as a possible remedy. Here they all were, playing tennis, and

everyone seemed delighted. 'If they'd just let us out for a week' – felt the young men. David could not look up as he stirred his tea. What was the good of them? This, he felt, everyone should be wondering. But the party would indeed have been dull without them, there would have been no young men. Nobody wished them elsewhere.[80]

Thus, Captain Vermont and the subalterns remain unappalled and disinterested regarding the burning of the barrack, and perhaps disengaged from its wider implications. David, Gerald, Smith, Carmichael and Timmie are seen as superfluous to ongoing affairs. David's question – 'What was the good of them?'[81] – which the other characters do not hear, is unexplored and unanswered, and its subject ('them') remains without further explication. And with everybody seemingly 'delighted' at the tennis party which would 'have been dull without them … nobody wished them elsewhere',[82] the characters reduce the depth of the horizon of their orientation in the world and turn away from the reference point of the wider predicament. The routine of the habitual tennis party thus aids their ontological security and the diminishment of external sources of anxiety, which are both bound up with the distancing of the event which remains under-represented and under-defined in the text. As such, the subalterns' relation to the Royal Irish Constabulary Barrack is curtailed in the narrative commentary, which further disconnects those at the tennis party from any coherent relation to the immediacy of the supposed War. As in this scene, then, when The Troubles seems to form the referential focus of conversation, the phenomenon is not referenced clearly by a character. Similarly, when the narrative device assumes the task of 'filling in', or providing the voice of the collective subject (as is apt of extra- and heterodiegetic narrative devices of high realism), it proliferates the circumlocution which the characters display and thus occludes, rather than confirms, the wider cultural event. The narrative operation, in such terms, chaotically and confusingly implies an ongoing war whilst concurrently deferring its presence.

The narrative focus then turns to Gerald and Lois's affair. Directly following the previously quoted passage concerning the barracks and the army, it is related that 'Lois had been worried chiefly because Gerald had illusions about her'.[83] With this, all of the previous dialogue concerning the attack at the barrack and the narrative device's interjections on that subject come together in a single sentence that Gerald utters: 'Well, we all feel a little rotten about that barrack.'[84] In this sentence, the event that has not been talked about by any of the characters, but has been ceded by the narrative device, is related by a character. The casual reader will probably have accepted the discrepancies between what is uttered in dialogue and what is related by the narrative device (or simply consign such difficulties to 'Bowen's style') and allow Gerald's statement coherence. It remains unclear, however, if Gerald witnessed the event, and so the possibility remains that he is performing for Lois and merely repeating the army's ideological line (let's not forget that 'no one could quite understand why Captain Vermont and the subalterns did not seem more appalled and interested').[85] Lois, eager for such events to be made real and witnessed, responds that he should not feel ashamed: 'Don't!,' she says,

> do you know that while that was going on, eight miles off, I was cutting a dress out, a voile that I didn't even need, and playing on the gramophone? How is it that in this county that ought to be full of such violent realness, there seems nothing for me but clothes and what people say? I might be just as well in some kind of cocoon.[86]

Even at a distance of eight miles, the event lacks presence for Lois as its reality cannot be felt or registered. Its impact and violence is all too absent, and so Lois, like most other characters in the novel, lacks a coherent language in which to represent the supposed event.

As with this particular instance, it is clear that Lois has little to no access to national affairs in her adolescence, and so the relationship between gender and the novel's plot becomes pertinent. Indeed, later when driving Mr Montmorency home in the cart, Lois rails against her cocooned exclusion, by virtue of her gender, from social affairs, as well as the perceived nationalist project, which she dubs as an endeavour with no intrinsic solution: 'What is it exactly that they mean by freedom? What does it affect? What is it besides an excuse for war? ... Then to fight's absurd; ... It's a hopeless kind of beginning.'[87] Notwithstanding, Lois remains alone with her avid concerns as Mr Montmorency does not respond; like those at the tennis party, Mr Montmorency has also reduced his orientation in the world to trivial affairs. And on immediate re-entry, the narrative device neither confirms or disavows the implied event which has held the focus of Lois and Mr Montmorency's conversation, signifying instead the 'unsaid [which] would exercise now a stronger compulsion upon their attitude'.[88] Without access to the realities which assail her country, Lois's isolation is reinforced by the narrative operation as the implied event is held in abeyance. With the unsaid kept in suspension, the historical reality of the Troubles remains absent through a narrative operation which resists ascribing meaning, as well as assuming a position of equivalence, to an extratextual historical process of colonization and decolonization. As a result, it is perhaps overdetermined to substantiate *The Last September* as 'a type of coming-of-age story for both Lois and her country',[89] or to suggest that Bowen is 'trying to locate the Ascendancy as the centre and the focal point of the War of Independence'.[90] As Esty suggests, the novel's antidevelopmental plot of frozen youth caught in an anachronistic social class ensures that the bildungsroman allegory of national and personal formation occurs 'in an objectified or estranged form'.[91] As suggested here, a component of that estranged form concerns how the narrative operation dislocates Lois and the inhabitants of Danielstown from the monumental history of Ireland in the 1920s by absenting the presence of the latter story in the text.

Lois is not alone in her attempts to have circumstances explained. Marda repeats Lois's efforts, though she too fails to get a coherent response from Mr Montmorency. She inquires, 'How far do you think this war is going to go? Will there ever be anything we can all do except not notice?'[92] Nevertheless, Mr Montmorency breaks down the coherence of the supposed event. He responds 'as though beneath the pressure of omniscience', 'A few more hundred deaths, I suppose, on our side – which is no side – rather scared, rather isolated, not expressing anything except tenacity to something that isn't there. And deprived of heroism by a wet smother of commiseration.'[93] Under pressure to respond to an ill-defined omniscient power – which perhaps prompts a need to acknowledge the war, perhaps it is an ethical injunction to respond to atrocity and death, or perhaps a demand to displace Marda's overdetermined assertion of the presence of war (the most forthright in the novel) – Mr Montmorency denotes a lack in the identity in 'our side', in turn collapsing the sense of a coherent force which is opposed to another and fighting for clear and obvious outcomes. Similarly, their implied affective state – a 'wet smother of commiseration' which deprives them of heroism – induces a variety of possible causes. To begin the list of obvious (and divergent) examples which might apply here to 'our side', this commiseration could occur as an after-effect of British involvement in the First World War, Anglo-Irish or Irish involvement in the First World War, British involvement in Ireland or the relations of the Anglo-Irish in Ireland. Mr Montmorency's statement remains without further explanation and is left suspended in the text, dispersing, in turn, any unitary identity to Marda's denoted war.

When it then comes to what is regarded as a critical episode in the novel – the scene in the mill where Marda is shot by an apparent IRA gunman[94] – it is unsurprising to find a similar resistance to representation at play in the narration of the event. Lois and Marda, while walking with Mr Montmorency, are focalized as happening upon an abandoned and ghostly mill. They enter it without Mr Montmorency and find a man sleeping. After they unintentionally wake him, the narrative device relates that the man, while pointing a pistol at them, 'sat looking ... with calculating intentness, like a monkey, then got up slowly'.[95] A dialogue is then presented between the three in the mill:

'Don't be silly,' said Marda. 'Go to sleep again. We're not –'

'Are there any more of yez?'

'One – not interested either. Better let us go now, there will be less talk.'

'We're just out for a walk,' said Lois, surprised at her own voice.

'Indeed,' said the man 'It is a grand evening for a walk, no doubt. Is it from Castle Trent y'are?'

'Danielstown'.[96]

At this point, the narrative device re-enters and, after briefly focusing on Lois, relates that 'the man, who did not cease to regard them with uneasy dislike, asked which way they had come, whom they had met, if they had observed any movement of soldiers about the country'.[97] In dialogue, 'the man' remains unprobed as to his identity and remains unidentified, with the exception of his gender, in the passages of narrative commentary which follow. Thereafter, the narrative focus switches to Mr Montmorency who is sitting alone and smoking outside the mill. He is presented as coming to terms with the fact that he loves Marda more than he does Francie, his wife. As such, the subsequent events in the mill remain unrepresented, and with the man holding Lois and Marda at gunpoint, an intimacy and privacy is manifested as particular to his control of the public sphere. As Mr Montmorency rehearses the revelation of his love for Marda, a shot is heard, 'making rings in the silence'.[98] The narrative focus remains with Mr Montmorency who becomes immediately concerned for Marda's welfare. He goes to meet them as they exit the mill, and they, upon meeting him, pretend that nothing has happened. Marda downplays the event: 'I have lost some skin ... Just, a pistol went off – you heard? – by accident.'[99] And she does not suggest that she was the target of a shooting: 'Look at my beastly hand – I was holding on to the door.'[100] When Mr Montmorency demands that he be allowed enter the mill, Lois says, 'We swore.'[101] This declaration goes without interrogation as Marda explains, 'Someone went upstairs backwards, not very sensibly, not having eaten much for four days. There was some plaster, the pistol went off, naturally.'[102] Mr Montmorency twice more repeats his demand to be allowed entry and Lois reiterates the oath which herself and Marda apparently took. The situation diffused, Mr Montmorency does not enter and the secret of the man's identity remains intact. Lois and Marda's conversation thereafter does not turn to what happened inside the mill, but instead they engage the question of Mr Montmorency's romantic interest in Marda. Lois finishes their conversation by repeating the demand that the events of the mill are not told elsewhere, thus maintaining the privacy of the man in the public domain: 'A swear *is* a swear, isn't it, even in England?'[103]

As a result of its circumlocutory presentation and investment in non-representation, the narration of this scene refrains from closing in on a specific signified. The man's manner of speech might seem to suggest an Irish accent, and his suggestion that 'they had better keep in the house while y'have it' indicates his knowledge of the ongoing conflict. Yet neither his manner of speech (which is a literary imitation of voice, and mainly differentiated here through the use of a 'z' for the plural form and the contraction of 'you are' to 'y'are'), nor his advice to Lois and Marda, fully reveals his involvement in the Irish Republican movement. Both his manner of speech and his advice require a critical intervention to make them mean more than they relate, without the intention of which the man remains unconfirmed as an IRA gunman in the text. As J. Hillis Miller suggests concerning the ethics of reading in *Topographies*, 'the barrier forbidding further progress beyond what is now presented [is] no more than a trope, a rhetorical artifice. "*If* it [literature] had a voice, it would say", but of course it does not have a voice.'[104] Following Miller's logic, the man's identity, as a result of Bowen's tantalizing mode of representation, is undecidable. Moreover, as his gun ironically doubles as his penis (Marda and Lois catch the man in the 'calm of sleep'; they are not scared but 'embarrassed by this curious confrontation'; neither of them had seen a pistol at this angle; it was short-looking scarcely more than a button'; like a 'monkey' with an erection, his 'pistol maintained its direction'[105]) the threat which he poses, both in the mill or as a potential rebel with a gun in a war, is underplayed and subverted in the representation of this scene. And this ironic ambiguity between the gun and the penis signals another reasoning, beyond a masculine control of the public sphere, for the intimacy and privacy of the scene and Lois and Marda's awkward behaviour after the event: 'There never was anybody, we never saw anybody,' says Lois; 'we are neither of us good at explosions,' Marda suggests.[106] Furthermore, because 'the man' is only partially penetrated by the narrative operation, and because the scene of the apparent shooting is not narrated during the moment of the event, nor narrated after the event by those who witnessed it, no determined connection is made to The Troubles. Likewise, the oath ('We swore') which Lois and Marda apparently took is not revealed and so remains a structural secret of the narrative.

Thus, in and after the event which supposedly testifies to an IRA encounter, there is no textual testimony to confirm this phenomenon, leaving its presence unqualified in the text. At the moment it creates it as a possibility, the narrative operation interrupts its potential to operate referentially concerning the wider context of the Troubles. Like Pascale Casanova's translation, Bowen's text renders 'political and national issues into its own terms – aesthetic, formal, narrative, poetic – and at once affirms and denies them',[107] thus manifesting an affinity and an incommensurability between literary text and national origin as a deterministic explicative tool. In such terms, the war, rather than being 'off-stage' as Peter Kalliney writes, remains an absent presence which is deferred by the narrative of *The Last September*. Kalliney suggests, regarding this same event in the mill, that 'the narrator simply blocks direct access to the scene, allowing what is ostensibly the most important moment in the story to happen behind the dramatic curtain'.[108] And so Kalliney writes that 'here, in Revolutionary Ireland, nearly all the action is displaced and rerouted, happening on the fringes of the coming-of-age plot'.[109] Continuing with the stage metaphor, Kalliney suggests that 'yet we would be mistaken if we conclude that the narrative totally supresses the violence happening, for the most part, offstage'.[110] The reading tended above differentiates from Killiney's, and other such readings of Bowen's novel,[111] by disputing the applicability of the stage metaphor to the analysis of narrative fiction, which, as understood here, is constituted by narrative presentation and structural absences, ellipses, omissions and secrecies. In such terms, the war is not 'offstage' but remains an absent presence which is bypassed and deferred in the text because the narrative is replete with structural secrecies (secrets without secret, crypts without depth, as Derrida denotes these events particular to the institution of literature)[112] which are specific features of Bowen's oblique unrolling of events. In this instance, the identity of the man, the event in the mill, the ironic ambiguity as to whether the pistol or the penis 'went off, naturally',[113] and Lois and Marda's subsequent oath, remain secrets in the text. While the stage metaphor duly caters for the explication of the novel in terms of the War of Independence, and thus facilitates the 'completion' of Bowen's absences, gaps and ellipses with historical detail, such analysis foregoes the structures particular to the modernist novel, which in the case of Bowen's text have the particular effect of leaving the presence of the War of Independence unqualified in the narrative. Inherent to the fabric of *The Last September*, Bowen's structural secrecies, which both invite interpretation and resist deterministic qualification, always remain enigmatic in terms of a specific meaning or referent which would occur beyond the text, and thus establish a proximity as well as an irreducible distance between text and extratextual history.

Gerald's death, recognized in criticism as an IRA assassination,[114] is similarly under-represented in the text. It is related that

> the world did not stand still, though the household at Danielstown and the Thompsons' lunch party took no account of it. The shocking news reached Clonmore that night, about eight o'clock. It crashed upon the unknowingness of the town like a wave that for two hours, since the event, had been rising and toppling, imminent. The news crept down the streets from door to door like a dull wind.[115]

The narrative continues in this evasive manner until a dialogue is presented. In that dialogue, which focalizes Mrs Vermont, Denise and Percy, it is ambiguous as to whether Mrs Vermont or Denise asks, 'Didn't anyone hear anything, any firing? I mean, didn't it make a noise?',[116] and it is similarly ambiguous as to who provides the information that Gerald is dead: 'Why did they get just Gerald?'[117] Percy responds indirectly to the initial question – 'Well, we've got to get after 'em haven't we'[118] – leaving 'them' unidentified before prompting Mrs Vermont and Denise to go to bed. The narrative device relates the moment they fall asleep and a later moment when Betty awoke 'to hear herself say: "What I mean is, it seems so odd that he shouldn't really have meant anything"', thus echoing Captain Vermont's and Mr Montmorency's earlier sentiments concerning the lack of identity in our side.[119] As a result, the moment of Gerald's death is both denied qualification in the narrative and annulled by a character soon after, and thus unrepresented and stripped of its meaningfulness. Mr Daventry belatedly confirms that 'the officer – Lesworth – was instantly killed', but, regarding the killing, it is only related that 'the enemy made off across the country'.[120] And when Sir Richard is presented as recognizing the potential assailants, the explanation is underwritten and oblique:

> But Sir Richard had slipped away quietly; he was an old man, really, outside all this, and did not know what to do. He was wondering, also, about the Connors. Peter Connor's friends – they knew everything, they were persistent: it did not do to imagine.[121]

And so what Peter Connor's friends knew remains another structural secret in the text. The total effect of these narrative operations defer Gerald's death as an event which belongs to a wider event (which is also deferred), and as a moment in the history of a national war. This resistance to representing the contours of the War of Independence which the novel institutes has the effect of curtailing the monumentality of the war in both its moment (the fictional time of the novel) and its aftermath (the moment of writing). What results from the burning of Danielstown at the end of the novel is the monstrosity of an unknowable future: 'the door stood open hospitably upon a furnace', achieved 'by the executioners bland from accomplished duty'.[122]

On this latter clause, it is worth pointing out, as Ellmann does, an ambiguity in the word 'executioner'. With a nod to Maria Edgeworth's *Castle Rackrent* (1800) and Sheridan Le Fanu's *Uncle Silas* (1864), Ellmann notes that 'in previous Anglo-Irish Novels, the term "execution" had been used to mean the seizure of the property of bankrupt landowners ruined not by revolution but by the costs of their man-eating estates'.[123] Bowen is perhaps updating the word 'executioner' to fit the contours of modern history; contrastingly, if understood in the sense Ellmann's uncovers, the word adds another nuance, one not wholly determined by revolutionary impulses, to the dispossession of Danielstown. Moreover, it connects the destruction of Danielstown to an ongoing legacy of Big House dispossession, which, despite their ongoing misfortune, the Anglo-Irish continue to endure. Like the doubling of the gun with the penis in the scene in the mill, this final scene also presents concurrent and jarring narrative strands, subtexts which contradict the coherency of the main narrative, and invites the reader to choose one or the other or both. As the novel ends with Sir Richard and Lady Naylor in motion fleeing across the 'open and empty' country,[124] their present and future, though they are homeless, remain undecided and under-defined. Despite their increasing marginalization, they are not a wholly disempowered elite. And notably, there is no present denoted in the text which marks the exit of the former colonial power and the beginnings of the postcolonial state. Such is the case when Bowen returns to write of Ireland in *A World of Love* in the 1950s: the Anglo-Irish are still in Ireland, and the major cultural event haunting the characters is the First World War. The 1916 Easter Rising, the War of Independence and the Irish Civil War all remain under-defined and absent in the narrative.

Irish modernism/Irish *modernism*

The Last September thus defers what it seems to present as it resists representing a specific historical signified. The narrative device's abrogating presentations, the gaps opened by what the characters do not say, and the manner in which male and female social spheres are penetrated, occlude the presence of The Troubles, the War of Independence, in the novel. As such, the narrative operation subverts the general tenets of omniscient narration to create an instability in the authority of that mode of representation. Though both extra- and heterodiegetic – in the sense that the former signifies a narrative device which is above or superior to the story and the latter signifies a narrative device which does not participate in the story – the narrative operation stalls the possible omniscience of these positions. Similarly, new narratological terms such as 'voice of a collective subject' (Culler) and 'telepathy' (Royle) fall short of accounting for the effect of Bowen's narrative operation. The narrative device of *The Last September* obscures the identity of the collective subject which it might relate as well as its own potential for telepathy. The respective narrative re-creations and supplementations of what characters have just said provokes an experience of the uncanny; what was seemingly simple or familiar a sentence prior is quickly made strange in narrative time by circumlocutory enunciations, in turn fracturing the possibility of a neat homology between its content and Ireland's War of Independence.[125]

Notwithstanding, it is too reductive to label the novel 'a narrative of Irish national ambivalence',[126] or to suggest that Bowen defers Ireland for political reasons.[127] Bowen's Irish modernism establishes the possibility of reading a historical situation but not without distorting the presentation of that situation, thus creating a tension between imitative representation and abstraction as it sides with neither. As such, *The Last September* does not conveniently host referential modes of reading particular histories, yet it does not deny the validity of those respective histories either. The Troubles, the War of Independence, is deferred because it is both, as a result of the narrative strategy, an absent presence which is both a haunting and a trace of an elusive historical signified. A hint of an Ireland is given, but it is a trace which always lacks self-present meaning in the text. As Lois awakens to discover: 'or how, after every return – or awakening, even, from sleep or preoccupation – she and those home surroundings still further penetrated each other mutually in the discovery of a lack'.[128] Refraining from gathering a referent under the form of a stable signifier, then, the narrative operation creates the possibility for literary alterity to become manifest. If thus considered as Irish modernist literature, *The Last September* performs a resistance to its Irish moniker. But rather than denying or disavowing that moniker, it both reveals and conceals its possibility through its narrative technique and, in turn, leaves its status open rather than foreclosed. Ireland will thus remain as a hint never to be achieved in the novel, in turn making *The Last September* untranslatable to determined forms of methodological nationalism wherein decolonization features as the equation of colonial emancipation with national liberation.[129]

The Last September, then, when read as an Irish modernist novel, establishes an affinity and a difference between Irish modernism and Irish postcoloniality. As is the case with Bowen's novel, the preoccupation with, to use Jean-Michel Rabaté's terms for Irish modernism, language and seeing reality differently, as well as refashioning history, puts it beyond theorization as symbiotic with Ireland's postcolonial history. If read as a parallel project to, or originated and shaped by, Irish postcoloniality, the modernist preoccupations it manifests – with language, narrative and seeing differently – are made to correspond to the metanarrative of Irish monumental history, an effect of which is that Irish modernism is weighted as *Irish* modernism, thus catering for the recognition and critical appraisal of *The Last September* as a 'powerful record of cultural memory which conveys the historical trauma of war'.[130] In the terms tended throughout this chapter, Bowen's Irish modernism (or Bowen's Irish *modernism*), which defamiliarizes and distances extratextual historical realities, is both similar and different to the cultural memories it supposedly transmits, and so it poses problems to deterministic historicist reading strategies. Operating then as both a tranquil locus and an intractable site of semantic opacity upon which to locate accounts of national memory, the text poses an ethical warning against our critical tendency to posit Irish modernism as homologous to state history and, in turn, the critical predilection to scale from the micro example through to the macro argument.

4

Kate O'Brien's 'flawed' modernism

If Elizabeth Bowen is a liminal Irish modernist, Kate O'Brien is a liminal modernist *tout court*. Long regarded as a romantic realist, one whose novels explore the desires of a central character, O'Brien has largely been absent from modernist discussion since the institutionalization of the term. After various recovery projects, however, as well the intersection of Irish studies with expanded definitions of modernism, O'Brien's writing has recently become relative to, and a feature of, modernist discourse. Her explorations of feeling, gender, queerness and sexuality, as well as the politics of modern Ireland, now constitute an important chapter in the history of Irish modernism, one which has reinforced politicized definitions of the term. As Michael Cronin suggests, 'Her fiction clearly shares a modernist vision of sexuality as a vital force with the potential to radically transform the self and revolutionize society.'[1] And Gerardine Meaney has written that her work is 'simultaneously but distinctly, Irish modernist and feminist'.[2] O'Brien's modernism, prominently traversing Irish, Spanish and other European landscapes, thus coincides with definitions of Irish modernism as directly related to the history of the nation state and the politics of Irish and European modernities.

Now that O'Brien has entered the equation of Irish modernism, and modernism more generally, her writing, long regarded as flawed, open-ended, strange and uncanny, also begs exploration of how it relates what it relates, and thus as a formal modernism and, building on Meaney's proposition, as a distinct mode of Irish modernism. As an Irish modernist, O'Brien's corpus is rarely investigated in terms of the aesthetic precepts of high or late modernism. At first blush, 'make it new', as Ezra Pound's war cry went, would seem elsewhere to O'Brien's writerly agenda. In comparison to James Joyce, Samuel Beckett, Flann O'Brien or Bowen, for example, Kate O'Brien's writing is less evidently concerned with fragmentation, scepticism or the mobilization of epistemological doubt as aesthetic strategies. Her works generally seem to correspond to Roland Barthes's description of a moderately symbolic literature, one which functions as a general sign and closes in on a signified.³ As this chapter will show, however, her novels, when put under close scrutiny, exhibit peculiar formal tendencies, the manner of which add complexity to understandings of O'Brien as an Irish modernist. The following explores those formal tendencies and establishes new criteria for understanding O'Brien's modernism in aesthetic as well as political terms. It shows how the formal procedures developed in her novels – particularly *Mary Lavelle* (1936), *Pray for the Wanderer* (1938) and *The Land of Spices* (1941), three novels which mark O'Brien's first foray into a representation of the twentieth century – approximate and distance certain extratextual histories through their omniscient narrative strategies. This predicament, and a new vantage point for observing O'Brien's moderately symbolic modernism, becomes particularly apprehensible in terms of a widely regarded flaw in her narrative procedures.

Kate O'Brien's flaw

Various critics have designated O'Brien's writing as flawed, an occurrence which seems to operate across her corpus. Anne Fogarty has given an overview of this circumstance:

> The literary output of Kate O'Brien … is of interest because of its flawed and hybrid character. Her novels are compelling because they are misshapen, open-ended and lacunary. It is their imperfect meshing of women's romance with social critique which leaves the reader both with an impression of the probing acuity of O'Brien's fictions and also with an abiding sense of their imbalance. In entering the literary domain of Kate O'Brien, one makes the acquaintance of a social world permanently out of kilter and at odds with itself.⁴

Indeed, O'Brien's oeuvre has attracted such criticism since its first appearance. Evelyn Waugh, in his 1938 review of *Pray for the Wanderer*, described it as a 'book of very high quality',⁵ but not without noting that its literary quality is contentious. Waugh writes that 'Miss O'Brien seems in danger of one of the greatest faults the novelist can commit: of regarding conversations for their general instead of their particular interest'.⁶ He writes that 'the views expressed would be interesting in a magazine article on the subject, not because a certain character is moved to express them at a certain time and place. … Her views about modern Ireland are of first-class interest but they are best presented implicitly in the action of her book'.⁷ Acknowledging that same novel's potentially flawed character, Adele

M. Dalsimer writes, 'If *Pray for the Wanderer* fails aesthetically, it is a provocative failure.'[8] In suggesting as much, Dalsimer does not comment further on how the novel fails and what makes it nonetheless provocative and relevant.

This trope of 'failed but relevant' looms over O'Brien's oeuvre, but it does not seem to affect its critical pertinence or prowess. Rather, it contributes to the appeal of the writing and, among other factors, makes it worthy of investigation. For example, Eibhear Walshe has written in his introduction to *Ordinary People Dancing* that

> there is no doubt that O'Brien's writing is, in part, flawed, uneven and complex, yet I would argue that it is these very complexities and flaws that make her fiction so revealing. It is revealing because it is informed by O'Brien's struggle to articulate cultural and aesthetic debates subversive to the Ireland in which she wrote. O'Brien's is a voice rarely heard in Independent Ireland, the voice of an intellectually informed, sexually dissident, (col)lapsed Catholic. The disturbances and conflict within her novels are consequent of this isolation and therefore worth examining.[9]

For Walshe as well, then, the potency of O'Brien's literature seems to lie within its flaws. Concerning their source, Walshe, like Terry Eagleton's historically deterministic comment that the realist novel could not happen in Ireland because there was no social stability to support its fruition,[10] inscribes a material base: post-independent Ireland. Thus, as is regularly the case with definitions of Irish modernism, the macro example of the metanarrative of Irish history serves to explicate the form of the micro unit of the literary text. The struggle to articulate cultural and aesthetic debates subversive to post-independence Ireland was not a problem specific to O'Brien, however, and it does not wholly account for the supposed defect in the writing. Similarly, the suggestion that her writerly voice is that of the intellectually informed, sexually dissident, (col)lapsed Catholic is one of biographical conjecture. O'Brien's own struggle, though perhaps of biographical intrigue, does not equate to that which makes the novels interesting and says little of the oddness that makes the writing revealing. Notwithstanding, O'Brien's writing has become regarded as a radical literature[11] – 'each novel a Trojan horse smuggling in forbidden topics, such as adultery, lesbianism and venereal disease';[12] and 'a radically subversive act which undermines the bases of the Establishment'[13] – despite, as Michael Cronin has suggested, that she remained deeply committed to bourgeois liberalism.[14] As such, more recent criticism on O'Brien has moved beyond concern with this supposed flaw to locate her writing as reactionary to and within the politics of her life and times, often collapsing the question of form to bring the historical traces and spectres in O'Brien's narratives of individual development to the foreground when denoting her modernism. Aintzane Legarreta Mentxaka, for example, completely rebukes the critical reception of O'Brien's writing as flawed – Legarreta Mentxaka wryly suggests that 'it is an unfailing source of amusement to wait for the inevitable admission [that O'Brien's writing is flawed] in an essay'[15] – and notes that the blended styles, hybridity and meshed construction of *Mary Lavelle* signals that novel's modernism. Despite such apposite ripostes, O'Brien's earlier critics were not necessarily wrong to highlight the formal oddities across her uncanny fictions, which have not yet experienced the same critical uptake that Bowen's work, for example, has undergone as a result of the new modernist studies, a fate which seems linked to the form and style of O'Brien's writing (indeed, Legarreta Mentxaka outlines problems of cohesion in her analysis of *Mary Lavelle*).[16] And unlike Joyce's explosion of the novel, Beckett's *désœuvrement*, Flann O'Brien's destruction or Bowen's estranging, Kate O'Brien's repeated investment in overarching omniscience signals a maintenance, rather than a subversion, of nineteenth-century realist forms. As such, what the perceived failure(s) is/are and how the novels maintain their pertinence as a result remains under-articulated and relevant, particularly as it concerns O'Brien's Irish modernism.

Waugh is perhaps the most explicit on the structure of O'Brien's flaw when he notes that 'the view' that is being presented in *Pray for the Wanderer* lacks specificity to the characters of that novel. In making this critique, Waugh tacitly suggests that the issue is a problem of narration. If the views are not implicit in the action, and if the novel would benefit by presenting them therein, then Waugh is insinuating that O'Brien's narrative operations create a discord between what is presented and the characters who supposedly say and think what they are presented as saying and thinking. As Waugh implies, the flaw would be that the view is expressed at a narrative level which is above the characters, thus at the extra- and heterodiegetic level of narration. In her analysis of *The Land of Spices*, Mary Breen writes that 'control of the narrative is never withdrawn from the omniscient narrator'.[17] The same could be said for the majority of O'Brien's writing. Indeed, Legarreta Mentxaka uses the term 'overseer-narrator'[18] to describe the narrative device of *Mary Lavelle*. Such devices are used throughout O'Brien's fiction to refer the thoughts and feelings of the characters and to relate their memories and past lives and take control of all that is recounted. In contrast to the opening chapters of Joyce's *Ulysses*, for example, where cultural memory occurs through the experiences of the two central characters, O'Brien offers a narrator's discourse on history and the past. Thus, unlike Joyce, who locates cultural memory in the space and time of his protagonists' environments and minds (as well as through his narrative devices), O'Brien often wholly situates cultural memory in and through her narrative devices, and beyond the action time and setting of her novels. In this sense, O'Brien's novels deploy narrative devices with an impossible and godlike narratorial capacity. And it is in relation to such terminology, as mentioned in the last chapter, that Jonathan Culler and Nicholas Royle respectively debunk and displace omniscience as a critical concept. While Culler's and Royle's respective subversions of the term remain apposite, omniscience is retained here as O'Brien's narrative devices go beyond consensual or telepathic relations with her novels' characters and settings. As her narrative devices provoke dislocations between form, content and setting, they oversee and transcend, rather than act as pervasive presences in relation to, that which is related in the texts. O'Brien's narrators in such terms are very similar to Culler's description, as cited in the previous chapter, of nineteenth-century extra- and heterodiegetic narrators.[19] The three novels that form the focus of analysis in this chapter – *Mary Lavelle*, *Pray for the Wanderer* and *The Land of Spices* – all present omniscient narratives of this type. *Mary Lavelle* and *Pray for the Wanderer* finish on, more or less, the same note: the love plot fails as a result of a deployment of a logic of the past, which is prior to the time, and outside the setting, of the respective novels. In *The Land of Spices*, Reverend Mother and Anna Murphy both seem to be beginning a new future after working through traumatic pasts. For both characters, the past that is overcome, and the coherence of the present that is subsequently denoted, is related by the narrative device on their behalf. As Waugh implies, an initial reservation that the critic might have with these narrative strategies concerns the presentation of the memories of the past which affect the outcomes of the respective novels. O'Brien's omniscient narratives flout a demonstration that subjective memory would require a certain inheritance, as opposed to an 'assuming of', in order to be narrated; and thus, her novels present information omnisciently without drawing self-reflexive attention to any problems inherent in such modes of representation. Yet, as O'Brien's critics have noted, theses modes occur as problematic because they establish an imbalance between the mode of narration and the characters and places represented, the latter occurring at the behest of the narrative structure. As such, an omniscient narration of a character's memories in a totalizing narrative structure disobeys what Jacques Derrida describes as the law of inheritance. In *Spectres of Marx*, he writes,

> If the readability of a legacy were given, natural, transparent, and univocal, if it did not at the same time call for and at the same time defy interpretation, we

would never have anything to inherit from it. ... The critical choice called for by any reaffirmation of the inheritance is also, like memory itself, the condition of finitude. The infinite does not inherit, it does not inherit (from) itself.[20]

An omniscient narrator, then, if this injunction is followed, could never unequivocally assume the remembrance of something on behalf of a character. In doing so, it defies the secret which is immanent to inheritance: 'an inheritance is never gathered together, it is never one with itself'.[21] Yet, this transgression of narrator and character relations is undertaken in the omniscient narrative strategies in *Mary Lavelle*, *Pray for the Wanderer* and *The Land of Spices*.

It thus seems necessary to read O'Brien's narrative operations suspiciously in order to understand this potential 'flaw' in her writing. Particularly, this chapter performs a reading of her texts in which the demand for the suspension of disbelief in fictional narrative is both accepted and refused, thus assuming both sides of Barthes's perverse reader, which, following Sigmund Freud, Barthes describes as the cleavage of the reading subject in two. Typically, the reader takes pleasure in the text despite being aware of the illusion it creates ('*I know these are only words, but all the same*'[22]). If O'Brien's 'flaw' is implicit to her technique, then suspending belief, and assuming the distinction between content represented and the technical apparatus of representation, allows for an analysis of how her texts are constructed and a broader elucidation of the supposed structural flaws in her fiction.

Moreover, in a manner of perverse reading, this chapter subverts what is obvious about O'Brien's texts to show how analysis of the 'flaw' of overarching omniscience in her writing enables a different understanding of her modernism. Specifically, the impossibility of total inheritance of memory and the past in O'Brien's writing, which lends the work its 'flawed and hybrid' status and which makes it 'misshapen' and 'permanently out of kilter and at odds with itself',[23] stems from the deployment of false memories by extra- and heterodiegetic narrative devices which feign the simple recounting of characters' lives in the production of narrator's discourses (interestingly, O'Brien provided resonant and tacit aesthetic coordinates for this position in her UCD lecture: 'Proust has taught us that the memories we sit down to, that we select and seek, are false'[24]). The apparent disingenuousness of these performances both caters for O'Brien's feminist, individual development and queer interventions into the politics of modernity and manifests an irreducible difference between her modes of narration and the characters and settings that are narrated. And as will be demonstrated in these pages, it similarly entails an approximation and a structural distancing of Ireland's historical condition. O'Brien's productive 'flaw', it is suggested here, thus constitutes a distancing effect which invites analysis of the relationship between her narratives and their corresponding content, as well as the relationship between fiction and its purported referents.

Mary Lavelle's ghosts

A romance novel published in 1936, *Mary Lavelle* is set in 1922 and the eponymous protagonist is a governess recently arrived in Altorno to the Areavega family, whose son, Juanito, is Mary's love interest. The Civil War in Ireland is registered as being in progress. Luisa, Juanito's wife, will have recorded on her behalf that 'She admired the Irish Spaniard hero, de Valera, thought the civil war in Ireland tragic but inevitable, and the Treaty compromise a grave mistake'.[25] Within this broader social and political situation, Mary gathers herself on more than one occasion by smiling to the ghost (a term which is repeatedly used and does not signify a decedent in the novel) of her fiancé, John, who is from and lives in Mellick, O'Brien's recurrent fictitious Irish town/county, where Mary is also from. And Mary feels no yearning for the ghost or the landscape which it envelopes; in the final words of the chapter entitled 'San Geronimo', Mary is presented as

> relaxed against the window-pane. She was beginning to like the taste of the favorito. John would certainly forbid such strong tobacco. She smiled again to his ghost. She had no pang or longing, and was too young to reflect on their lack. It was good to be here and to observe this view.[26]

Mary thus smiles in spite of the fact, as is suggested on Luisa's behalf, that John inhabits a country torn by civil war, which Mary is presented as knowing; and there is 'no pang or longing' arising from what young age cannot recognize as 'lack'.[27]

On another occasion at the beginning of the novel, whilst looking at a photo of John, Mary 'smiled back at him and his intense familiarity somewhat neutralised her mood by exacting an orthodox reaction of sentimentality'.[28] 'Dearest' Mary says to John's ghost before she 'reluctantly put the photograph away' to attend to her duties as a governess.[29] As in this instance, Mary is smiling ('again') to what the narrative frames as John's ghost, this time feeling an orthodox sentimentality. Elsewhere she holds John's letters and she picks up John's photo, but Mary is never conflicted by his situation in war-torn Ireland in 1922, which is established as an absent presence, and bypassed, in the text. Such lack and orthodox sentimentality render Mary's love for John, and her relation to the civil war in Ireland, ambiguous, in turn paving the way for the development of her sentiments for Juanito. Simultaneously, this lack of overt feeling for John and Ireland raise the possibility that O'Brien is mounting, like Bowen, a gendered critique of Irish politics, a critique, that is, of nationalist politics that foreground the gun and the army and occludes women's participation in national affairs. Legaretta Mentxaka makes the convincing case that the novel's politics are most adequately elucidated through Basque, Spanish and European cultures and histories (which outlines another mappable distance of Irish modernism) and, in doing so, suggests that *Mary Lavelle* is 'intent on silencing Irish nationalism',[30] a feat particularly observable through the oblique representation of John and Mellick in the novel. The critique tended here expands on O'Brien's feminist negation of the cultural dynamics of the Free State to show how her omniscient narrative strategies also entail a structural distancing of the conditions of post-independence Ireland, one which renders the latter spectral in the novel.

As a ghost, John is never directly encountered in *Mary Lavelle*. It is suggested that he engages in written correspondence with Mary but there is no access to, or presentation of, his writings. Some ephemeral words of his are recorded in the narration – 'Damn Aunt Cissy!'; 'It scares me to feel so happy'; 'Look there, my love … and see why I'm so crazy'[31] – but John is not represented in dialogue or in epistolary form, even though he is integral to the moment of the novel. Yet, John's spectre will create the sense of Mary being watched from the past and the future. She has accepted his proposal of marriage and will live with him in Mellick, making John, like Mellick, a static, non-ageing, transhistorical presence in the novel, one registered as a simulacrum: as a ghost, photograph or letter. Serving a structural purpose, John's background in Mellick is presented to establish Mary's character, the story of a past that precedes her moment in Spain, the time of the narrative and her inevitable future. In the 'Introduction' to the novel, it is suggested that Mary 'knows her eventual place, and will be content to fill it'.[32] Contrastingly, it is also related that Mary is 'an individualist who does not mind temporising'.[33] Thus, the spectres of John, Mellick and the Irish Civil War are formal devices in the text which are deployed in contrast to Mary's procrastinatory character to create doubt and guilt concerning her feelings for Juanito. As Derrida writes, a spectre is always coming back: 'At bottom, the spectre is the future, it is always to come, it presents itself only as that which could come or come back.'[34] And so the ghosts of John, Mellick and Ireland will loom over the text as the signs of a determined future, no matter what happens in Spain. The haunting of *Mary Lavelle* by spectres from Ireland thus occurs as a necessary ploy in the plot development of the novel, as well as a means to launch its feminist politics. As Legarreta Mentxaka suggests, 'Mary's feminist politics can only be articulated through action, by her exercising of personal freedom': 'in choosing a job, in choosing a lover. She does both despite opposition, after overcoming her own doubts.'[35] As a result, the term 'ghost' in Mary Lavelle is produced in a narrative system which deploys a faint, secondary image of something (John, Mellick, Ireland) to assist more primary concerns: establishing the novel's feminist politics and recording the eventual failure of Mary and Juanito's affair. John, Mellick and Ireland are thus spectres which haunt the novel. Not real, not unreal, they are tropes implanted in the text which both facilitate the narrative operation; structural devices, rather than dialectic and historical entities, they enable the novel's temporal sequencing.

A particular example of this occurs as Mary's past is related in the following passage:

> In the convention of Mary's upbringing a suitably affianced girl is a happy girl and Mary was therefore by her own conventional assumption happy. Moreover, though without particularly noticing this, she did sometimes undergo the sensation of happiness. There were occasional premonitions of emotion too – as when loafing with John before the breakfast-room fire, they talked, he talked of the future, of married peace, of the house they would have and its garden, of the children who would grow and play there and of what those children would become, of growing old with her, of seeing their grand-children.[36]

This analepsis is deployed in relation to a first narrative which has previously been established. As the novel opens, the reader is aware that Mary is in Spain: 'The trunk of a "Miss", going over the Pyrenees, is no great matter.'[37] The subsequent record of Mary's past in Ireland, which is initiated as Mary's memory ('The name sent her dreaming back into what surely was reality'),[38] though it is related in the narrative commentary. As this excerpt reveals, the omniscient narrative device has access to Mary's past and future, to her interior life, the conditions of her happiness, her emotional capacities and her dreams and hopes for the future; its scope extends beyond direct telepathy or the voice of general consensus, as per Royle and Culler, respectively. Thus, a decision for the future is made before the time of the novel begins – 'of the house they would have and its garden, of the children who would grow and play there and of what those children would become, of growing old with her, of seeing their grand-children'.[39] Similarly, Mary's feelings concerning these arrangements are related in the narrative commentary: 'Her heart approved the goodness of this plan and she perceived how well it became the good and spirited man who purposed it with her. She liked his face when he talked in this vein; there was a penetrating sweetness in the way he would laugh over his unborn children.'[40] Particularly, the image of the unborn child creates a certain responsibility. It gives Mary and John a duty to each other and their children. The deployment of this memory of the future has the effect of confining Mary's romantic possibilities before she begins her life in Spain. And this is reinforced by the narrative commentary: 'She felt both honoured and touched; she felt surprised too that a scheme which is or has been everyone's should seem at the personal proof so special and exacting.'[41] Mary in turn becomes subject to a scheme that holds her within the bounds of a doctrine of happiness; and the narrative device presents this as her desire by relating a scenario in which she is shown to admire John's plans for the future. As mentioned, however, John never explains himself in *Mary Lavelle*. Some ephemeral lines of his are related, but he is never presented as pronouncing such promises. Thus, these recollections of the absent John – this relation of a past which inscribes the promise of an unborn future on behalf of Mary by the narrative device – loom as prosthetic, if not false, memories in the text. The narrative commentary establishes a moment prior to the time of the novel where Mary buys into an ideal of universal happiness; and the happiness she supposedly feels is explained for her in the narrative commentary yet unannounced by herself or the one (John) who supposedly promises to give it to her. Such is Waugh's critique of O'Brien: the action and the 'view' of the novel occur at the extra- and heterodiegetic level of narration. The narrative operation then appears flawed because, unlike Bowen's *The Last September*, for example, wherein the narrative device remains with the unfolding action and deliberately discords with the characters, O'Brien's characters appear at the total behest of, and lack autonomy from, her omniscient narrative devices. As such, Mary's moment in Spain is unsettled by a memory that is created through the narrative operation, and not in the action or time of her life there.

Simultaneously, the meaning of these memories face resistance in the form of the ghost. John is the figure who represents the past and on whom these dilemmas are built, yet he is also the spectre who returns to demand nothing. As a real and unreal presence, which is there and not there in the text, every appropriation of John from the moment of narration, the moment of Mary's time in Spain, will also be haunted by the non-speaking ghost. Invested with meaning in the narrative commentary, the ghost remains enigmatic by never confirming its intentions. It simply looms in the text as a trace. As Derrida writes of the experiencing of spectres,

> something that one does not know, precisely, and one does not know precisely if it is, if it exists, if it responds to a name and corresponds to an essence. One does not know: not out of ignorance, but because this non-object, this non-present present, this being-there of an absent or departed one no longer belongs to knowledge. ... One does not know if it is living or if it is dead. Here is – or rather there is, over there, an unnameable or almost unnameable thing.[42]

As a non-object and a non-present, the reproach of adultery and disregard of the unborn this ghost poses is that which the omniscient narrative makes it inhabit. But the ghost does not confirm the inevitability of such reproach. The irrefutable injunction which it carries (a commitment not to commit adultery, a commitment to the unborn) facilitates the telling of the story of a failed romance, and, ultimately, the narrative of Mary's self-development.[43] Concurrently, however, Mary's relationship with Juanito does not end in failure because of a commitment Mary made to her fiancé. John does not hold Mary back in the novel; she sleeps with Juanito as she knows that John will have to reject her not just because she has fallen in love with the Spaniard but because she has had sex with him. Similarly, if we consider Legarreta Mentxaka's excellent symbolist reading of the sex scene based on the bullfight – where Mary represents the Bull, Juanito the matador and Don Pablo the mortally wounded – Mary emerges as the victor pitying Juanito[44] and notably not lamenting John. And when confronted with John's ghost, Mary feels no pang and no longing, and the ghost poses no threat. The memory that Mary is forced to inhabit and abide by is thus 'out of kilter' with how she lives.[45] The narrative commentary creates the guilt by mobilizing the threat of John's ghost which will always return to demand nothing; and so Mary is found on two occasions smiling to the ghost, experiencing 'intense familiarity' but 'no pang or longing'.[46] Thus, John, the Civil War and Ireland all feature as tropes in the text which aid the construction of the novel's plot. Beyond their value as a plot tools, however, neither the historical condition of Ireland nor the Irish Civil War have any impact on the novel's events. And neither do the names of the Irish nationalists that appear in the narration. On one occasion, as the narrative commentary relates, Mary 'amusedly' hears the names 'Arthur Griffiths' and 'Patrick Pearse' in the oration of a Basque nationalist.[47] Notwithstanding, their context and meaning is left suspended and unanchored in the text. These historical figures and realities never intrude on, or cause consternation in, O'Brien's omniscient narrative of self-development.

In one sense then, O'Brien can be read as establishing a gendered critique of nationalist politics that occludes women's participation in national affairs by showing how Mary thrives, and can undergo self-development, once she is at a remove from that situation. Simultaneously, in its focus on the development of the individual along feminist and liberal ideals, O'Brien's omniscient narrative strategy assumes a certain history for the development of Mary's character. In the process, the narrative strategy reduces that history – John, the Civil War, Ireland – to empty simulacra which ultimately render an uncanniness to the novel's plot and its articulation: Mary's self-development, the novel's feminist politics and its exploration of queer sexualities (the latter represented most prominently through the character of Agatha Conlon) all occur in O'Brien's romance narrative as a result of the negation of John, Mellick and Ireland, which also appear, as a result of the 'overseer-narrator' (to borrow Legarreta Mentxaka's term again), as prosthetic memories in the text. In such terms, O'Brien's romance novel and its omniscient narrative strategy establishes a deliberate critique of the conservative politics of 1920s nationalist Ireland in feminist and sexual terms; moreover, through the characters of Don Pablo and Juanito, it allows for the explicit import of anarchist and Marxist politics into Irish and European romance literature.[48] Concurrently, Mary's development remains *overseen* by an external narrative authority which establishes the account of her maturation as a feature of the narrative strategy, which is beyond, and at a distance to, the observed action and time of the novel; and which has the paradoxical effect of maintaining Mary's development within an enclosed structure, a circumstance which, given its uncanny investment in Mary's freedom and confinement, lends to the appreciation of O'Brien work as oscillating between a mild and radical sexual politics. The story of Mary's development thus occurs at a double distance to the historical condition of post-independence Ireland: first, through its negation in the articulation of a feminist narrative of self-development; and second, through its spectrality in an omniscient narrative strategy. In such terms, then, O'Brien's omniscient narration becomes as much the event of *Mary Lavelle* as Mary's development, an operation that is repeated to a more extreme degree in *Pray for the Wanderer*.

O'Brien's riposte to censorship

In *Pray for the Wanderer*, O'Brien's 1938 novel, which is often regarded as her riposte to the Irish Censorship of Publications Board for the banning of *Mary Lavelle* (the reasoning for which was because the titular character has an affair with the married Juanito), Matt Costello, the main protagonist, is a successful writer whose recent novel has been banned by the Free State government on the grounds of blasphemy. Similarly, he has recently returned to Mellick, his hometown, from London after a failed relationship with Louise, his ex-partner, and so the melancholy which assails his character in the novel is presented as deriving from these negative events. *Pray for the Wanderer* is thus directly engaged with the political climate of post-independence Ireland, particularly Eammon de Valera's infamously conservative cultural policies; simultaneously, *Pray for the Wanderer* is an aesthetically and formally unbalanced novel and has been recognized in criticism as such: a double aspect of the novel which lends to its poignancy and unevenness. As Paige Reynolds has recently suggested, 'the unexpected lack of obvious correspondence among content, form and setting was in part what baffled and frustrated readers'.[49] Notably, as it concerns Irish political conservatism, O'Brien's riposte – which Anthony Roche regards as 'an extraordinary intervention in the politics of 1930s Ireland' and which he sees as marking 'a sustained engagement with the presence and politics of de Valera'[50] – occurs in Matt's thoughts, largely independent of action, and is narrated through free indirect discourse:

> There is no escape for a man from his own time, Matt reflected wearily, save in his own nature – in his use of memory and imagination. By these, by his unconscious reliance on them, Will for instance held this illusive oasis. He created his present out of what he knew and what he wanted – and was happy, and good, in a sad and evil world. That was something – that was decidedly a contribution, a courageous one. There were many men like Will. There could be many more – even under Dev's tricky constitution. Perhaps they were the innocent hope of the world.[51]

Here, Matt considers that, in terms perhaps typical of the writer of literary fiction, escape from one's historical moment occurs through recourse to mnemonic and fictive efforts,[52] and he is compared to Will, his brother, who 'created the present out of what he knew and what he wanted' through his unconscious reliance on memory and imagination.[53] In his ability to be happy and good in a sad and evil world, Will makes a courageous contribution to life in post-independence Ireland, 'even under Dev's tricky constitution'.[54] What thus makes Will and men like him the innocent hope of the world is their use of memory and imagination; and Matt, the writer whose profession is concerned with such pursuits, is presented as being outside this group, and so O'Brien establishes an ironic critique, after the banning of *Mary Lavelle*, of the role of the artist in post-independence Ireland: the recourse to faculties of recollection and imagination are only valuable to lay men and women in the Free State, and not necessarily the writer of fiction.

Similarly, later in the novel, when out with his nephew, in a supposedly internal monologue unrelated to the immediate action at hand, Matt ponders, 'Could he live in de Valera's Ireland, where the artistic conscience is ignored?'[55] And Matt's direct tract on de Valera and the Free State Constitution similarly appears as an interior monologue: 'Matt imagined, and imagined that de Valera too imagined, that Ireland, newly patrolled by the Church, would be unlikely to vote against the Holy Trinity.'[56] In each instance, then, the critique recorded and the 'presence' of de Valera's Ireland occur through a narrator's discourse in interior monologues that are largely independent of action and setting, and thus feature entirely as discrete diegesis and not, as Waugh's critique of the novel goes, 'because a certain character is moved to express them at a certain time and place'.[57]

A defence of the freedom of literary invention is later elaborated, though, similarly, Matt does not undertake this critique. In conversation during a drive back to Mellick from a lake, Matt, Nell and Tom discuss the act of writing. Tom describes Matt as 'the man of imagination' (one of two terms previously denied to him in what were seemingly his own reflections).[58] Tom suggests, with recourse to Plato, that imagination is the 'final essential of genius' and that 'Matt has it'.[59] Matt responds, 'The advantage of looking in your heart to write … is that you actually see nothing.'[60] To which Tom replies, 'Precisely. You just have to invent – which is your function.'[61] Tom reinserts this argument a little later in the same journey; while discussing Keats, Tom says, 'Keats found his poetry under his own hat. He didn't interview Nature – he invented her when he felt the call'; to which Matt responds, 'Yes, And the Elizabethans too.'[62] Here, Matt and Tom defend the artistic freedom of the writer: the 'nothing' from which the writer must 'invent' to fulfil their 'function' enables the production of literary material. This dialogue thus relates both a critique and a metacritique of the task and responsibility of fiction, which in turn serves both political and ethical purposes: political in a critique of the draconian cultural policies of de Valera's Ireland in its obstruction of the freedom of the writer, and ethical in the insistence that writing entails invention and that this is precisely the function of literary fiction.[63] This discussion, then, whilst constituting a defence of the freedom of literature, also serves as a forewarning of the narrative strategy of *Pray for the Wanderer*.

These critiques concerning de Valera's Ireland and the freedom of literature are undertaken both beyond and through Matt at the extra- and heterodiegetic level of narration and in dialogue. First, Matt is presented through free indirect narration as recognizing that memory and imagination are only valuable to lay men and women in the Free State; later, Matt is recorded as passively agreeing with Tom's assertions concerning the role and task of the writer. In such terms, the view established in the novel regarding the role of the writer and the freedom of literary fiction in the Free State is presented at Matt's expense, an intricacy that becomes observable when the reason for his melancholy is interrogated. The banning of his book and the demise of his relationship to Louise establish why Matt is unhappy in the novel; the latter occurrence, however, has determined his return to Mellick as it has made his life in London untenable. The banning of Matt's book by the Free State government, however, has not necessarily forced Matt to leave London. As it is later revealed, despite this critique of censorship in post-independence Ireland that is undertaken in the narrative discourse on his behalf, Matt's 'problem' in the novel is not necessarily de Valera's conservative politics, his writing or, as Roche suggests, 'the 1937 Constitution and the severe limits it placed on individual freedom'[64] (like Mary Lavelle's concern is not necessarily John, Ireland or the Civil War). Matt is a successful writer and one of his plays is on stage in London. As per O'Brien's preference for failed romance plots, his relationships with Louise, and later Nell, are the main sources for his consternation. Like *Mary Lavelle*, then, the narrative operation presents information concerning the main character while that character is either absent or partially present in proceedings, a by-product of which is a tension within representation that occurs between the narrative mode and the central character. The critiques concerning the relationship between literary writing and censorship that are established in the novel are thus both relevant and flawed. As Waugh's review suggests, the views would be best presented implicitly in the action of the book. Indeed, as it becomes evident in the novel's subsequent chapters, Matt's romantic life is the main subject of the novel. O'Brien's focus on the development of the individual along liberal ideals, and beyond the restrictive demands of national and social life, establishes a dissimilitude between her Irish modernism and Irish postcoloniality. The banning of Matt's novel at the hands of the Free State serves to launch the story of Matt's life in Mellick, but it becomes evident as the story develops that Matt continues in Mellick largely unperturbed by this event. The concerns of Irish life, as Brad Kent has suggested generally of Kate O'Brien, is 'tangential' to her recurrent thematic of individual development: 'Her plea for the freedom of individuals from externally imposed restrictions is not dependent on a locale.'[65] The novel's critique of the cultural climate of post-independence Ireland in turn remains relevant but falls short of occurring as immanent to Matt's dilemma and melancholy, a result of which is that Irish cultural politics ultimately features as an astatic and spectral presence in the text, not necessarily dictating its cause of play. As *Pray for the Wanderer* proceeds, the focus on individual development takes precedence ahead of Irish cultural politics, and the jarring disconnect between the mode of narration and character autonomy expands.

In the fourth chapter, a scene in which Matt is alone in his bedroom in Will's house, a kaleidoscope of narrative perspectives is deployed to relate how Matt and Louise's relationship ended. The scene includes the representation of a message that Matt is writing to Louise; the content of Louise's telegrams to Matt; the third-person narration of Matt's consciousness;[66] the representation of his movements in the room in which this scene takes place; a past and supposedly usual response that Louise often gave to Matt as he tried to praise her for their relationship;[67] narrative commentary on how Matt and Louise had felt about each other when they were together;[68] a twelve-page analeptic dialogue in which Louise and Matt argue about the end of their relationship; as well as the narration, at the end of the chapter, of Louise being asleep in London. Thus, in this scene in which Matt is presented as being alone in a room in Mellick, the variety of narrative perspectives which occur across different temporalities and spaces – both Louise's response to Matt's wish to thank her and their long dialogue derive from supposedly past conversations in London – signal a multivocal narrative perspective and a transnational and a trans-temporal focalization. The account developed in this chapter, then, occurs beyond its setting (Matt's room) and the present tense of the characters which form its content (Matt located in his room in Mellick, Louise located in London). And as it is presented outside of the action and time of the novel (Matt is supposedly 'reliving a hundred wild conversations of farewell'[69]), it becomes evident that this is not necessarily Matt's or Louise's account of the end of their relationship. Unlike Bowen's omniscient narrative device in *The Last September* which remains with the characters in specific geographical and temporal settings, the narrative scope of *Pray for the Wanderer* extends beyond telepathy and the geographical and temporal location of a singular or collective subject and pushes omniscience to its impossible and unbelievable limits. Consistency of representation is fragmented and sacrificed for the construction of an omniscient view of the debacle, one which becomes important to the development of the novel's failed-romance plot and not necessarily to its critique of the censorship policies of Free State Ireland. The scene ends with Matt tearing up the letter he has written to Louise, as well as four of her telegrams that he had kept, to suggest an end to his engagement with her, which is subsequently confirmed in narrative commentary in the fifth chapter – 'Everything was over, therefore: the affair was closed'[70] – thus paving the way for the development of his interest in Nell and the novel's romance narrative.

At the beginning of the fifth chapter, the narrative strategy returns to free indirect narration and Matt is presented as considering his future: 'When memory eased he would find a respectable way of advancing on old age. Here perhaps, after all, under the skies of home.'[71] Soon after, the seeds of Matt's interest in, and appreciation of, Nell are established. With this turn in narrative focus, Matt's concerns about whether or not he could live in de Valera's Ireland largely evaporate and the romance narrative accelerates. In the seventh chapter, the omniscient narrative device presents Una, Will's wife, as thinking that Matt is romantically interested in Nell – 'Una felt something in the air. There was something, which was absolutely nothing, about Nell in Matt's presence that arrested and entirely evaded, Una's intuition'[72] – thus confirming Matt's romantic interests in Nell beyond his own thoughts. Later in the same chapter, the narrative focus switches to Matt and it is related that 'in Nell very strangely, he saw a strange impossible hope'.[73] The possibility of Matt and Nell's relationship is thereafter heightened in the narrative and culminates with Matt proposing marriage, which Nell rejects because of her perception that Matt remains enamoured with Louise:

> There's only one thing you're determined upon, Matt – that Louise Lafleur is not to die! You're a great artist and she's your greatest creation. It hardly matters that the woman on whom you planted this superb conception, in whom you proved it, the actress still living and playing in London, has turned out to be exactly what she always was – normal and sensible like the rest of us.[74]

While Nell rebuts Matt's proposal, and the failed romance plot comes to its conclusion, her remarks in this instance about Matt's creation of Louise echo with how Matt is narrated throughout the novel. In the transition from the fourth to fifth chapters, the narrative operation installs the idea that Matt recognizes that his relationship with Louise has ended, and relates his initial interest in Nell. Matt is then presented as developing a romantic passion for Nell, a process mediated through the omniscient narrative strategy. Reinforcing it, Una is also presented as recognizing Matt's intentions. Crucially, Matt's proposal of marriage comes after he has seemingly worked through the demise of his relationship with Louise in chapter four. However, this working through occurs through the narrative strategy as it is related from a multivocal, transnational and trans-temporal perspective, and thus, like his critiques of de Valera and the Free State, beyond Matt's time and space as he is located in the novel. As such, it is not necessarily Matt who has undertaken this process of mourning concerning the end of his relationship with Louise. Nonetheless, he is immediately propelled into a romance plot and, apparently having overcome his difficulties, is presented as wanting to propose marriage to Nell. As such, the creation of meaning in the text occurs at the level of the narrative discourse rather than action or setting. Thus, Matt is autonomous neither in his proposition of marriage to Nell nor, it can be retrospectively introjected, in his reflections on Irish cultural politics. Rather, he occurs as an instrument in a romance narrative structure which overrides the characters and settings it represents.

To put it boldly, then, the only event worth noting in *Pray for the Wanderer* is the event of the omniscient narrative strategy. The novel presents the situation in which, as Gérard Genette describes, 'narrator > character'; 'the narrator knows more than the character, or more exactly says more than any of the characters knows'.[75] Similarly, it ironically confirms Shlomith Rimmon-Kenan's concerns with the ability of narrative fiction to show the action it represents: 'The notion of 'showing' is more problematic than it seems … no text of narrative fiction can show or imitate the action it conveys, since all such texts are made of language, and language signifies without imitating. Language can only imitate language.'[76] While it establishes the illusion of a form of mimesis, the action of *Pray for the Wanderer* is the effect of its narrative device. In this sense, Kate O'Brien's novel stands opposite Flann O'Brien's *At Swim-Two-Birds* wherein the characters overpower their narrator and author; no such overpowering is possible in Kate O'Brien's narrative strategy. The narrative overcoding of the novel's characters and setting with content which may or may not correlate to action and setting – which manifests an irreducible difference between narrative strategy and the characters represented – facilitates the blending of social critique with romance narrative in a narrator's discourse. And this discourse, paradoxically, enables both a strident critique of the conservative cultural politics of post-independence Ireland, as well as the negation of that critique through Matt's attraction to Nell, marriage and the family unit, cornerstones of the Free State constitution. *Pray for the Wanderer* thus points to O'Brien's ongoing uncanny aesthetic strategy, though particularly flawed in this instance, of blending social critique with popular literary forms through her experiments with omniscient narration; a particular feature of which is the deployment of Irish cultural politics to establish the dilemma of a central character while such politics later become tangential in her narratives of individual development. O'Brien's distinct brand of Irish modernism, in such terms, entails an approximation and a distancing of the impact of cultural and political affairs on her characters' lives, a feat more effectively achieved in what is perhaps O'Brien's most important novel: *The Land of Spices*.

The Land of Spices and disconnected narratives

O'Brien moves away from the failed romance plot for her 1941 novel, *The Land of Spices*, though she maintains the use of the cultural politics of Ireland for charting the direction of the novel. Set in an Irish convent, Reverend Mother is presented as becoming dismayed by the cultural nationalism of her colleagues and their desire to adapt European pedagogical practice to local requirements. As the novel begins, Reverend Mother has prepared her letter of resignation to leave the convent and its narrow nationalism. She decides to remain, however, in order to protect Anna Murphy, a young and vulnerable student who is suffering from a troubled familial situation. Long regarded as one of O'Brien's most polemical novels – for some, a portrait of the artist as a young woman – *The Land of Spices* tackles the relationship, amongst other issues, between the Catholic Church and queer sexualities, and thus directly partakes in a modernist preoccupation with the relationship between sexual orientation, desire and identity. Particularly, this polemic, like *Mary Lavelle* and *Pray for the Wanderer*, occurs through the formal operation of the novel, which relates Reverend Mother's and Anna Murphy's development narratives.

O'Brien's polemic on same-sex desire and relationships is made possible by, and constructed through, narrative analepses which relate Reverend Mother's past. These analepses are narrated from the outset and function to establish the possibility of Reverend Mother performing an intervention on Anna's behalf towards the novel's end, an act which establishes a queer bond between the two characters. In the first chapter, entitled 'The Holy Habit', Reverend Mother's memory, after Mrs O'Doherty's mention of *Bruges la Morte*, 'takes a curiously desolate plunge across many years. … It was twenty-five years since she had taken final vows in the chapel at *Sainte Fontaine* in Bruges',[77] which signifies a troubled past, not yet dealt with, that upsets her present:

> The vows taken at *Sainte Fontaine* when she was twenty had finally, she believed, sealed up girlhood and its pain, and the resolute young woman, gladly dedicated to God, did not pause to review herself as a continuous life, or to ask if the present is not the delicate vessel of the past.[78]

Similarly, 'she had not accounted herself especially happy in her time of novitiate at Sainte Fontaine,'[79] and, thus, in the time of the first narrative, 'she was momentarily a ghost where she stood and a ghost also where her memory revisited; divided within herself as too often she was'.[80] Resolving this unhappiness in Reverend Mother's past becomes integral to how the narrative proceeds. Despite the initial reference to Irish cultural nationalism, then, Reverend Mother's difficulty, as Kelly Sullivan suggests, 'lies not in external forces (Ireland, rising nationalism) but rather within her own soul'.[81] Or as Breen suggests, *The Land of Spices* 'excludes national and international crises and concentrates on personal ones'.[82] And Reverend Mother confirms as much: 'Our nuns are not a nation, our business is not with national matters. We are a religious order.'[83] Thereafter, like *Pray for the Wanderer*, the characters' respective familial difficulties (and not national traumas) form the central focus of the narrative, as does the development of the queer bond between the characters. Like the two earlier novels, then, the Irish cultural politics which O'Brien uses to launch her text becomes tangential, rather than central or parallel, to her double narrative of individual development, which is primarily dependent on the resolution of Reverend Mother's past.

Later in the novel, the repression of adolescent pain haunts Reverend Mother in the moment she learns that her father is dying: 'She was assaulted by the necessity once more at last to relive a scene which, since entering religion, she had not allowed her conscious mind to rest on. ... Assaulted by the necessity once more at last to relive a scene which, since entering religion, she had not allowed her conscious mind to rest on,'[84] a narrative anachrony follows and a scene from Reverend Mother's adolescence – one she apparently has not had the opportunity to 'relive' since entering religion[85] – is presented. A second narrative in relation to the first narrative (Reverend Mother is lying in her bed) is established and a series of analepses are deployed in response to the news that Reverend Mother's father is dying. The omniscient narrative strategy thus operates transhistorically as it focalizes a moment from Reverend Mother's past. As an external retroversion (to use Mieke Bal's narratological term) that takes place outside of the timespan of the first narrative, the narrative anachrony (the second narrative analepsis) is disconnected from the first narrative, an effect of which is that Reverend Mother is maintained as a 'ghost' between two temporalities (notably, O'Brien again uses the term 'ghost' to signify non-decedent characters narrated beyond the immediate action, time and place of the novel). In the time of the omniscient narrative, then, Reverend Mother's life is represented across a disconnected first and second narrative, and the narrative operation creates the illusion that the external retroversion is Reverend Mother's memory (it is related in the first narrative that 'she escaped a minute into the present'[86]) and that she is performing its remembrance. Thus, as 'the past would not lie still',[87] the anachrony is resumed and its content ultimately serves as material for the resolution of her character in the present/the first narrative. The anachrony, or external retroversion, thereafter relates the moment Reverend Mother 'saw Etienne and her father in the embrace of love' (the famous sentence which was responsible for the novel being banned in Ireland by the Censorship of Publications Board), the scene which is apparently 'the last scene of youth'.[88] This episode between Reverend Mother's father and Etienne acts as the fulcrum around which *The Land of Spices* turns; it is the pivotal moment which will begin the process of change in Reverend Mother's behaviour and countenance. As such, the disconnect between the first and second narratives becomes further evident at this point: as this scene comes *before* in the story but *after* in the narrative, it represents both a disconnected past and a future to be reconnected with concerning the development of the novel's plot. In such terms, Reverend Mother occurs as a fragmented character who will be assembled and reconstituted, rather than observed in a setting or a specific Irish historical locale, in narrative time and through the narrative strategy.

As the analepsis continues, a moment of change relative to this event is related which had separated Reverend Mother's adolescence from her adulthood: 'She remembered her savage awareness of total change within, and the cunning which she used to hide it, and her delight in that cunning. She saw now that her self-control was like that of a mad woman.'[89] The relation of this moment, which also comes before in the story but after in the narrative, operates as the moment of explanation for the woman Reverend Mother has become ('she found to her pleasure that her heart was hard'), her abandonment of her father and her subsequent decision to become a nun and lead a life in the Order of *Sainte Famille*. The opportunity of the Catholic Church thus initially enabled the means through which Reverend Mother could repress her experience of her father's homosexual liaisons; the resumption of the first narrative establishes Reverend Mother's awareness of these decisions alongside her regret that her father is dying ('Father, forgive me – I know not what I did'[90]). As it belatedly becomes clear, however, this sequencing of events, and the connection of these two disconnected narratives in a narrative strategy external to the character, is a necessary ploy regarding the plot which constitutes the novel's overall development; the feigned shift into the past undertaken in the anachrony is integral to a dramatic change in Reverend Mother's constitution. As such, the external retroversion, as it occurs in narrative time, though it comes before in the story, operates as the narrative ploy which alters Reverend Mother's adulthood, facilitates her ability to help Anna, and initiates an unspoken queer love between the two characters. With the narrative having thus developed in this direction, Reverend Mother's earlier distaste of her colleagues' cultural nationalism becomes an incidental and remote feature of the text, one which is elsewhere to the main thrust of the novel.

As becomes evident, the possibility of Anna's future is made to depend upon Reverend Mother coming to terms with this instance of homosexuality in relation to her acceptance of her father's death, which thus overrides her concerns with nationalist and national affairs. This alignment will make Anna's life possible after the trauma she suffers following the premature death of her brother Charlie. And more broadly, the narrative structure, and particularly its shuffling of *histoire* and *recit*, facilitates the novel's relation of what Fogarty calls a 'secret league of queer emotion'.[91] In a narrative analepsis (Reverend Mother 'remembered an evening six months ago'[92]) presented in dialogue in book three chapter one, Anna asks Reverend Mother if she can stay at the convent for Christmas; she does not want to return home as she has still not come to terms with Charlie's death. Both characters are presented in a dialogue which is denoted as six months prior to the first narrative of the novel. Thus again, a key scene in the novel occurs as an external retrospective, or a disconnected second narrative, which is made relative to the first narrative; similarly, it comes before in the time of the story and after in the time of the narrative, further establishing the sense that the narrative is composed of disconnected narrative fragments that are co-assembled in an omniscient narrative strategy which occur beyond the action and setting of the European convent located in Mellick in Ireland. As this analepsis between Reverend Mother and Anna ends, the narrative commentary signals, 'That was six months ago. Anna had decided to go home for Christmas; but the holidays, Reverend Mother understood, had not only been unhappy, but unpleasant.'[93] The analepsis thus reconnects with the first narrative and qualifies the action Reverend Mother will take on Anna's behalf.

The narrative strategy becomes evident as *The Land of Spices* draws to a close. As a result of Reverend Mother having supposedly worked through the suffering she experienced because of her father's homosexuality – formulated through the connection of two narratives in an omniscient narrative strategy – she is presented as finding the capacity to intervene on Anna's behalf against her grandmother concerning the acceptance of a scholarship. Thus, the resolution of Reverend Mother's past in the first narrative creates the situation in which

Anna's traumas can be resolved; Reverend Mother will not let Anna become hardened by an event in youth which will subsequently define her emotional and psychical demeanour. Anna's future thus depends on the resolution of Reverend Mother's past, which occurs as an effect of the narrative strategy and beyond the immediate action and setting of the novel (as does the resolution of Anna's present, which is dependent on the mourning of Reverend Mother's past). Importantly, because of these related resolutions, the narrative strategy facilitates the expression of the under-articulated and unspoken bond which features between Reverend Mother and Anna, and thus the 'novel's secret league of queer love' which, as Fogarty suggests of the text, 'gives space to same sex love that is otherwise prohibited from any outlet'.[94] While Fogarty suggests that 'the nun steers the young girl's life, but does so from afar',[95] the reading tended here suggests that this queer affection occurs as a result of the specific shuffling of *histoire* and *recit* that occurs through the narrative procedure as it establishes the situation in which – as a result of a nun mourning her past alongside a pupil mourning the death of her brother – Reverend Mother and Anna can arrive at the juncture of a fresh departure through an indirect and remote emotional connection, one which exceeds, and is not bound by, the cultural politics of Mellick or Ireland. In such terms, the alignment of detail and character plot lines, rather than any specific event or occurrence particular to this European Catholic convent in Ireland, caters for the unvoiced expression of queer feeling that is created between the two protagonists. As such, O'Brien's distanced omniscient narrative strategy, which like *Mary Lavelle* and *Pray for the Wanderer* occurs at a remove from the action, place and time of the respective novels, enables the meshing of social critique with narratives of individual development to create surreptitious queer perspectives, and otherwise difficult to voice cultural, social and political commentaries that are implanted on, rather than imitatively represented in or dictated by, the space of the Irish and European convent.

Another dimension to O'Brien's modernism

This returns us to the question of O'Brien's Irish modernism, which, in a moderately symbolic language, constitutes a feminist and queer critique of modernity as well as a dislocation between form and content as a consequence of the 'flawed' aspect of her omniscient narrative strategies. In the analysis developed in this chapter, O'Brien's modernism and her critique of modernity is built on a supposed flaw in her writing, a hypothesis which runs the risk of suggesting that O'Brien is a bad writer and that she flukes an uncanny formal modernism only through the lens of a suspicious and perverse reading strategy. O'Brien, however, repeats the same narrative 'flaw' across her novels in a systematic manner, a reoccurrence which accounts for the strange relationship that is instituted between form and content across her work, and is linked to how her writing, particularly in *Mary Lavelle* and *The Land of Spices*, achieves its feminist and queer critique of modernity, as well as its oblique relation to Ireland. Thus, if the 'flaws' are considered as integral to O'Brien's narrative performances – and it is difficult to argue against reading them as such given their coherency and systematic repetition – then a consideration of the relationship between the 'flawed' aspect of O'Brien's writing (that is, her penchant for narrative telling rather than an observational style which maintains a unity of action, space and time) and her feminist and queer perspectives enables an elucidation of how the latter are constructed and encoded in her texts, as well as a delineation of the specific form of O'Brien's Irish modernism and its relation to Irish history. As the analyses tended here suggest, the 'flawed' aspect of O'Brien's omniscient narratives highlights how the perspectives developed in her novels – Mary's feminist development, Matt's critique of post-independence Ireland's censorship policies, the exploration of same-sex love and queer feeling in *The Land of Spices* – occur through the aesthetic structures, rather than in the action, of her omniscient narratives of failed romances and individual development. A structural effect of which is that Irish cultural nationalism and Irish history, which appear in the narrative commentary beyond the time and setting of the novels, are a means and a trope for launching these narratives of individual development rather than a dialectical or informing force which underpins, shapes or determines their outcome. In *Mary Lavelle*, the failed romance plot and the narrative of the titular character's development are established against the absent presence of John, Mellick and the Civil War. In *Pray for the Wanderer*, the banning of Matt's novel by the Free State serves to establish discussion around censorship under de Valera's government, but the novel's failed romance plot ultimately extends beyond the relevance of that content to its overall trajectory. And in *The Land of Spices*, the cultural nationalism of Reverend Mother's colleagues is deployed to launch the narrative of her staying at the convent to protect Anna Murphy; ultimately though, Reverend Mother's past in relation to her father's homosexuality in Bruges facilitates the development of the unspoken queer bond developed between the protagonists. In such terms, the 'flaw' or irregular shape of O'Brien's writing is not necessarily determined by Ireland's uneven development, and neither do her characters particularly suffer from this trauma (Mary is unperturbed by

John and Ireland; Matt's consternations arise from his romantic relationships; and Reverend Mother's and Anna's traumas derive from familial situations). Moreover, the political dimensions of post-independence Ireland that occur in *Mary Lavelle* and *Pray for the Wanderer* do not emerge through an engagement with the material world in the novels' represented realities but appears through the overarching position of the omniscient narrator's discourse. There is thus very little represented or temporally located action in the novels which occurs in a parallel or micro-thru-macro scalar relationship with the historical realities of postcolonial Ireland; the action of the novels occurs in and through the temporal manipulations of the omniscient narrative strategies. In such terms, O'Brien's failed romance plots and narratives of individual development, meshed with feminist and queer perspectives, occur at a certain remove from Free State cultures and histories. Though Ireland is suggested, the dynamics of its historical condition remain underdetermined, spectral and vestigial in these texts, which, as Fogarty suggests, 'upturns the expectations of the nationalist novel, which posits a congruence between individual and nation'.[96] In turn, telling at an omniscient remove (which, as Bowen has demonstrated, has a place in modernism), and playing with the limits of that narrative structure, enables O'Brien's uncanny exposition of feminist and queer modernities, and the distance of her Irish modernism. Her interventions into the politics of modernity thus occur through, not despite, her distant omniscient narrative strategies, which subtly draw attention to how, and by what aesthetic means, they are constructed, and which affirm and deny, and absent and defer, certain extratextual histories.

5

John McGahern and the limits of Irish modernism

John McGahern is very rarely considered a modernist or in relation to Irish modernism. Emerging after a decade of literary sterility in Ireland, McGahern's writing marks for many a departure from the experimental forms of high and late modernism. Long lauded as one of Ireland's major writers of the second half of the twentieth century, his work – as well as the output of his peers, including Jennifer Johnston, Edna O'Brien and William Trevor – is often cited for its turn towards naturalist and social realist forms,[1] and its registration of the cultural and social landscape of post-independence and contemporary Ireland.[2] Joe Cleary, for example, includes McGahern in a group of naturalists that 'cultivated a bleak naturalist aesthetic to present an anomic conception of small town and rural Ireland that countered the official pastoral versions of state and Church propaganda'.[3] For Cleary, it is with this same group of writers that 'the whole function of the writer was re-cast so that they increasingly saw their role in terms of individual dissent and critique: the artist not as visionary representative of "a risen people" but as solitary and alienated victim of an arthritic society'.[4] McGahern, in such terms, is not a cosmopolitan writer whose work maps the development and movement of global capital and imperialism. Nor is his work distinctly concerned with crises in language and representation, the refashioning of history and the seeing differently of reality, and thus the aesthetic precepts of modernism (elusiveness, fragmentation, self-reflexivity). The exuberance and overdetermination of James Joyce and the indigence and sobriety of Samuel Beckett are ostensibly elsewhere to McGahern's honed, moderately symbolic language that lends itself to the recording of past and present social circumstances. As per this largely dominant critical perception, McGahern, to date, has not been prevalent within conversations of Irish modernism – as is evidenced by recent edited collections dealing with this critical terrain – despite the expanded formal, geographic and temporal remit of the term.

This chapter tests the boundaries and terms of Irish modernism by considering McGahern's writing within its scope. McGahern's work clearly expands the remit of Irish modernism if cultural output in modernity is a modus operandi for defining modernism. As per the new modernist studies, the development of inter, mid-century, rural and vernacular modernisms make McGahern an obvious candidate for analysis in terms of expanding definitions of modernism. Particularly, the criteria for intermodernism, as put forward by Kristin Bluemel, provides an entry for McGahern's consideration within modernist discussion: intermodernists 'represent working-class and working middle-class cultures', are 'often politically radical, or "radically eccentric"', and are 'committed to non-canonical, even "middlebrow" or "mass genres"'.[5] Though McGahern does not correspond directly to Bluemel's criteria – or the temporal scope for intermodernism: 'interwar, wartime and immediately postwar years'[6] – his writing easily maintains positive associations with an intermodernist remit: features of his corpus include the representation of working-class and working middle-class cultures, a radicalism in terms of the moral order of mid-century Ireland, and a seeming commitment to mass genres. Similarly, Bluemel, with Michael McCluskey, puts forward terms for rural modernity, to which McGahern also broadly corresponds. As the other of urban modernity, rural modernity, through terms such as 'country, pastoral, nationalism, nostalgia, conservatism ... admit[s] more complex and contradictory data into the critical narrative of modernism and modernity',[7] and thus 'rural regions, communities, classes and figures can originate and sustain histories of and criticism on modernity and the modern'.[8] Indeed, a host of criticism on McGahern has laid the groundwork for this potentiality; he is often regarded as one of the finest surveyors of specific facets of twentieth-century Irish life, his writing representing the end of a certain form of rurality and the development of a certain modernity in Ireland.

Concurrently, then, the relationship between McGahern's writing and Ireland's modernity invites critical attention in terms of the representational strategies of modernist writing. Built up through inexpression, McGahern's novels maintain and respect the silence that constituted so much of what is now understood as the difficulty and solitude of Irish society and country life during the mid-twentieth century as it faced its own failures of sovereignty following independence. Engaging and deferring the dynamics of that modernity, his fictional worlds are often bitter and repressed realities which are always pregnant with the explosive tension of what is not being said. The peculiar quality of the writing exhibits a capacity to convey so much through what it leaves out and, in doing so, gently eases the pressure of the era with which it deals. Concerning that process, in his introduction to *Creatures of the Earth*, McGahern writes, of the short stories collected there, that 'unless they were reinvented, re-imagined and somehow dislocated from their origins, they never seemed to work. The imagination demands that life be told slant because of its need of distance'.[9] McGahern's 'telling slant' and 'need of distance' is also particular to his novels, which until recently, have been under-examined for how they represent what they represent. Reinvented, reimagined and dislocated from (the presence of) their origins, his fiction establishes a certain 'distance' – to take McGahern at his word – from the social worlds out of which they seemingly emerge. Often read as providing a window on the actually lived world, McGahern's narrative procedures, complex operations in themselves, thus beg analytic attention in terms of what they have been made, critically speaking, to represent: post-independence Irish society and rural life.

With modernism now operating as both a mode of cultural production in modernity, and an array of aesthetic strategies which include alienation, estrangement and the mobilization of epistemological doubt, the temporal expansion of modernist studies invites the interrogation of new modernisms in expanded (economic, geographic, temporal) and extant criteria (aesthetic, formal, linguistic). This chapter analyses McGahern's writing in relation to Irish modernism in such terms. It focuses on *The Barracks* (1963), *The Dark* (1965), *Amongst Women* (1990) and *That They May Face the Rising Sun* (2002) to take account of the range of narrative forms and focuses that McGahern undertakes across his career. Specifically, it interrogates the aesthetic operations of these novels to analyse if and where Irish modernism ends – both as a mode of narration and as a historical and stylistic phenomenon – and if McGahern can be included in that discussion. As the final study in a sequential analysis of high to moderate modernisms, and now an apparent turn to naturalism and realism after modernism, and thus the end or limit of a certain version of (Irish) modernism, this chapter explores the critical distinctions and tensions between concepts of realism, naturalism and modernist experimentation.

The Barracks and the construction of McGahern's referent

At first blush, McGahern's premier novel manifests an aesthetic strategy at quite a distance from the concerns of high modernism. *The Barracks* is a third-person narrative which recounts Elizabeth Reegan's ordeal with cancer. Married to a disgruntled Garda Sergeant, a bitter veteran of Ireland's War of Independence, the narrative focalizes Elizabeth's life and has access to her thoughts and memories. Set in a police barracks, an environment in which McGahern famously lived during his childhood, the story echoes his well-documented youth, a major feature of which was his father's poor treatment of his own mother before she died of cancer when he was six years old. As a formally and stylistically direct novel, *The Barracks* has paved the way for criticism on McGahern to place heavy emphasis on his biography and the social reality in which he lived and grew up, thereby validating the pertinence of historicist and materialist paradigms as apposite modes of analysis concerning this body of writing, as well as justifying the emergence of a branch of McGahern criticism which sees his writing as referentially representing specific facets of twentieth-century Irish life. Indeed, it is difficult not to refer to the various accounts of McGahern's life when considering the potential impetuses for his fictions. His 'story' has been documented in his non-fictional writings, various interviews as well as other national and international media, and is now very well known. Eamon Maher, for example, sees McGahern's fictions as striking to the core of the social and religious realities of his lifetime,[10] and Eamon Grennan finds in McGahern the 'best cartographer of the physical and metaphysical landscape our generation, and Ireland as a whole, has moved across over the past sixty years'.[11] The formal structures of the writing seem to support these arguments given that McGahern's supposed naturalism is a form of mimesis ably suited for the representation of historical realities. Grace Tighe Ledwidge, for example, writes that the tragedy of Elizabeth 'unfolds in the bleak, postcolonial world of mid-twentieth-century rural Ireland. It is a world marked by economic stagnation where mass emigration has devastated the poorer regions of the country. It is a time when the stability of the Irish family is viewed by Church and state as essential to the success of the new Republic.'[12] Thus, with the referent in the case of much of McGahern criticism almost unanimously mid-twentieth-century Irish society, as well as his childhood, adolescence and adulthood,[13] McGahern provides a compelling case for the analysis of mid-century and rural modernisms and modernities in Ireland.

Specifically, *The Barracks* explores the role of the housewife in mid-century Ireland and thus mounts a gendered critique of that society, one established through Elizabeth's impending death due to cancer. Elizabeth deals with her illness alone as her husband, for the most part, refuses to acknowledge and engage with her situation. This is most pertinently brought to the fore at the novel's end, after Elizabeth has died, where her husband is passive regarding his wife's death and continues his life as before. The ending thus consolidates the isolation that Elizabeth has been forced to undergo in a society in which the rural housewife relies on familial company for activity and solace. Regarding the novel's narrative strategy, Elizabeth's management of this trauma is narrated in two distinct ways: she is presented as repressing the reality of her illness through a focus on habitual activity; and she is presented as exploring her past for meaning before she dies. Regarding the former, when confronting her illness without support, and undergoing an existential crisis,[14] Elizabeth resorts to habit to forget and repress her illness. Habit in the form of forgetting thus provides her with a means of 'knowing-how' and coping,[15] and her focus on routine and the quotidian assuage the play of her imagination and, consequently, her fear of death. On the latter point, which is significant for understanding how the novel blurs distinctions between realism and modernism, Elizabeth recovers meaning and finds momentary calm in what are presented as her memories, particularly her recollections of her past life with Halliday, the doctor that she met and fell in love with many years before in London. In the third chapter, after Elizabeth finds herself in crisis following her first consultation concerning her suspected cancer,[16] an evocative memory comes to her mind:[17] 'And then a single voice of memory broke across her agitation and she grew calm to listen.'[18] Elizabeth remembers Halliday asking her, 'What the hell is all this living and dying about anyway, Elizabeth? That's what I'd like to be told?'[19] Thereafter, Elizabeth experiences more evocative memories, which ultimately have the effect of provoking a change in the narrative operation of the novel.[20]

The Barracks until this point is presented in the third person, the focus of the narration has been on Elizabeth and she has been the only character to which the narration has had internal access. Every other character in the novel is experienced through their participation in dialogue. The recounting of this scene, however, marks a shift in the narrative procedure. The narrative remains in the third person, but access to Johnny Halliday's consciousness is also represented: 'He didn't care whether he shocked her or not. He had given up all hope of his life ever getting strength and purpose through her. No, no, no he argued with himself, she'd not be always there in the evenings when he'd come home tired.'[21] Coterminous with Halliday's represented consciousness, the narrative also relates the internal voice of a past (in relation to the 'first narrative' of the novel) and younger Elizabeth: 'She was still in subjection to him, but she'd recover. She'd smash that subjection, she'd hate him, he was the cause of all her suffering; when she'd got completely free of him she'd never see him again.'[22] The narration is still in the form of the third person but, as in this particular scene, with expanded scope and knowledge. As the scene ends, the narration shifts back to its previous third person focus on the elder Elizabeth:

> 'What is all this living and dying about anyway?' came almost as flesh of her own thought at last in this small-town café, but it had been Halliday's question in the beginning, it had never been hers alone. Even if she hadn't cancer she was still growing old and it was more than time to face up to the last problems; but weren't they so inevitable and obvious that they were better ignored? Were the real problems faced and solved or rather declared insoluble or were they not simply lived in the changes of her life? She could live her life through in its own mystery, without any purpose, except to watch and bear witness. She did not care. She was alive and being was her ridiculous glory as well as her pain.[23]

In this passage, which directly follows the remembrance of Elizabeth's life with Halliday, there is a noticeable change in Elizabeth's demeanour as she begins to accept her illness. Particularly, this change in demeanour becomes manifest after a change in the mode of narration. When the process of memory changes from the passive form of evocation and habit to the active form of searching and recollection, the focalization of the narration expands and has access to the inner conscience of Elizabeth and Halliday. A process of remembrance is thus undertaken on behalf of Elizabeth in omniscient form, and the expansion of the scope of narration would suggest that this operation has been necessary to host this memory. A new narrative situation – a second narrative is produced in relation to the first narrative – creates the possibility for Halliday's voice to emerge. Elizabeth's change in demeanour is thus achieved after an expansion in focalization and a shift to omniscient narration, an effect of which is that the narrative operation foregoes the coherency it had previously established. Following the deployment of this memory, the narration reverts to the third person and focalizes Elizabeth finding comfort in the remembrance of this past encounter with Halliday. Elizabeth's exploration of memory thus prompts this shift in narrative perspective which caters for the creation of Halliday's voice in the novel and the presentation of a locus from which peace can be derived.

Meaning in *The Barracks* is thus generated through the active recourse to forgetting and remembering, where remembering involves a fragmentation of the narrative operation. When Elizabeth is overwhelmed by her situation, she is presented as engaging in habit memory whereby she generates meaning in the repression of recollection and searching. Contrastingly, when Elizabeth is narrated as recalling memories, meaning is generated through an analeptic narrative process which entails a fracturing of the aesthetic procedure. As a result, Elizabeth's story is assembled from different sources and through different narrative modes. Elizabeth, in turn, is not a coherent subject imitatively represented in the narrative, but one whose subjectivity is assembled through the narrative strategy (a performance pushed to a more extreme and radical degree by McGahern in *The Dark*). In such terms, it is not necessarily the friction between remembering and forgetting which allows Elizabeth to create meaning as she faces death, but the nuanced control of both in a third-person narrative which sacrifices consistency of representation to perform the different narrative operations required for the telling of this story of domestic life in rural Ireland. The introduction of Halliday, through an expanded focalization towards omniscient narration, allows for Elizabeth to remember a loving relationship in London which operates in stark contrast to her difficult marriage in rural Ireland. This critique of gender dynamics and roles in rural Ireland is thus made possible through a narrative operation which foregoes a consistency of representation in the telling of its polemic. The formal structures of the writing of *The Barracks*, then, extend beyond a belated and imitative referential representation of mid-century Irish life as McGahern constructs his referent in a fragmented narrative form which straddles realist and modernist distinctions.

Responding to such tendencies in this corpus, criticism focused on McGahern's aesthetic strategies has suggested that his fiction can be peculiar when it comes to the writing of history and biography.[24] Denis Sampson, for example, sees 'the true adventure' of his fiction as consisting 'in the engagement of the imagination with the everyday'.[25] More recently, Stanley van der Ziel and Richard Robinson have respectively situated McGahern's writing within a tradition of nineteenth- and twentieth-century writing. van der Ziel shows how 'aesthetic principles and ideas McGahern found in the writers he admired are reflected in his own fiction',[26] and Robinson undertakes the task of showing how McGahern's writing conceals and reveals its modernist traces, and evaluates the extent to which 'literary modernism ... is belatedly assimilated into McGahern's work'.[27] Similarly, Niamh Campbell suggests that McGahern's 'writerly atmosphere', while it 'looks like chronicle, so subtle the lyric effects that produce it are invisible', is 'really the result of a long career of emphasis and development'.[28] Concerning his thinking about the writing process, McGahern often preferred to deal with his 'aesthetic and procedural priorities'[29] and was largely shy concerning the referent of his fiction.[30] van der Ziel points out that McGahern

> maintained that it was not only futile but counterproductive to look for the historical or biographical elements in a work of art because 'Often it seems to me

that the effect of much biographical criticism is to return fiction to the original confusion out of which clarity was won.'[31]

This gesture concerning the dissimilitude of art and history does not directly correspond to the aesthetic of a writer who is claimed as engaged in representing a set of familial, personal and social circumstances external to literary writing. As Frank Shovlin suggests, 'the reversion to biography is an all too common methodological distraction when it comes to critical reading of McGahern's work'.[32] While his novels engage the cultural dynamics of mid-century and contemporary Ireland, the representation of reality is simultaneously rendered as a hermeneutic enigma which demands multiple modes of interpretation, narration and translation, an undertaking which becomes most deliberate with *The Dark* (1965).

The Dark and McGahern's 'important' mode of narration

In an interview in 2002 with *Hotpress*, McGahern suggested that *The Dark* 'is probably still my most important book',[33] but he did not overly elaborate on why this is so. Undoubtedly, its presentation of scenes of clerical and parental sexual abuse were and still are a provocation to an Irish society overseen by Church and State which covered up so many heinous crimes and scandals. Simultaneously, *The Dark* is also McGahern's most adventurous and complicated narrative performance. This double aspect of the novel begs close attention for how it relates what it relates, and thus the relationship between mid-century Irish life and the aesthetic operation of the novel. Like *The Barracks*, *The Dark* is narrated with a focus on one individual, Young Mahoney, whose life is traumatized by an abusive patriarchal figure. Unlike the seemingly coherent third-person narrative which *The Barracks* presents, the narrative of *The Dark* is presented in first-, second- and third-person modes, as well as free indirect narration. The fractured account of Young Mahoney's life thus makes clear that a politics of narration is at play, the impetus and meaning of which remains enigmatic in criticism.[34] The narrative mode seems linked to a real history of trauma; these details find support in McGahern's *Memoir*, an account that Dermot McCarthy has deployed to read *The Dark* autobiographically.[35] Simultaneously, a host of the novel's preoccupations diverge from a strictly imitative and referential representation of traumatic experience, as evidenced by the novel's aesthetic and ethical concerns: namely, the aestheticization of traumatic experience, self-aestheticization, the ethics of writing trauma in literary language, as well as its modernist impulses. Considering this dual aspect of the novel, the following reading argues that *The Dark* scrutinizes traumatic experience and the possibility of its literary representation through a procedure of narrative fragmentation which, due to its different and varied concerns, is beyond deterministic accumulation to an anterior extratextual signified.[36]

In doing so, this reading provides a different understanding of a narrative procedure which has long perplexed critics. McCarthy, for example, notes that an aspect of *The Dark* which has 'drawn particular critical attention' is 'a narrative voice that modulates through all three persons for no clear programmatic reason'.[37] When discussing this feature of the narrative, particularly the second-person voice, McCarthy gives it a programmatic agenda: 'Almost half of *The Dark* is narrated from a second-person point of view which should be understood as inflected by both a retrospective temporality and a "confessional" ethos'.[38] McCarthy explains this shift to the second-person perspective in *The Dark* by noting that it appears after chapter five (the scene in which Young Mahoney masturbates) and creates a 'narrative fission in which the confessional "I" … divides, becoming the penitent "you" and the narrator-confessor who addresses "you"'.[39] This is slightly overstated, however, given that chapters one and two are narrated from a third-person perspective, and that chapter three is presented in free indirect narration (indeed, most critics of the novel direct focus to its surprising inclusion of the second-person voice and overlook its relation to first-person, third-person and free indirect narration in the overall narrative structure). In such terms, there has already been a narrative fission, before the emergence of the first-person voice, from the beginning of the novel. In this reading of *The Dark*, I suggest that the second-person voice is part of a self-reflexive aesthetic strategy of fracture and fragmentation that, along with its scrutiny of traumatic experience, both explores and disperses the tenets of identity formation. This *anti-bildungsroman* process, as both van der Ziel and Robinson have respectively suggested, can be located in modernist terms as occurring 'beyond mid-century generic exhaustion' and, particularly, as emerging from the 'post-Trilogy *nouveau roman* period in which selfhood has been evacuated and subjectivity erased'.[40]

The first two chapters of *The Dark* are related from a third-person perspective. The narrative presents scenes displaying elder Mahoney's brutality, the suffering of his children at his hands and the tortuous reality which the family inhabit; and the narrative device has access and is sympathetic to the emotions of a central character, Young Mahoney ('He') and a group of which Young Mahoney is a member ('They'). In these two chapters, the children are presented as succumbing to Mahoney's reign of terror. In the first, Young Mahoney is humiliated and nearly beaten by his father and is left trying to regain calm in an outside lavatory. In the second, the siblings humour him and fall into his trap by accepting his offer of a boat trip even though they know he will turn foul again. The presentation of these moments from a third-person perspective suggests that the narrative strategy assumes a distance to these events to separate the voice which recounts the proceedings from the individuals it records. Simultaneously, in relating their 'smiles' – 'There they'd listen silently, with grave faces: but once they'd turn to each other they'd smile cruelly'[41] – it communicates that its sympathies lie with the children and against the elder Mahoney. In turn, the deployment of third-person narration appears to be integrally linked to the traumatic content that is related. As Cathy Caruth's influential account of trauma and its narration goes, the traumatic event is not fully perceived in its happening and is only grasped, while remaining inaccessible, after the fact.[42] Distorting the possibility of historical representation, trauma obscures the referencing of the past, which is no longer simply formed in the first-person of the past simple tense ('I was'). Rather, trauma remains present and does not become a past which can be directly narrated by the self. In such terms, the third-person narrative operation of chapters one and two, as a result of the content they relate, can be understood as a symptom of the effect which trauma has on the ability to narrate traumatic events and as a strategy for dealing with those events: symptomatic in the sense that the events are not recounted through a first-person 'I', strategic in the sense that the narrative operation, as a result of Young Mahoney and his siblings' failures at rebuke, creates a separation between the voice that remembers the events and the individual that is the focus of those events. The same strategy is deployed in chapter four when Father Gerald is introduced. Like those events concerning Mahoney as an ominous force, the scenes in which Father Gerald poses a threat and is unchallenged are recorded in a third-person voice that will refer to Young Mahoney as 'he' and his siblings as 'they', thereby creating a distance between the narrative voice and the helpless subjects (Young Mahoney and his siblings). In such terms, then, the deployment of third-person narration in each of these chapters seems linked to a traumatic history of parental and clerical abuse and harassment. The narrative operation thus creates the means by which the later 'I' of chapter five is separated from the person and group that both suffered and witnessed the violent and traumatic events of chapters one and two (in turn disrupting any simple conceptualization of *The Dark* as a methodical coming-of-age story where the subject's relationship to society develops following a cause-and-effect chronology). In doing so,

McGahern's novel shows the potential effects of a real history of trauma (and the resulting disidentification this entails). Simultaneously, it demonstrates how trauma can be written in the novel form. The opening chapters of *The Dark* render both the possible impact of a real history of abuse, as in Caruth's referential terms for traumatic experience, as well as a mode of writing, a controlled aesthetic strategy, which translates and represents the effects of, and simultaneously displaces and distances, an originary trauma, as in Jacques Derrida's terms for writing which defers presence through the proxy of the sign. From the outset, then, McGahern's novel is both concerned to approximate certain histories of abuse, while it simultaneously lays bare its use of the literary artifice necessary for the construction of a representation of traumatic experience.

A more extreme performance of this predicament is evident in chapter three, in which free indirect narration is deployed:

> The worst was to have to sleep with him the nights he wanted love, strain of waiting for him to come to bed, no hope of sleep in the waiting – counting and losing the count of the thirty-two boards across the ceiling, trying to pick out the darker circles of the knots beneath the varnish. Watch the moon on the broken brass bells at the foot of the bed. Turn and listen and turn. Go over the day that was gone, what was left done or undone, or dream of the dead days with her in June.[43]

In a manner similar to the use of the third-person perspective in chapters one and two, the deployment of free indirect narration for the presentation of this scene can be understood as symptomatic of, as well as a strategic means of dealing with, the traumatic content related. Symptomatic in the sense that the memory of the event falls outside of the category of subjective experience; strategic in the sense that the remembering is not undertaken by one who would be the heir to the events in the same way as a remembering 'I'. Similarly, a separation from the 'I' that is recorded in dialogue with Mahoney in this scene is achieved through the deployment of free indirect narration, the use of which disrupts the ascription of the memory to an individual; even if the narrative recounts an 'I' in dialogue – 'Soon, I'll be able to go to sleep'[44] – this 'I' is not necessarily the voice that records the scene. In such terms, the trauma of these events can be understood as necessitating free indirect narration because of the need for non-identification and separation from the 'I', 'You' and 'He' which first-, second- and third-person narrative voices create.

Concurrently, like the opening chapters, this chapter is also concerned with the aesthetic representation of trauma, and the *writing* of traumatic content. As the above passage attests, as well as others,[45] it is a highly aestheticized scene, one that invokes the poetic capacities of language and delights in the allure of its sonorous qualities. The effect of relating this content in such language draws attention to its status as a scene of literary fiction. Presenting an instance of parental sexual abuse in a language which is pleasing makes explicit the problematic of representing trauma in literature. Seamus Heaney responds to this particular aspect of McGahern's writing: 'Take a novel by John McGahern where there is a kind of undertow of suffered life and a certain desolation, but there's also the cello music of the writing itself.'[46] The delight in language that is an integral part of the writing and reading process (regardless of whether the text is conceived as 'readerly' or 'writerly', in Roland Barthes's terms) defers the referential capacities of the literary representation of trauma. As Barthes writes, 'writing is: the science of the various blisses of language',[47] a bliss, as McGahern demonstrates, that does not disappear in the rendering of particularly traumatic content. Similarly, the deployment of free indirect narration in this instance, rather than a first-, second- or third-person voice, which will always simultaneously belong to other forms of writing, draws attention to the literariness of the text. The deployment of highly aestheticized language and free indirect narration in this chapter, as well as in the final chapter of the novel – 'the memories of the nightmare nights in the bed with the broken brass bells came'[48] (note McGahern's alliteration here) – thus serves a dual purpose: to separate the narrative content from the possibility of ascription to a remembering individual (which, like the other narrative voices, ultimately disrupts and fractures Young Mahoney's narrative) and to expose the impossibility of ethically representing trauma in literature because of the pleasure derived from literary language and form by writer and reader. *The Dark*, in such terms, continues to represent traumatic experience through a medium which is also concerned to demonstrate its aesthetic intentions, making its narrative content both similar and different to an extratextual traumatic experience, as well as the cultural memories which it might be read as transmitting.

The fragmentation of the subject continues with, rather than finds resolution in, the deployment of the first-person voice in chapter five; and like the earlier chapters, the shift to first-person narration is directly linked to the content related: a scene in which Young Mahoney masturbates and thereafter suffers guilt because of the act. The close relationship between masturbation and the emergence of the first-person voice in the novel marks a departure from traumatic experience as a determining force in *The Dark*'s movement between different narrative voices, even though Young Mahoney is afraid of betraying Catholic doctrine. Specifically, while demonstrating the inner turmoil felt by Young Mahoney as he follows Catholic dogma concerning auto-affection, this scene simultaneously suggests that masturbation is a necessary act of aesthetic self-constitution, a circumstance which becomes observable with recourse to Derrida's reflections on Jean-Jacques Rousseau's masturbation, an account which lends a more nuanced rationale to the occurrence of the first-person voice with adolescent auto-affection in *The Dark*.

The scene begins with Young Mahoney engaged in masturbation: 'She stirs to life, I have her excited, she too is crazy, get hands under. One day she must come to me. I try to pump madly on the mattress, fighting to get up her nightdress, and get into her, before too late, swoon of death into the softness of her flesh.'[49] The first non-quoted use of the personal pronoun – 'I have her excited' – occurs in relation to a non-present other that is summoned through the act of masturbation. In the case of male masturbation, as Derrida writes in his critique of Rousseau's *Emile* in *Of Grammatology*, the woman's absence rouses the feeling of total ownership of the object of one's desire; masturbation, or 'the dangerous supplement', cheats maternal nature and celebrates both the absence and the immediacy of the other.[50] Thus, for Derrida, as for Young Mahoney, the 'dangerous supplement' involves the transgression of 'nature' in which, as Derrida suggests with Rousseau, 'one corrupts oneself' in 'affecting oneself by another presence',[51] which also brings about a certain shame. Following the act, Young Mahoney displays guilt as he imagines confessing his sins: 'Bless me father, for I have sinned. It's a month since my last confession. I committed one hundred and forty impure actions with myself. A shudder started at what the priest would say.'[52] This particular form of reproach will remain consistent with masturbation throughout *The Dark*. Like Derrida's Rousseau, Young Mahoney 'will never stop having recourse to, and accusing himself of, this onanism that permits one to be himself affected by providing himself with presences, by summoning absent beauties. In his eyes it will remain the model of vice and perversion'.[53] Importantly, however, this shame comes with an ironic and detached admission of guilt:

> Flushed cheeks was all that was left to show what I had done, and the sock. Pull it off, the wool was wet, but it'd dry. Only for the discovery once of the sock's uses the sheet would stain grey and stiff as with starch and Mahoney might notice.
>
> The clock beat on the lowest of the shelves, twenty past three. A great clattering army of stares were black on the yew tree outside the window, and it was time to get up and dress and go downstairs.[54]

Young Mahoney's shame thus becomes a spur for reflection on selfhood: 'I'd never be a priest. I was as well to be honest. I'd never be anything. It was certain.'[55]

In this sense, masturbation is concerned with the other through which the self is formed; it constitutes a narcissistic engagement with otherness in the constitution of the self. As Derrida points out, 'Rousseau neither wishes to think ... that this alteration does not simply happen to the self, that it is the self's very origin',[56] and that it establishes a break from maternal nature. The act of masturbation, Derrida suggests, is an integral moment in the adolescent transgression of nature and the constitution of the self: 'Affecting oneself by another presence, one corrupts oneself [makes oneself other] by oneself.'[57] For this reason then, masturbation is, like writing, an act of self-constitution: 'It is myself who exerts myself to separate myself from this force that nature has entrusted to me.'[58]

It is unsurprising, then, after the act of masturbation and the (ironic) admission of guilt, that, at the end of the chapter, the narrator breaks the promise he made as a boy to his (now dead) mother:

> On the road as I came with her from town loaded with parcels and the smell of tar in the heat I'd promise her that one day I'd say Mass for her. And all I did for her now was listen to Mahoney's nagging and carry on private orgies.
>
> I'd never be a priest. I was as well to be honest. I'd never be anything. It was certain.
>
> There was little to do but sit at the fire and stare out at the vacancy of my life at sixteen.[59]

The last two lines signal that the transgression of maternal nature has happened; Young Mahoney is 'honest' with himself that he will 'never be a priest' and that he will not fulfil what he before perceived as his mother's wish for him to say Mass for her.[60] Instead, he views 'my life at sixteen'.[61] Importantly then, the constitution of the self in *The Dark*, achieved alongside the deployment of first-person narration, coincides with masturbation and a break with 'maternal nature', and is not necessarily determined by a traumatic history: as Derrida suggests, 'the dangerous supplement ... destroys very quickly the forces that Nature has slowly constituted and accumulated'.[62] As in chapter twenty-two, for example, when Young Mahoney is about to take a writing exam: 'It was impossible not to laugh too, it was comic, the whole affair exaggerated, I was going to no crucifixion on a mountain between thieves but to a desk in a public building to engage in a writing competition'.[63] Or in the same chapter when, during the lull of orgasm followed by masturbation, Young Mahoney relates: 'I'd hang around till I was calmer, brush my clothes clean. The exam was tomorrow. It was far away as tomorrow now, I didn't care.'[64] Both instances, then, attest to a transgression of the education system, or, as Derrida writes, 'the art of pedagogy ... [which]

allows the work of Nature time to come to fruition.'[65] Significantly, the first-person voice is deployed in those self-constituting acts of transgression against 'nature' and, in the case of the former, a moment of aesthetic self-consciousness. Young Mahoney recognizes that his fate does not lie in crucifixion as a saviour between thieves but rather – in an echo of Vladimir in *Waiting for Godot* and, by extension, Saint Augustine – his fate is uncertain and heterogeneous to predetermined morals and narratives: 'Do not despair, one of the thieves was saved; do not presume, one of the thieves was damned.'[66] The first-person voice, far from performing any ideal union of selfhood, confirms that the other, like language, which becomes Derrida's central point, has already deposited its trace inside us as we announce ourselves in the first-person. The coincidence of masturbation and self-aestheticization thus points to the difference of *The Dark*'s (and Derrida's) 'I' with itself. The novel's scenes of seeming calm are thus also, rather than ideal self-union, continuous moments of identity creation. This in turn negates the possibility that a coherent first person 'I' precedes the occurrence of the third-person voice and free indirect narration in the first four chapters. Proceeding the third-person voice and free indirect narration, the first-person voice signals, beyond the traumatic content related earlier in the novel, a subject continuously undergoing processes of self-formation, in turn amplifying, rather than resolving, the fragmented and disparate subject which the overall narrative operation of the novel presents. This aspect of the text thus complicates an understanding of its mode of representation as wholly determined by an abusive and/or violent history. The novel is undoubtedly linked to a certain and specific history of trauma in Ireland. Simultaneously, however, as the use of the first-person voice and its link to masturbation signals, *The Dark*'s fragmented mode of narration, extends beyond, and maintains diverging concerns to, a determining historical or traumatic reality which would anchor its play.

Following the act of masturbation/self-constitution in chapter five, Young Mahoney becomes resituated in the external world of the family environment in chapter six; but the narrative voice does not return to the distanced voice of the third person, or that of the voiceless under personal duress. Further fragmenting the subject, the second-person voice is deployed to negotiate the difficulties of domestic life after the constitution of the self has begun. It first occurs in a scene in which Young Mahoney comes to the aid of his sister who is being beaten by their father: 'You'd watched it come to this, hatred rising with every word and move he made, but watched so many times it was little more than habit.'[67] Young Mahoney thereafter intervenes on behalf of his sister – '"Hit and I'll kill you," you said and you knew nothing'[68] – and quells the violent episode but remains the host of his father's savage taunting: 'The violence had been easier far than the jeering and mockery.'[69] In the initial sentence quoted here, Young Mahoney is both active and passive. In the first half of the sentence – 'You'd watched it come to this, hatred rising with every word and move he made'[70] – Young Mahoney has reached a climax and is in the thrall of explosion. In the second half of the sentence – 'but watched so many times it was little more than habit'[71] – he is presented as distant and passive. As the violence increases, Young Mahoney knows the elder Mahoney's actions are wrong and so he has the confidence to challenge him. But as the violence dies and the situation diffused, Young Mahoney slips into inactivity – 'You hadn't the strength even if you'd wanted. The whole kitchen and was sick and despairing. Hatred had drained everything empty'[72] – and succumbs to the elder Mahoney's savage taunting: 'I'd have smashed you to pieces, do you hear that, to pieces, you pup, and you'd have tried it, you pup.'[73] The second-person voice thus records how Young Mahoney, like in chapters one and two, endures Mahoney's reign of terror but, unlike those chapters, not without having made a threat on his life. The event recounted in this chapter is not a total success, yet neither is it a total failure. Its content falls between those scenes narrated by a distanced voice (third-person or free indirect narration) which registers events in which Young Mahoney was abused, passive and hurt, and those narrated in a first-person voice which registers acts of self-aestheticization and self-constitution.

The second-person voice similarly features in chapter seven when Young Mahoney is presented as attending confession because he wants to take action against himself for having corrupted himself in the act of masturbation. It is also deployed in chapters twelve to sixteen when Young Mahoney, during his stay with Father Gerald, is presented as tackling the various injustices that are done to his sister Joan and himself. Correspondingly, it features in chapter twenty-eight, when Young Mahoney mediates the unknown of the future during his visit to the university.[74] Directly related to the content presented, then, the second-person voice represents the subject caught between activity and passivity and strength and weakness. An active and accusatory 'you' signals a split subject, one caught between moral turmoil and the impetus to take action, and thus one that succeeds and fails. In this sense, the second person voice, like the use of the third-person perspective in the opening chapters, potentially occurs as a symptom of a real history of abuse and trauma; simultaneously, it features as an aesthetic strategy which translates the effects of, and ultimately displaces and distances, an originary trauma. In the latter terms, it directly contributes to, along with the deployment of the other narrative perspectives, the deliberate and continued fragmentation of *The Dark*'s subject, a process which dissolves the central tenets of the *bildungsroman* – the development, growth and progress of an individual in tandem with the dynamics of a specific modernity – and readily locates the novel within a late modernist aesthetic scepticism (this latter circumstance is particularly signalled in the final chapter through the use of free indirect narration which, as mentioned, McGahern deploys as a strategy of non-identification and self-dissolution).

In turn, *The Dark* presents a rigorous narrative schema, one which both potentially bears the effects of lived traumatic experience (its narrative splintering perhaps deriving from the affect of a traumatic history) and, contrastingly, one which, as it displays the signs of its own construction, uses the formal tools of the novel and literature to produce an account of individual development amidst a traumatic history. In this sense, the narrative operation can be understood as displaying the strategies and symptoms of the trauma victim, as well as a means of rendering an untranslatability to the novel's form. In such terms, the aesthetic strategy of *The Dark* maintains a proximity and an irreducible distance to a coherent extratextual referent which could be located as determining its cause of play (McGahern's biography, life in rural or mid-century Ireland). Or, as in Pascale Casanova's terms, 'literary space translates political and national issues into its own terms – aesthetic, formal, narrative, poetic, – and at once affirms and denies them'.[75]

Consequently, McCarthy's suggestion that there is 'a narrative voice that modulates through all three persons for no clear programmatic reason'[76] requires revision.[77] As Robinson suggests, 'McGahern's gesture towards a splintering of selfhood is actuated by something more than the ludic desire to experiment'.[78] As demonstrated here, the relation between each narrative voice and the content presented occurs as part of a deliberate and self-reflexive aesthetic strategy which is concerned with negotiating traumatic experience, the ethical problems of rendering trauma in fiction, and the aspects of individual development that are not wholly determined by, and remain divergent to, traumatic histories: free-indirect narration is deployed to render traumatic experience and to highlight the ethical challenges of undertaking such representations in literary form and language; the first-person voice is used in the presentation of events of aesthetic self-consciousness and self-constitution as well as transgressions against 'nature'; the second-person voice is employed to present the subject's negotiation between a will to act and an inability to act; and the use of the third-person voice signals both the potential effects of a history of abuse, as well as a mode of writing, a controlled aesthetic strategy, for narrating traumatic experience. And by morphing through these different narrative voices with their respective agendas, the narrative operation of *The Dark* manifests the scars of its construction and blurs, in the process, any simple distinction between a referential realism and a modernism energized by alienation, estrangement and epistemological doubt. *The Dark*, as David Malcolm succinctly suggests, 'inhabits the borderland between the relatively invisible conventions of realism and the foregrounded art of other kinds of fiction',[79] a circumstance which, as we will continue to see, makes McGahern an exemplary case for rendering fluid the critical distinctions between concepts of realism, naturalism and modernist experimentation, and thus for probing and rethinking the limits of Irish modernism.

McGahern's analepses: *Amongst Women* and *That They May Face the Rising Sun*

McGahern's next two novels *The Leavetaking* (1974, revised 1984) and *The Pornographer* (1979), like *The Barracks* and *The Dark*, are focused on a main character, though neither repeat the experiment of divided narration of the latter. Both *The Leavetaking* and *The Pornographer* present relatively coherent first-person narratives. Like *The Barracks*, they respectively include instances where the narrative focalization lapses from identifiable positions to thwart the seemingly coherent narrative operations previously established. This is particularly evident in a scene in *The Leavetaking* when, without any sign of a change in narration, the first-person voice of the narrator parasitically inhabits the first-person voice of the father in a manner which creates the effect of father speaking within son, and son speaking within father, throwing into question the origin, ownership and prerogative of the memory presented in the narrative.[80] Like the narration of Johnny Halliday in *The Barracks*, the process of remembrance in question involves the inhabitation of another character's voice – a character external to the action of the novel – in order for the required effect to be achieved. Following these four novels, McGahern's focus switches from the individual to the family and community with *Amongst Women* and *That They May Face the Rising Sun*.

Amongst Women marks a shift in narrative style in the John McGahern oeuvre. Moran and his position as the patriarch of his family form the central focus of the novel and thus the family unit in rural mid-century Ireland is the novel's object of exploration. The narrative is presented in a distant omniscient voice which rarely has access to the thoughts and emotions of the individual characters it shows.⁸¹ This strategy becomes particularly evident in the second scene, a narrative analepsis which presents the last Monaghan Day on which McQuaid visits Great Meadow and which establishes the background to Moran's character and disposition. McQuaid and Moran remember their activity in the War of Independence in dialogue; they flatter each other regarding their roles played in the war before ultimately disagreeing on the subject of life under Church and Government in the Free State, which in turn spells an end to their relationship and elucidates the nature of Moran's subsequent bullish silence. This analepsis establishes how Moran has become disconnected from local society, as well as his unflinching beliefs and need for total control over his immediate affairs. Thereafter, and throughout *Amongst Women*, Moran is observed exerting power over the house in the form of imposed habit, through which he offers his children both entrapment and security in Great Meadow. With the exception of Luke who abandons the family home, all eventually renounce outside affairs which cannot be assimilated to Moran and Great Meadow. Even Michael, who after Luke has the most fraught relationship with Moran, decides to visit Great Meadow for better or for worse. Just as McQuaid and his peers denounce a critical and recollective engagement with the founding of their society in favour of a habitual and stable nationalist memory, Moran's children in their temporary returns, with the exception of Luke, choose the safety of habit and that which they know: 'Beneath all differences was the belief that the house was essentially one. Together they were one world and could take on the world. Deprived of this sense they were nothing, scattered, individual things.'⁸²

As much as *Amongst Women* performs an exploration and interrogation of a patriarchal family in mid- to late-twentieth-century Ireland, it is not a chronological and innocent representation of a series of events which maps the historical progression of one event following another. After the first scene, in which Moran's daughters announce that they will celebrate Monaghan Day for his benefit, and beginning with the same narrative analepsis which features McQuaid's visit and his subsequent falling out with Moran, a very long narrative anachrony (a series of sequential analepses punctured by ellipses) is undertaken. All subsequent scenes, until the end of the novel, as they present the image of a reality in which familial habit led by the father is normalized, will form the content of this anachrony as the novel makes its way back to the 'present moment', or first narrative, from which it begins. Throughout, the narrative device provides commentary which structures the presentation of character dialogue and the direction of the narrative. In such terms, the narrative operation establishes its own apparatus of memory. The scene between Moran and McQuaid, in which the realities of the War of Independence are recounted, forms an allusion to a past prior to the first narrative. As an allusion, it is made to relate to the present tense moment of the first narrative and manifests that the narrative is a doubly temporal sequence. As Gérard Genette suggests, in narrative fiction, there is the time of the story recounted and there is the time of the narrative.[83] Thus, a time scheme which operates as a memory is invented in terms of another: the first narrative (itself translated, or told 'slant', from elsewhere). Concurrently, the presentation of scenes from an earlier past – for example, the recollection of aspects of the War of Independence in the narrative commentary before Moran and McQuaid's dialogue – signal another temporal position. The narrative commentary creates the memory of a scene within a scene that is already an allusion to the past, and is thus creating another 'first narrative' as Genette describes it: 'An anachrony can assume the role of first narrative with respect to another that it carries.'[84] The novel thus builds layers of memory in narrative time.

The social realism of *Amongst Women* is constructed through such means, a method very similar to aspects of Proust's *À la recherche du temps perdu* (*In Search of Lost Time*), a work in which the fashioning of analepses and prolepses gives modernist fiction its great and complex work of narrative memory. In that novel, as Genette observes, the figuring of the analepses is sometimes done in a manner wherein 'the narrative ... avoids acknowledging its own footprints'.[85] The effect of this avoidance, or 'negligence', as Genette writes, 'consists of forgetting the analeptic character of a section of narrative and prolonging that section more or less indefinitely on its own account, paying no attention to the point where it rejoins the first narrative',[86] and so the reader of *À la recherche du temps perdu* becomes exiled in the open past of the analepses. *Amongst Women*, though not as extreme in structure as the various volumes of Proust's magnum opus, can be understood in similar terms.

As mentioned, the novel opens with the Moran sisters recreating Monaghan Day for their father before the narrative begins the anachrony (or the progressive series of analepses punctured by ellipses) which constitutes the narrative fabric of *Amongst Women*. Though the narrative does reconnect with its point of departure (the revival of Monaghan Day) in a covert manner, this series of analepses almost has the effect of exiling the reader in the open past until, at the very end, with the brief mentioning of the revival of Monaghan Day, an opaque form of narrative reconciliation is performed. Most of the narrative of *Amongst Women* is relative to two previously related scenes: the first scene in which the daughters revive Monaghan Day, and the second scene (the analepsis presenting a previous Monaghan Day) which follows that in narrative time but anterior to it in terms of the supposed historical time of the opening scene. The former of these scenes, which is the first 'first narrative' and the present tense moment from which the novel embarks, changes in status and becomes a future temporality as the narrative anachrony which shapes the novel is undertaken. As it returns to this moment, the narrative operation is almost negligent concerning its own structure until it is retrospectively announced towards the end of the novel that 'the attempt to revive Moran with [Monaghan] Day had been futile'.[87] Thus, the narrative does not reconnect with the moment from which it embarks but links up with a narrative retrospection, related in the past tense, of that moment. In this sense, the narrative anachrony never rejoins the opening scene, the 'first narrative', satisfactorily. The first scene, by the end of the novel, becomes an ellipsis, a gap in memory between the analepses which form the fabric of the novel. In turn, the relation of past scenes to a seemingly 'present tense' moment, which features both as a first narrative and an ellipsis, entails that *Amongst Women*'s pivotal moment features as both a presence and later an absence in the novel. It thus disrupts expectations of completion as the narrative anachrony does not rejoin where it begins. As the narrative proceeds beyond that moment to relate Moran's death, the end of *Amongst Women* constitutes a new first narrative: 'The failure to change anything only strengthened their determination not to let him slip from them. They began to be in Great Meadow more than in their own homes.'[88] After Moran's death is related, his daughters' shift their attention to their brother and 'the men who lagged well behind on the path and were chatting and laughing pleasantly together', which announces a different present and future, one beyond and independent of Moran. As such, the social realism of *Amongst Women* is constructed through a series of achronological narrative fragments, the ordering of which subtly reveals how the novel's realism is produced. The narrative procedure, in turn, diffuses simple dichotomies between realism and modernism, and complicates the objectivity of the realist eye that gazes through the fourth wall, as well as understandings of McGahern's writing as constituting a window on the historical realities of mid-century Irish life. Like *The Barracks* and *The Dark*, then, the narrative structure of *Amongst Women* is not without a certain method of translation, one which establishes a proximity and an irreducible distance between its content and 'the original confusion out of which clarity was won'.[89]

That They May Face the Rising Sun institutes a similar narrative procedure to *Amongst Women*. The novel focuses on the quotidian affairs of a lakeside community and, like *Amongst Women*, its action is related by an omniscient narrative device, the scope of which encompasses the individuals that comprise that community and its transition towards an observable modernity at the end of the twentieth century in Ireland. And like *Amongst Women*, narrative analepses are used to establish the background of some of the novel's central characters, a particular example of which occurs early in the novel with the introduction of Bill Evans. Joe Ruttledge, who could loosely be described as the novel's main character, is presented as knowing the 'outlines of such a life',[90] and as one who can empathize with Bill Evans's gruff and taciturn manner. The narrative procedure until this point has only displayed access to Ruttledge's thoughts. In expanding its focus to elucidate Bill Evans's character, a story is presented of a domestic servant – male, no more than seven or eight years of age – who was beaten publicly by the Christian Brothers for a minor mistake.[91] This story/memory is not ascribed to Bill Evans, but it is suggested that it might be a part of his past:

> He would have known neither father nor mother. As a baby he would have been given in to the care of nuns. When these boys reached seven, the age of reason, they were transferred to places run by priests or brothers. When he reached fourteen, Bill Evans was sent out, like many others to his first farmer.[92]

Though the story might appear to be Ruttledge's, it features as an analepsis without ascribable origin and is suspended in the narrative. The account of the beating follows in the same manner:

> One morning a boy turned quickly away from a table and found the Dean unexpectedly in his path and went straight into him with a tray. Plates and bowls went flying. The soutane was splashed. Only the students who were seated close to the accident saw what happened next, and even they weren't certain. In the face of his fury it was thought that the boy broke the rule of silence to try to excuse the accident. The beating was sudden and savage.[93]

Following this, in sympathy and in an effort to confront this trauma, Ruttledge is presented as probing Bill Evans about his past. First he asks about his work on a farm and supposes that 'they didn't treat you very well', to which Bill Evans responds, after a period of seeming ignorance, 'Why are you asking me this, Joe?'[94] Ruttledge ignores Bill Evans's rebuke and slightly diffuses the situation before asking, 'Weren't you in a place run by brothers and priests before they sent you to the first farm?'[95] Ruttledge notices Bill Evans discomfort but persists: 'Before the priests and Brothers weren't you with nuns in a convent with other small boys? Weren't you treated better when you were small and with nuns?'[96] Bill

Evans expresses torment and cries out, 'Stop torturing me.'[97] Ruttledge becomes ashamed and realizes that his efforts towards healing and sympathy are useless, and so he apologizes to Bill Evans.

This analepsis/memory ignites the understanding that caters for the momentary entertainment and immediate expulsion of this conversation between Ruttledge and Bill Evans. Ruttledge, however, can only ask speculative questions in the conversation because the memory, as it occurs in the narrative as an open analepsis that does not link directly with a first narrative, has neither 'beginning nor end, departure nor arrival, origin nor destination'.[98] Its deployment in the narrative makes it independent of the characters, and thus the memory does not link Ruttledge or Bill Evans 'any more than it conjugates or mixes them'.[99] It creates the possibility for Ruttledge to probe Bill Evans on his past, and so it produces a shared proximity between the two characters which creates an intimacy that propels their short conversation. Ruttledge effectively terminates the conversation by asking, 'Weren't you in a place run by brothers and priests before they sent you to the first farm?'[100] Yet the failure of Ruttledge's gesture is arbitrary in terms of the effect that the analepsis creates. It conjugates and momentarily transports them to another relation with each other, and it establishes the possibility of insight during a brief liaison, but it does not create a situation in which one can ask for and grant forgiveness on behalf of another to another. This is Ruttledge's mistake, and he is ultimately presented as recognizing it as such, as his probing has the effect of removing the momentary intimacy shared between the two men.

Thus, despite its apparent passing through beings and bringing them into new relations with one another, memory as open analepsis does not serve as the means by which past violations can be interrogated and then pardoned. Rather, as in this scene, it brings characters in and out of new relationships with one another and engenders relationships generated on an interactive understanding of the past so as to make new and future relationships possible. This installed memory which creates a situation in which Bill Evans can be respected by his community in silence and on his own terms thus occurs in the novel as a narrative tool which creates the possibility for Ruttledge to empathize with Bill Evans. In turn, the brute nature of Bill Evans's actions can be reconciled with an awareness of traumatic histories and he can be assimilated into the fabric of the community which the novel represents. In these terms, the narrative creation of memory is required to establish a necessary empathy towards an otherwise uncouth character. The question of forgiveness, simultaneously, is suspended because this memory is a creation-without-origin of the narrative, as

McGahern's covert self-reflexive mode demonstrates. The analeptic character of this section of narrative is unacknowledged and has the effect of, as Genette says, 'prolonging that section ... indefinitely on its own account',[101] a result of which is that the reader becomes momentarily exiled in the open past of the novel, a site of otherness opened by the narrative which the characters do not own and are unable to close or reconcile. In turn, this memory, as a creation of the narrative, and as a fragmented and discontinuous structure, necessarily fails because it does not belong to any of the characters. Building on the modernist premise that language can do anything and is still artifice, this narrative operation exposes itself as such and must fail for that reason, despite the positive effect it has on the characters. The open analepsis, in these terms, is a necessary, though failed, narrative ploy which creates the possibility of engaging with a past that cannot be represented. In the opening scenes of his last novel, then, McGahern is already straddling the boundaries between realist convention and modernist hesitancy and scepticism, upsetting any stable distinctions between the two.

McGahern and Irish modernism

With *Memoir* (2005), McGahern closes in further on the long-suspected referent of his fiction: his and his society's life in mid- to late-twentieth-century Ireland. The strategies of the novels analysed in this chapter are largely displaced in *Memoir* for a first-person narrative voice to which all the detail recounted is made relative. The narrative begins with the narrator locating himself as living in Leitrim as an adult, and it relates, through a long narrative anachrony, his childhood and adolescence in that same region. Towards the end of the text, at the conclusion of that anachrony, the narrator states, 'This is the story of my upbringing, the people who brought me up, my parents and those around them in their time and landscape.'[102] Whilst *Memoir* relates the story of those people in their time and landscape, it is also the story of those people in the time of McGahern's narrative anachrony – a created structure in relation to a first narrative, itself a translation, a telling slant, a winning from confusion of experience – and in the landscape of his language. *Memoir*, too, then, is not without an ideological narrative structure and mode of representation (one that draws from the armamentarium of literary devices and tricks) that manifests a particular way of seeing and displaces the reality of the object it purports to represent; and which, in turn, establishes a proximity and an irreducible distance between the people who brought McGahern up and the people he represents in his book. McGahern hints at this predicament in *Memoir* when reflecting on the types of stories and writing that piqued his interest when young and ultimately inspired him to become a writer: all stories 'reflect the laws of life in both its sameness and its endless variations. I now searched out those books that acted like mirrors. What they reflected was dangerously close to my own life and the society that brought me up, as well as asserting their own differences and uniqueness.'[103] McGahern's comments here are relative to form as much as content. Applied to his own writing, the mirror of McGahern's modes of representation continue to reflect something dangerously close to his society, thus reflecting its sameness, whilst asserting their difference and uniqueness by means of their endless variations of reflection. Sameness, in such terms, is only affirmed through the multiple variations of reflection. *Memoir*, then, is another link, rather than a finality, in the chain of McGahern novels that, through their different modes of representation, engage reality as a hermeneutic enigma which requires continuous interpretation, interrogation and translation.

Each text, in turn, remains untranslatable in terms of the other, as well as accounts of McGahern's life, despite their shared similarities. The biographical details of McGahern's life, for example, provide a historical apparatus for seeing *The Dark*'s Young Mahoney as similar to *The Leavetaking*'s Patrick Moran, *Amongst Women*'s Luke, and *That They May Face the Rising Sun*'s Ruttledge, as well as *Memoir*'s narrator. Likewise, *The Barrack*'s Reegan is similar to *The Dark*'s Elder Mahoney and *Amongst Women*'s Moran and *Memoir*'s Daddy. However, like Beckett's Malone, Molloy, Moran and Unnamable, these characters are dissimilar not only in name; they are narrated from different perspectives, in different scenarios and with different agendas. For example, the oedipal fantasies which are persistent in *The Dark*'s protagonist and *The Leavetaking*'s and *Memoir*'s respective narrators are not dominant in the remit of *The Pornographer*'s narrator or Ruttledge in *That They May Face the Rising Sun*; indeed, this fantasy reaches its height, and occurs as the dominant mode of seeing in *Memoir*, a text which professes to tell the story of the writer's parents in their place and time though it was written and published a long time after McGahern's real-life parents had died.[104] The sum of these novels' worlds, in turn, does not amount to a totality or close in on a signified which precedes the texts. Like Proust and Jean Genet, McGahern allows his life to be read as text, where text, to reference Barthes again, is structured but off-centered and without closure. Each text constitutes a fragment of narrative fiction, none of which forms a privileged centre through which the play of the others can be anchored. As Peter Brooks writes, 'at any time one goes over a moment in the past, the [narrative] machine can be relied upon to produce more narrative – not only differing stories of the past, but future scenarios and narratives of writing itself'.[105] In this sense, the seemingly same raw material is repeated in McGahern's novels, each time embellished, recreated and refashioned in different narrative voices, and all the while claiming no hold over the potential referent(s). The capturing or recording of the past is relinquished for the institution of a method which ensures that the possible referents of the fiction are supplemented and thus deferred and displaced as they are rendered differently in narrative. As such, each text remains untranslatable in Barbara Cassin's invocation of the term: 'The untranslatable is rather what one keeps on (not) translating';[106] it is continuously translated and never absolutely translated.

Does McGahern, then, belong to a history of Irish literary modernism, enforcing, or operating just beyond, the limits of that term, or does he remain a naturalist or a realist writer, extraneous to Irish modernism, despite his work being formally intricate as well as corresponding to a history of modernity in Ireland? As this chapter has endeavoured to show, McGahern's writing straddles modernist versus realist distinctions and renders their criteria as fluid and overlapping. The divided narrative of *The Dark* produces a fragmented story which is beyond accumulation to a coherent subjectivity or anterior origin, a feat which, had the novel been published a few years earlier and in a different literary climate, might have led to its inclusion in modernist discussion before the twenty-first century. Regarding his other novels, particularly those analysed here, his literary method involves intricate narrative operations that can easily go unnoticed in the reading of his fiction; understated shifts in the respective narrative procedures which create the illusion of a belated and imitative form of representation are so subtle that the effects on narrative proceedings are difficult to detect. Unlike Proust's overt analepses which often do not reconcile with the narrative they are a part of, McGahern's novels do not deliberately make a point of exhibiting their formal play. Such is the case in the story of Elizabeth Reegan where the third-person narrative device of *The Barracks*, which seemingly only has access to Elizabeth's conscience, narrates an anachrony with access to the conscience of Johnny Halliday. And in both *Amongst Women* and *That They May Face the Rising Sun*, the respective narratives include analepses that do not belong to any one character but are interjected by the respective narrative operations and serve as structural devices. The manipulations of narrative that are required to produce these imitations appear as artifice when analysed as such, and thwart the supposed innocence and objectivity of the realist eye as it looks through the fourth wall. In this sense, it seems misguided to consider McGahern's aesthetic mode as signalling a return to nineteenth-century naturalist and realist forms.

Recent work on McGahern by Richard Robinson and Stanley van der Ziel has created a heightened awareness of McGahern's rewriting and manipulation of a host of literary strategies from the modernist and other canons. Though neither Robinson nor van der Ziel label McGahern a modernist, what emerges from their accounts, as is intended to emerge here, is a fiction that is aware of the structural artifice that is necessary for the construction of literary representations. In these terms, McGahern's literary method can be understood as subtly exposing its own realist endeavours and, thus, on aesthetic, formal and literary grounds, as extending a history of Irish modernism which constitutes a jarring proximity and an irreducible distance between textual production and modernity in Ireland.

Epilogue

The analyses performed in the preceding five chapters have explicated certain forms of untranslatability occurring as a result of the respective aesthetic strategies of the authors in question. An effect of the untranslatable – which signifies that which cannot be translated and that which always remains to be translated – in each case is an irreducible distance between the aesthetic forms of these works and the historical realities which are often said to underpin or determine these texts. Samuel Beckett's writing, when thought in terms of Roland Barthes's writing degree zero, entails an unknown element to the word which remains open to a variety of definitional possibilities and thus untranslatable to specific historical occurrences. The problem of the pseudonym relative to the O'Nolan/O'Brien/na gCopaleen corpus, as well as the metafictional strategies of the early fictions, dismantle the possibility of locating any origin which might be denoted as determining their play; and thus the multiple names and the procedures of the novels remain untranslatable to a specific and tranquil locus. The narrative procedure of Elizabeth Bowen's *The Last September*, the novel so often read as representing Ireland's moment of decolonization, resists giving meaning to Ireland's War of Independence as it abrogates and circumvents the contours of that cultural event through its narrative procedure. As Ireland remains a hint never to be achieved in the novel, its narrative remains untranslatable to nationalist projects and projections. Kate O'Brien's fictions, through their peculiar use of omniscient narrative strategies, manifest their literariness simultaneous to their recounting of stories of individual development and interventions in social and political problematics; with the latter often occurring at the level of narration rather than character and setting, O'Brien's fictions establish these narratives of individual development through a dislocation between form and content. The relationship between what is narrated and the characters and settings that form the subject of those representations remains untranslatable because of the 'flawed' manner in which these stories are told, an effect of which is that O'Brien's fictions occur beyond, and at a distance to, the determinations of historical and material realities. And John McGahern's fictional modes manifest the structural artifice necessary for the production of literary representation and engaging reality as a hermeneutic enigma; through his respective narrative modes, McGahern's fictions obscure distinctions between autobiography, history and literature, in the process rendering the content of the respective fictions untranslatable to a determined origin.

As outlined in the introduction to this book, Irish modernism has been defined, broadly speaking, as a postcolonial phenomenon whereby the literature and cultural practice corresponding to the term is read in relation to, and as representing, Ireland's status in late-nineteenth and twentieth-century colonial and postcolonial modernities. Following a deracinated modernism which emerged in the mid-twentieth century, our recent version of Irish modernism has brought to light how modernist aesthetic practice can be read as bound up with various local and historical contexts, the structures of global imperialism, and as relating stories of the oppressed and making heard the voices of the hitherto silent. A consequence of such definitions of Irish modernism has been the assumption of literature's apparent invitation to be read as qualifying certain historiographical metanarratives and thus as a belated, encoded and imitative representation of the past. Critics and readers of literature thus accept its request for the suspension of disbelief and read literature as telling various stories of past events and phenomena. As has been suggested in the chapters of this book, the texts which are, and can be made, relative to Irish modernism also involve intricate formal and stylistic operations which are perverse in relation to nationalist projects and projections and refrain from allowing the positing of any easy symbiosis between their respective narrative modes and the dynamics of a specific modernity. At stake, then, in this bind is an ethics of reading arising from the relation of the critic to the literary object. As Ross Chambers writes, the critic is an 'interpretive subject', 'a position that manifests the dependency of identity on otherness'.[1] Because of this necessary sovereignty in relation to the other, the task of the interpretive subject involves being seduced by, and responding to, that which will never reveal its intentions and that which cannot be coerced into strict identitarian categories. As the critic endeavours to control the scene of literature, the act of reading is already fated to negotiate with what Jacques Derrida calls the paradox of the secret inherent to literature. The structural gaps and omissions inherent to the (modernist) literary text, which it is the wont of the historicist critic to qualify with historical detail, are also, in Derrida's language, the secrets without secret of the text.² Thus, the structural gaps and omissions of any literature, of which modernist literature is often particularly replete, remain enigmatic and beyond accumulation to any literary critical method. In such terms, literature never refrains from extending an invitation to be read but never reveals why it does so or what exactly it intends to signify. Importantly, this gesture is not a resuscitation of the perceived tenets of New Criticism, wherein the artwork remains an autonomous and hermetically sealed artefact. The role of the secret in literature signals an ethics of indeterminacy, one built on the iterability of the text. As Derrida suggests concerning the singularity of the work of literature, every text retains its own iterability and therefore differs from itself. Because texts are constituted by networks of signifiers, they demand to be reread infinitely and differently each time. Each text thus inscribes an ethics of reading which demands that the iterability of the text is made sovereign. Moreover, as J. Hillis Miller writes, the ethical moment of reading 'cannot ... be accounted for by the social and historical forces that impinge upon it. In fact, the ethical moment contests these forces or is subversive to them.'³ It is, as Hillis Miller suggests, 'a much more fundamental "I must" responding to the language of literature in itself'.⁴ Or, as he describes in *Topographies*, it involves a recognition that

> the fundamental means of the argument, prosopopoeia, becomes ... the barrier forbidding further progress beyond what is now presented as no more than a trope, a rhetorical artifice. "*If* it had a voice, it would say", but of course it does not have a voice.⁵

For this reason, the reading of literature, ethically speaking, cannot be the study of a symptom or historical fact which is more real than literature and which literature simply communicates as such. As Paul De Man suggests, 'Literature is fiction not because it somehow refuses to acknowledge "reality", but because it is not *a priori* certain that language functions according to principles which are those, or which are *like* those, of the phenomenal world.'⁶ Thus, if literature, and not history, is to be read ethically, it is first towards this indeterminacy that the act of reading must also direct itself before and if claims of historical representation can be made. In ignoring this ethical demand, literature is made, as Hillis Miller says, 'no more than a minor by-product of history, not something that in any way makes history'.⁷

As a certain version of Irish modernism will always remain concerned with those terms of canonical modernism – aesthetic hesitancy, fragmentation, mobilization of epistemological doubt, scepticism – this circumstance concerning the ethics of reading will remain a feature of how that canon is negotiated and defined. And as W. B. Yeats's, James Joyce's and Beckett's radically symbolic modernisms keep the tenets of canonical modernism in play within the discourse of Irish modernism, other seemingly moderately symbolic literatures – such as Bowen, Kate O'Brien and McGahern – remain to be interrogated for how they relate what they relate, and in terms of an ethics of reading, as they are made relevant to the canon of Irish modernism.

In saying as much, it hangs in the balance whether the methodology proposed throughout this book is applicable across the Irish modernist canon. De Man, for example, has suggested that, because the rhetorical structure of the text undermines its meaning, every work of literature deconstructs itself, and that it is thus the task of the critic to demonstrate this process. Notably, Derrida did not understand deconstruction in the same way; he preferred instead to respond to certain 'dated' problematics within specific texts, which did not always lead to a 'deconstruction' of the texts under scrutiny. In his readings of Charles Baudelaire, Paul Celan and Joyce, for example, Derrida responded to the texts in question to reaffirm and repose the meaning of the institution of literature. The works analysed here were chosen for particular intricacies which they had already manifested in criticism. In this sense, this book has sought to respond to those already evident intricacies and sedimented problematics within certain corpuses and bring their implications to bear on current formulations of Irish modernism. Unlike De Man's proposition, then, the analysis undertaken here has depended on specific formal problematics in particular texts to outline the distance of these works to historical realities and the thrust of certain metanarratives. The methodology proposed here would be disingenuous if applied to Edna O'Brien's *The Country Girls* (1960), for example (if McGahern is here made relative to the question of Irish modernism, then Edna O'Brien must also be considered within these criteria given her achievement and prominence in twentieth- and twenty-first-century literature). As a work with a particularly direct narrative structure that closes in on a specific signified, and which is largely unconcerned with the vagaries of form and language, *The Country Girls* remains bound up with a very specific cultural history and it seems disingenuous and unnecessary to try to subvert that relationship for the version of Irish modernism that is proposed here. In a nutshell, the narrative mode of *The Country Girls* – or, to provide other examples, Patrick Kavanagh's *The Green Fool* (1938) or Brendan Behan's *Borstal Boy* (1958) – remains, broadly speaking, translatable, in a certain sense of the term, to Irish history and modernity.

Simultaneously, Irish modernism, as a narrative mode, does not necessarily end just because certain examples of Edna O'Brien's, Kavanagh's or Behan's respective writings remain beyond productive assimilation to the methodology proposed here. As cultural production in modernity remains a key means of defining modernism, there is no reason why such writers cannot be integrated to a different narrative of Irish modernism. Moreover, this book has privileged literature, and particularly the novel, to make a specific argument about Irish modernism. All the other artistic practices and modes of cultural production which can be made relative to the term surely expand its remit and the possibility of its narration along different and multiple lines, the variety of which points to a plurality of Irish modernisms. The narrative of the distance of Irish modernism as proposed throughout these pages is just one of those potentialities, and one which is not necessarily confined to the authors discussed here.

In their recent special issue of *Irish Studies Review*, Deaglán Ó Donghaile and Gerry Smyth contest Joe Cleary's assertion that Irish modernism is now part of a receding history by invoking the recent examples of Eimear McBride and Mike McCormack as having received media attention which nominated their outputs under the banner of Irish modernism. They suggest, 'It's interesting to consider what a resurgence of "Irish modernism" might portend for an understanding of post-crash Irish culture.'[8] In this instance, 'Irish modernism' is reassumed for its relation to a specific economic and historical base, thus continuing the mode of narration that has long been deployed in the definition of the term. This reassumption of the term is also coincident with a turn to aesthetic and formal difficulty in contemporary literature, as Eimear McBride's *A Girl is a Half-Formed Thing* (2014) and Mike McCormack's *Solar Bones* (2016) make manifest. Similarly, Anna Burns's *Milkman* (2018) is hesitant and resistant in relation to a specific signified as it abrogates and circumvents in its own nuanced manner the contours of a certain cultural landscape. As such, with the expansion of the scope of Irish modernism into the twenty-first century based on these works of fiction – all of which present oblique aesthetic strategies in relation to historical metanarratives concerning the development of the nation state and the history of modernity – the proximity and the distance, and the affinity and the difference, of Irish modernist production to a specific modernity remains a pertinent line of questioning for the field.

In turn, the narrative of the distance of Irish modernism as established here, and which is pushed to its limits with McGahern in this study, maintains its applicability to cultural production in the twenty-first century and into the domain of contemporary literature. With this development, the relation between Irish (modernist) literature and the history of Ireland's modernity, at the conclusion of Ireland's *Decade of Centenaries*, remains dissimilar and open, always resisting closure. When thought alongside the politics of the *Decade of Centenaries* which has prioritized canonized and marginal cultural production in the investigation and rearticulation of Irish history, the example of Irish modernism demonstrates that the relationship between literature and the history of modernity is not as clear as an equivalence, a homology or a parallelism, an effect of which is that Irish literary modernism, because of its sometimes distance to specific historical events and phenomena, will always resist becoming a tranquil locus through which the past can be remembered. As the unassimilable material of Irish modernist literature makes it similar and different to the cultural memories it supposedly transmits, the relation between Ireland, its history in modernity and its twentieth- and twenty-first-century literature remains enigmatic, thus prompting an ethics of commemoration regarding the instrumentalization of literature in the present and deferring the problematic of how we define Irish modernism well into the future.

Notes

Introduction: The vicinities of Irish modernism

1 Ezra Pound, 'The non-existence of Ireland', in *Pound/Joyce: The Letters of Ezra Pound to James Joyce, with Pound's essays on Joyce*, ed. Forrest Read (New York: New Directions Books, 1967), 32.
2 Ibid.
3 Ibid., 32–3.
4 Ibid.
5 See Oona Frawley, 'Introduction: James Joyce, cultural memory and Irish studies', in *Memory Ireland Volume 4: James Joyce and Cultural Memory*, ed. Oona Frawley (New York: Syracuse University Press, 2014), 1–9.
6 See e.g. *Irish Modernism: Origins Contexts, Publics*, ed. Edwina Keown and Carol Taaffe (Oxford: Peter Lang, 2009); *The Cambridge Companion to Irish Modernism*, ed. Joe Cleary (Cambridge: Cambridge University Press, 2014); *Science Technology and Irish Modernism*, ed. Kathryn Conrad, Cóilín Parsons and Julie McCormick Weng (New York: Syracuse University Press, 2019); *A History of Irish Modernism*, ed. Gregory Castle and Patrick Bixby (Cambridge: Cambridge University Press, 2019); and *Irish Modernisms: Gaps, Conjectures, Possibilities*, ed. Paul Fagan, John Greaney and Tamara Radak (London: Bloomsbury, 2022).
7 For example: the Freud Project at IMMA, 2016–21, promises to pay attention to Lucian Freud's relationship to Ireland and Irish modernism; an exhibition entitled 'The Birth of Modernism in Irish Art 1920–60' was held between April and August 2019 in Dublin Castle, and on 25 September 2019 the Irish Cultural Centre in London hosted an evening dedicated to the theme 'Irish Modernism – A Brief History'. Similarly, the term is gaining traction in print and internet media: Irish writers Eimear McBride and Mike McCormack have respectively been described as reviving and resurrecting Irish modernism (J. P. O'Malley, 'Eimear McBride revives Irish modernism', *Independent*, 12 September 2016; Stephanie Boland, 'Bedad he revives: Why *Solar Bones* is a resurrection for Irish modernism', *New Statesman*, 4 July 2016), and Irish painter Mary Swanzy has been denoted as Irish modernism's unsung hero (Liz Cullinane, 'Mary Swanzy – the unsung hero of Irish modernism', *Independent*, 21 October 2018).
8 Gregory Castle and Patrick Bixby, 'Introduction: Irish Modernism, from emergence to emergency', in Castle and Bixby, *A History of Irish Modernism*, 4.

9. See e.g. Susan Stanford Friedman's *Planetary Modernisms: Provocations on Modernity across Time* (New York: Columbia University Press, 2015).
10. Barry Sheils, *W. B. Yeats and World Literature: The Subject of Poetry* (New York: Routledge, 2015), 4.
11. Tom Walker, 'The culture of art in 1880s Ireland and the genealogy of Irish modernism', *Irish Studies Review* 26, no. 3 (2018): 305.
12. Franco Moretti, *Distant Reading* (New York: Verso, 2013), 35–6.
13. Frawley, 'Introduction', 8.
14. Sean Latham and Gayle Rodgers, *Modernism: Evolution of an Idea* (London: Bloomsbury, 2015), 32.
15. Jessica Berman, *Modernist Commitments: Ethics, Politics, and Transnational Modernism* (New York: Columbia University Press), 7–8.
16. Castle and Bixby, *A History of Irish Modernism*, 4.
17. Jonathan Flatley, *Affective Mapping: Melancholia and the Politics of Modernism* (Boston: Harvard University Press, 2008), 32.
18. Ibid.
19. Julie Taylor, 'Introduction', in *Modernism and Affect*, ed. Julie Taylor (Edinburgh: Edinburgh University Press, 2015), 1.
20. Lauren Arrington, 'Irish modernism and its legacies', in *The Princeton History of Modern Ireland*, ed. Richard Bourke and Ian McBride (Princeton: Princeton University Press, 2016), 249.
21. Lauren Arrington, 'Irish modernism', *Oxford Research Encyclopedia of Literature*, 27 February 2017. Available online: https://oxfordre.com/view/10.1093/acrefore/9780190201098.001.0001/acrefore-9780190201098-e-237.
22. Mark Wollaeger provides a detailed analysis of this predicament in his 'Introduction' to *The Oxford Handbook of Global Modernisms* (Oxford: Oxford University Press, 2012).
23. Jean Michel-Rabaté, 'Editor's introduction', *Journal of Modern Literature* 38, no. 2 (2015): vi.
24. Enda Duffy, 'Critical receptions of Irish modernism', in Cleary, *The Cambridge Companion to Irish Modernism*, 196.
25. Ibid.
26. Ibid.
27. Ibid.
28. Ibid.
29. Ibid., 197.
30. Richard Begam and Michael Valdez Moses, 'Introduction', in *Modernism and Colonialism: British and Irish Literature, 1899–1939*, ed. Richard Begam and Michael Valdez Moses (Durham: Duke University Press, 2007), 5.
31. Ibid.

32 Joe Cleary, 'Introduction', in Cleary, *The Cambridge Companion to Irish Modernism*, 9.
33 Deaglán Ó Donghaile and Gerry Smyth, 'Introduction: Remapping Irish modernism', *Irish Studies Review* 26, no. 3 (2018): 299.
34 Fionna Barber, 'Irish modernism', *Routledge Encyclopedia of Modernism*, 1 October 2016. Available online: https://www.rem.routledge.com/articles/irish-modernism (accessed 4 February 2020).
35 Castle and Bixby, *A History of Irish Modernism*, 12.
36 Stanford Friedman, *Planetary Modernisms*, 196.
37 See Declan Kiberd, *Inventing Ireland* (London: Vintage, 1995). Kiberd presents a narrative structure 'which briefly sketches political developments, so that readers who wish can briefly map literature against the blunter realities of history' (ibid., 7). Literary and artistic practice, as such, become mappable in relation to political development.
38 See Emer Nolan, *James Joyce and Nationalism* (New York: Routledge, 1994). Nolan remarks, 'The modernity to which Joyce responds, then, is not transnational or universal, and the major trends in Joyce criticism have occluded the particularity of Irish historical experience as it determines and is reflected in his fiction' (ibid., xii).
39 Important predecessors to Kiberd's and Nolan's work are the volumes of *The Field Day Anthology of Irish Writing* and *Nationalism, Colonialism and Literature*, ed. Seamus Deane (Minnesota: Minnesota University Press, 1990).
40 Walker, 'Culture of art', 305.
41 Frawley, 'Introduction', 8.
42 Rónán McDonald and Julian Murphet, 'Introduction', in *Flann O'Brien and Modernism*, ed. Rónán McDonald, Julian Murphet and Sascha Morell (London: Bloomsbury, 2014), 2.
43 Susan Osborn, '"How to measure this unaccountable darkness between the trees": The strange relation of style and meaning in *The Last September*', in *Elizabeth Bowen: New Critical Perspectives*, ed. Susan Osborn (Cork: Cork University Press, 2009), 51
44 Neil Corcoran, *Elizabeth Bowen: The Enforced Return* (Oxford: Oxford University Press, 2004), 13.
45 Ibid.
46 Jacques Derrida, *Of Grammatology*, trans. Gayatri Chakravorty Spivak (Baltimore: Johns Hopkins University Press, 1998), 158.
47 J. Hillis Miller, 'Presidential address 1986. The triumph of theory, the resistance to reading, and the question of the material base', *PMLA* 102, no. 3 (1987): 288.
48 Ibid., 289.
49 Ibid.
50 Ibid.

51 Roland Barthes, *Image, Music, Text*, trans. Stephen Heath (London: Fontana Press, 1987), 158.
52 Ibid., 159.
53 Ibid.
54 Ibid.
55 Astrid Erll, *Memory in Culture*, trans. Sara B. Young (London: Palgrave Macmillan, 2011), 153.
56 Colin Graham, *Deconstructing Ireland: Identity, Theory, Culture* (Edinburgh: Edinburgh University Press, 2001), 67.
57 Ania Loomba, *Colonialism/Postcolonialism* (New York: Routledge, 2015), 52.
58 Rabaté, 'Editor's introduction', vi.
59 Walker, 'Culture of art', 307.
60 David Lloyd, *Anomalous States: Irish Writing and the Post-Colonial Moment* (Durham: Duke University Press, 1993), 2.
61 Paul Saint-Amour, *Tense Future: Modernism, Total War, Encycolpaedic Form* (Oxford: Oxford University Press, 2015), 37.
62 Ibid., 41.
63 Ibid.
64 Rónán McDonald, 'The Irish Revival and modernism', in Castle and Bixby, *A History of Irish Modernism*, 51.
65 See Erll, *Memory in Culture*, 152–3. Particularly, Erll distinguishes three aspects of mnemonic mimesis: (1) 'the prefiguration of a literary text by a memory culture', (2) 'the literary configuration of new memory narratives' and (3) 'their refiguration in the frameworks of different mnemonic communities' (ibid., 152–3). In explaining this process, Erll cites Ricoeur: 'For Ricoeur, literary world-making rests on a dynamic transformation process – on the interaction among the "prefiguration" of the text, that is, its reference to the already existent extratextual world (mimesis1); the "textual" configuration, with its major operation of emplotment, which creates a fictional world (mimesis2); and the "refiguration" by the reader (mimesis3)' (152). Erll then writes that 'in this approach, literature appears as an active constructive process in which cultural systems of meaning, narrative operations, and reception participate equally, and in which reality is not merely reflected' but, as Erll suggests through Ricoeur, 'poetically refigured' and 'iconically augmented' (152). Erll then alters the terminology slightly to aid the conceptualization of literature as a medium of cultural memory. Instead of literature being prefigured by an extratextual reality, Erll suggests that the literary text is prefigured by a memory culture (152). Thus, instead of a textual configuration leading to new fictional worlds (mimesis2), Erll suggests 'a literary configuration produces new memory narratives' (152). And, thus, as Erll writes,

'literature actualizes elements which previously were not – or could not be – perceived, articulated, and remembered in the social sphere' (153).
66 In focusing on the novel, this book makes an argument about Irish modernism which, in order to be thought through the other artistic forms which comprise that canon, will have to be adapted to the particularities of the form at hand. Otherwise, Irish modernism again risks capaciousness and under-theorization.
67 Arrington, 'Irish modernism'.
68 Cleary, *The Cambridge Companion to Irish Modernism*, 4–5.
69 Fredric Jameson, 'Modernism and imperialism', in Deane, *Nationalism, Colonialism and Literature*, 51.
70 Paul Saint-Amour, 'The Medial humanities: Toward a manifesto for meso-analysis', *Modernism/modernity Print Plus* 3, no . 4 (2019). Available online: https://modernismmodernity.org/forums/posts/medial-humanities-toward-manifesto-meso-analysis (accessed 11 December 2019).
71 Ibid.
72 Moretti, *Distant Reading*, 60.
73 Ibid.
74 Ibid., 48.
75 Or, as Sheils writes, with modern poetry in mind and directly critiquing Moretti on this issue, 'such a perspective can only be the iteration *outside* the text of what is already going on *inside* the text. After all, much modern poetry is notoriously rebarbative, hostile to the simple-minded incursions of anything like the "single direct reading", and, simultaneously, both less and more than itself' (*W. B. Yeats and World Literature*, 22).
76 See Rebecca Walkowitz, *Born Translated: The Contemporary Novel in an Age of World Literature* (New York: Columbia University Press, 2015).
77 Pascale Casanova, *The World Republic of Letters*, trans. M. B. Debevoise (Cambridge: Harvard University Press, 2007), 86.
78 Ibid. In the French text, Casanova writes, *'L'espace littéraire retraduit dans ses termes spécifiques – esthétiques, formels, naratifs, poétiques – les enjeux politiques et nationaux: il les affirme et les nie dans le même movement.' La République mondiale des lettres* (Paris: Editions du Seuil, 1999), 124.
79 Ibid.
80 Ibid.
81 Derrida, *Of Grammatology*, 154.
82 Ibid., 154–5.
83 Sheils, *W. B. Yeats and World Literature*, 19.
84 Barbara Cassin, 'Introduction', in *Dictionary of Untranslatables: A Philosophical Lexicon*, ed. Barbara Cassin and Emily Apter (Princeton: Princeton University Press, 2014), xvii.
85 Ibid.

86 Cassin writes, 'We began with the many (our plural form indicates this: "dictionary of untranslatables"), and we remain with the many: we have addressed the question of the untranslatable without aiming at unity, whether it is placed at the origin or at the end' (ibid., xix).
87 Martin Heidegger, *Hölderlin's Hymn 'The Ister'* (Bloomington: Indiana University Press, 1996), 65.
88 Ibid.
89 Emily Apter, *Against World Literature: On the Politics of Untranslatability* (New York: Verso, 2013), 3.
90 Emily Apter, *The Translation Zone: A New Comparative Literature* (Princeton: Princeton University Press, 2006), 210.
91 Jacques Derrida, *Monolingualism of the Other; or, The Prosthesis of the Origin*, trans. Patrick Mensah (Stanford: Stanford University Press, 1998), 61.
92 James Joyce, *A Portrait of the Artist as a Young Man* (London: Penguin, 2000), 215.
93 Ibid., 214.
94 Jean-Michel Rabaté, *The Pathos of Distance: Affects of the Moderns* (London: Bloomsbury, 2016).
95 Douglas Mao, 'The new critics and the text-object', *ELH* 63, no. 1 (1996): 237.
96 David James, 'Introduction', in *Modernism and Close Reading*, ed. David James (Oxford: Oxford University Press, 2020), 5–20.
97 Susan J. Wolfson, 'Introduction: Reading for form', in *Reading for Form*, ed. Susan J. Wolfson and Marshall Brown (Seattle: University of Washington Press, 2006), 14.
98 'Manifesto of the V21 Collective: Ten theses'. Available online: http://v21collective.org. The V21 Collective's manifesto laments Victorian studies as having fallen prey to 'positivist historicism', which does little more than 'exhaustively describe, preserve, and display the past'. In their opposition to the 'fetishization of the archival', 'an aspiration to definitively map the DNA of the period' and 'an endless accumulation of mere information', the V21 Collective has promoted a turn to formal analysis and theoretical reflection in Victorian studies. The V21 Collective thus critiques the misrepresented idea that history finds 'its academic antithesis in theory, and just as often in form' and suggests that 'framing "theory" as a monolithic other is intellectually lazy and allows positivist historicism to become ever-more habitual and unreflective'. In riposte to such anti-theoretical 'default' historicisms, the V21 Collective sets out to reinvigorate Victorian studies through new formalisms to analyse the politics of form and in the process recentre 'formal analysis as the province of literary critical knowing'.
99 Cara L. Lewis, *Dynamic Form: How Intermediality Made Modernism* (Ithaca: Cornell University Press, 2020), 6.
100 Ibid., 9.

101 Jacques Rancière, *Mute Speech*, trans. Gabriel Rockhill (New York: Columbia University Press, 2009), 170.

1 Samuel Beckett and the contexts of modernism

1. Samuel Beckett, *More Pricks Than Kicks* (London: Faber and Faber, 2010), 71.
2. Samuel Beckett, *Murphy* (London: Faber and Faber, 2009), 29.
3. Samuel Beckett, 'Homage to Jack. B Yeats', in *Jack B. Yeats: A Centenary Gathering*, ed. Roger McHugh (Dublin: Doleman Press, 1971), 75–6.
4. *The Letters of Samuel Beckett, 1929–40*, vol. 1, ed. Martha Dow Feshenfeld and Lois More Overbeck (Cambridge: Cambridge University Press, 2009), 324.
5. Ibid, 530.
6. Ludovic Janvier, *Samuel Beckett par lui-meme* (Paris: Seuil, 1969), 18.
7. See James McNaughton, *Samuel Beckett and the Politics of Aftermath* (Oxford: Oxford University Press, 2018). McNaughton dubs Leo Bersani's and Ulysse Dutoit's reading of *Endgame* as an existential drama – where it is found logical 'to understand procreation as murder' – as 'unsettlingly grotesque … once we allow that the play contradicts this concluding logic with awareness of recent political history's horrors' (ibid., 8). Similarly, see Emilie Morin, *Beckett's Political Imagination* (Cambridge: Cambridge University Press, 2018). Morin suggests, 'When reflecting on the challenges raised by Beckett's writing, scholars have tended to be somewhat more partial to the questions outlined by Blanchot than to those discussed by Adorno, and have generally avoided the granular and meandering narratives of the political' (ibid., 10). Or see Séan Kennedy, 'Introduction: Beckett in History, Memory, Archive', in *Samuel Beckett: History, Memory, Archive*, ed. Séan Kennedy (Basingstoke: Palgrave Macmillan, 2009): 1. Kennedy suggests, 'Beckett had himself suggested that "the artist who stakes his being is from nowhere", and this bold statement set the terms of engagement for a generation of scholars predisposed to read his own work in philosophical terms.'
8. Kennedy, 'Introduction: Beckett in History, Memory, Archive', 1.
9. Patrick Bixby, *Samuel Beckett and the Postcolonial Novel* (Cambridge: Cambridge University Press, 2009), 35.
10. Ibid., 37.
11. Richard Kearney, *Transitions: Narratives in Modern Irish Culture* (Manchester: Manchester University Press, 1988), 269.
12. C. J. Ackerley S. E. Gontarski, eds, *The Grove Companion to Samuel Beckett* (New York: Grove Press, 2004), xv.
13. Maurice Blanchot, 'Où maintenant? Qui maintenant?', *La Nouvelle Nouvelle Revue Française* 10 (1953): 678–86.

14 Pascale Casanova, *Samuel Beckett: Anatomy of a Literary Revolution*, trans. Gregory Elliott (New York: Verso, 2009), 9.
15 Andrew Gibson, 'Samuel Beckett: History, Memory, Archive (review)', *Modernism/modernity* 18, no. 4 (2011): 926.
16 McNaughton, *Samuel Beckett and the Politics of Aftermath*, 3.
17 Ibid.
18 Séan Kennedy, 'Introduction', in *Beckett and Ireland*, ed. Séan Kennedy (Cambridge: Cambridge University Press, 2010), 3.
19 McNaughton, *Samuel Beckett and the Politics of Aftermath*, 3.
20 Theodor Adorno, *Aesthetic Theory*, trans. Robert Hullot-Kentor (London: Bloomsbury, 2013), 6.
21 Ibid., 209.
22 Prominent Beckett critics – such as McNaughton, Morin and Shane Weller – have adopted this theoretical lens to explicate the relation between Beckett's work and the political histories of his times. McNaughton builds on Adorno as the 'first critic to hone the eerie physical literalism in Beckett's depictions of postwar degradation' (*Samuel Beckett and the Politics of Aftermath*, 7) to present Beckett as a politically engaged writer, one whose stylistic choices reinforce that engagement and thus contribute to what can be denoted as 'Beckett's political aesthetic'. For McNaughton, 'words or concepts employed with aesthetic, philosophical, or colloquial meanings suddenly suggest overwhelming political and historical power that impinges on bodies and lives' (ibid., 2), and so 'Beckett's direct encounter with contemporary politics', and his 'formal responses to and engagement with … political context in his creative work' can be demonstrated (ibid., 3). In *Beckett's Political Imagination*, Morin positions Adorno as instrumental to exploring the political coordinates of Beckett's writing: 'From Adorno's perspective, the historicity of Beckett's work revolved around its resistance to clear-cut referents, and its apophatic mode conveyed a proximity to horror, war and genocide' (ibid., 5). As Morin suggests, Beckett, with Kafka, gestures towards 'a new political art'. Building critically on Adorno, Morin reacts against 'a widespread reluctance to acknowledge the work's political coordinates', which can thus offer insights 'into a transnational history marked by important mutations within Western liberal values and murderous colonial and civil wars' (ibid., 22). For Shane Weller, *Language and Negativity in European Modernism* (Cambridge: Cambridge University Press, 2019), Beckett's linguistic negativism 'anything but attempts to evade a confrontation with the worst' (ibid., 104); 'Adorno is surely right to argue that Beckett's postwar work is political in a manner that locates it on the left, even if, for historico-aesthetic reasons, that work can offer no positive vision of utopia' (ibid., 122). As per these accounts, then, Adorno stabilizes an account of Beckett's writing as responding to and determined by the historical realities from which it emerges. And whilst no account produces

an image of the writer along the lines of a Sartrean commitment, whereby the artist bears a serious responsibility to society and produces socially useful ends – see Jean-Paul Sartre, *Qu'est-ce que la littérature?* (Paris: Gallimard, 1964) – Beckett is nonetheless reinvigorated as a politically conscious writer, one who records, and had and has unique things to say about, history through his oblique prose and drama.

23 Kennedy, 'Introduction', 1.
24 McNaughton, *Samuel Beckett and the Politics of Aftermath*, 109.
25 Séan Kennedy, 'Does Beckett studies require a subject? Mourning Ireland in the *Texts for Nothing*', in *Beckett and Ireland*, 23.
26 Bixby, *Samuel Beckett and the Postcolonial Novel*, 36.
27 Rónán McDonald, 'Beckett and Irish studies', in *Beckett and Ireland*, 23.
28 David Lloyd, 'Frames of referrance: Samuel Beckett as an Irish question', in *Beckett and Ireland*, 38.
29 Steven Connor, *Beckett, Modernism and the Material Imagination* (Cambridge: Cambridge University Press, 2014), 187.
30 Jean-Michel Rabaté, *Think, Pig!: Beckett at the Limit of the Human* (New York: Fordham University Press, 2016), 178.
31 Emilie Morin, *Samuel Beckett and the Problem of Irishness* (Basingstoke: Palgrave Macmillan, 2009), 163.
32 Andrew Gibson, 'Afterword: Beckett, Ireland and elsewhere', in *Beckett and Ireland*, 197.
33 Gibson, 'Samuel Beckett: History, Memory, Archive (review)', 927.
34 Ibid.
35 Gessner Niklaus, *Die Unzulänglichkeit der Sprache* (Zurich: Juris, 1957), 32.
36 See Elizabeth Barry, 'Translating nationalism: Ireland, France and military history in Beckett's *Mercier et Camier*', *Irish Studies Review* 13, no. 4 (2005): 514; Emilie Morin,'Samuel Beckett, late modernism and the paradox of distance', in *A History of Irish Modernism*, ed. Gregory Castle and Patrick Bixby (Cambridge: Cambridge University Press, 2019).
37 Samuel Beckett, *Mercier and Camier* (London: Faber and Faber, 2010), 13.
38 Samuel Beckett, *Mercier et Camier* (Paris: Editions du Minuit, 1970), 29.
39 For more on Beckett's involvement in Gloria SMH, see James Knowlson, *Damned to Fame: The Life of Samuel Beckett* (New York: Grove Press, 1996).
40 Beckett, *Mercier and Camier*, 5.
41 Beckett, *Mercier et Camier*, 12.
42 Beckett, *Mercier and Camier*, 5.
43 Beckett, *Mercier et Camier*, 12–23.
44 Beckett, *Mercier and Camier*, 5.
45 Beckett, *Mercier et Camier*, 13.

46 Beckett, *Mercier and Camier*, 8.
47 Beckett, *Mercier et Camier*, 19.
48 Beckett, *Mercier and Camier*, 8.
49 Beckett, *Mercier et Camier*, 19.
50 Beckett, *Mercier and Camier*, 8.
51 Beckett, *Mercier et Camier*, 19.
52 Beckett, *Mercier and Camier*, 8.
53 Beckett, *Mercier et Camier*, 19.
54 Beckett, *Mercier and Camier*, 10.
55 Beckett, *Mercier et Camier*, 24.
56 Beckett, *Mercier and Camier*, 10.
57 Beckett, *Mercier et Camier*, 24.
58 Beckett, *Mercier and Camier*, 82.
59 Beckett, *Mercier et Camier*, 168.
60 Beckett, *Mercier and Camier*, 82.
61 Beckett, *Mercier et Camier*, 168.
62 Gustav Flaubert, *Bouvard et Pécuchet* (Paris: Gallimard, 1999).
63 Beckett, *Mercier and Camier*, 4.
64 Samuel Beckett, *Mercier et Camier*, 11.
65 Beckett, *Mercier and Camier*, 17.
66 Jacques Rancière, *Mute Speech*, trans. Gabriel Rockhill (New York: Columbia University Press, 2009), 173.
67 Or as Barry suggests, *Mercier et Camier* 'provides an outlet for some very mixed feelings about Ireland and his new home' ('Translating nationalism', 506).
68 Beckett, *Mercier and Camier*, 45.
69 Beckett, *Mercier et Camier*, 89.
70 Ibid., 91.
71 Steven Connor provides a totalizing account of the differences between *Mercier et Camier* and *Mercier and Camier* in *Samuel Beckett: Repetition, Theory, Text* (Cambridge: Blackwell, 1988).
72 Beckett, *Mercier et Camier*, 166.
73 Ibid.
74 Beckett, *Mercier and Camier*, 81.
75 Beckett, *Mercier et Camier*, 29.
76 Beckett, *Mercier and Camier*, 13.
77 Ibid., 82.
78 Ibid., 39.
79 Beckett, *Mercier et Camier*, 59.
80 Rancière, *Mute Speech*, 170.
81 Ibid., 175.

82 Ibid., 174.
83 Feshenfeld and Overbeck, *The Letters of Samuel Beckett, 1929–40*, 254.
84 Pascale Casanova, *The World Republic of Letters*, trans. M. B. Debevoise (Cambridge: Harvard University Press, 2007), 41. Casanova writes that Beckett 'can be understood only in terms of Irish literary space' (a dubious point, one which this chapter later questions) and that to understand his work 'it must be situated in relation to his native literary space within world literature and his own position within this space'.
85 Ibid.
86 Rabaté, *Think, Pig!*, 191.
87 Rancière, *Mute Speech*, 175.
88 Roland Barthes, *Writing Degree Zero and Elements of Semiology*, trans. Annette Lavers and Colin Smith (London: Vintage, 2010), 54.
89 Ibid.
90 Ibid.
91 Ibid., 54–5.
92 Ibid., 82.
93 Samuel Beckett, *Molloy* (London: Faber and Faber, 2009), 23.
94 Ibid., 40.
95 Ibid., 65.
96 Ibid.
97 Bixby, *Samuel Beckett and the Postcolonial Novel*, 181.
98 Ibid., 162.
99 Beckett, *Molloy*, 14.
100 Ibid., 58.
101 In *Samuel Beckett and the Material Imagination* (Cambridge: Cambridge University Press, 2014), 187, Connor suggests that, regarding this same passage from *Molloy*, 'Beckett's world is both ineluctable and indefinable, extending beyond memory and experience, but also refusing to be levered or rounded out into anything like the condition of "a world"'.
102 Samuel Beckett, *Malone Meurt* (Paris: Minuit, 1951), 115.
103 Samuel Beckett, *Malone Dies* (London: Faber and Faber, 2009), 63.
104 Nancy Cunard, ed., *Authors Take Sides on the Spanish War* (London: Furnell & Sons, 1937).
105 Within this, Bixby suggests that 'no doubt the context produces a certain amount of ambiguity, but a reading attuned to the intertextual relationships played out in Beckett's oeuvre will identify the phrase as the rallying call of Irish republicanism, especially as expressed in the Fianna Fail anthem, "Legion of the Rearguard"'. Thus, Malone's 'sloganeering tears a declaration of political commitment from its original context and transforms its significance, but not without recalling the trials of Irish

history which continue to haunt the speech of Beckett's characters' (*Samuel Beckett and the Postcolonial Novel*, 165–6). Regarding the same passage in *Malone Meurt*, Sinéad Mooney, in *A Tongue Not Mine: Beckett and Translation* (Cambridge: Cambridge University Press, 2009), slightly loosens the bind to Irish history when she writes that 'the interpellation of English [in the French text] suggests the evocation of Beckett's "other" republic, the Republic of Ireland' (ibid., 150).

106 Mooney, *A Tongue Not Mine*, 150.
107 Beckett, *Malone Dies*, 63.
108 In *Samuel Beckett and the Problem of Irishness*, Morin writes that 'proximity to Irish culture and politics is asserted explicitly by means of English phrases' and that an 'untranslated reference to Irish nationalist orthodoxy enables Malone to produce a form of speech in and by itself' (70). Thus, as Morin suggests, 'viewed through the lens of Beckett's estranged speaker, the slogan is purely tokenistic and the idea of a collective experience is rendered meaningless' (71). In 'Up the Republic: Beckett, Writing, Politics', *Modern Language Notes* 112, no. 5 (1997): 909–28, Leslie Hill further dismantles the link between this passage and Irish politics in writing that it manifests an 'irreducible friction between discourse and writing, political statement and textual irony, since the effects of recontextualizing the slogan are complex and difficult to control' (912–23), and thus, 'Beckett's writing maintains, with respect to received political discourse, an irreducible distance or reserve' (911).
109 Barthes, *Writing Degree Zero*, 54.
110 For example, in *Samuel Beckett: Repetition, Text, Theory*, Connor demonstrates that 'Beckett's translation is concerned to bleed the two languages [French and English] together into a mixed or mongrel condition', where the act of 'translation for Beckett would always seem to be at one and the same time an act of confederacy, and of secession, which always distinguishes two languages in the act of uniting them' (124). In *A Tongue Not Mine*, Mooney suggests that 'we are forced into a realisation that Beckett's writings are never fully present to themselves, but are radically distracted from their textual moment' (19).
111 In this latter sense, the issue of translation in Beckett's work chimes with Rebecca Walkowitz's recent critical assessment of the 'born translated novel':

> Today's born-translated works block readers from being 'native readers', those who assume that the book was written for them or that the language that they are encountering is, in some proprietary way, theirs. Refusing to match language to geography, many contemporary works will seem to occupy more than one place, to be produced in more than one language, or to address multiple audiences at the same time. They build translation into their form. (*Born Translated: The Contemporary Novel in an Age of World Literature* (New York: Columbia University Press, 2015), 6.

112 Beckett, *Molloy*, 65.
113 Ibid., 23.
114 Walkowitz, *Born Translated*, 6.
115 Ibid.
116 Samuel Beckett, *The Unnamable* (London: Faber and Faber, 2010), 62.
117 Ibid., 132.
118 The latter history has recently been explored by Alan Warran Friedman, who points towards the spectrality of Surrealism in Beckett's later work, as well as the echoes between Beckett's early work – particularly *Dream of Fair to Middling Women* – and the aesthetic projects of the artists he translated for Cunard's anthology. See Alan Warren Friedman, *Surreal Beckett: Samuel Beckett, James Joyce, and Surrealism* (New York: Routledge, 2017).
119 Beckett, *Molloy*, 49.
120 Ibid., 48.
121 Ibid., 29.
122 Ibid.
123 Ibid., 49.
124 Ibid.
125 Beckett, *Malone Dies*, 63.
126 Beckett, *The Unnamable*, 25.
127 Ibid., 61.
128 Barthes, *Writing Degree Zero*, 83.
129 Ibid., 88–9.
130 Ibid., 88.
131 'What is lost in the domain of modernist stylistics,' as Rabaté suggests regarding writing degree zero, 'is a net gain for the ethics of the contemporary world' (*Think, Pig!*, 193). Thus, for Rabaté, as for Barthes, 'the blank and neutral writing is down-to-earth, it flows along with its endless store of popular idioms, which does not rule-out countless self-reflexive games' (ibid.). Importantly then, 'this writing can embody the new "morality of form" which Beckett craves for. Above all, it has very little to do with a committed literature explicitly discussing political events of the times and transforming the poet or novelist into a public intellectual. In short, it breaks with Sartre's model' (ibid.).
132 For an account of late modernism in relation to Beckett, see Morin, 'Samuel Beckett, late modernism and the paradox of distance', 379.
133 Ibid., 380.
134 Beckett, *Molloy*, 1.
135 Beckett, *The Unnamable*, 1.
136 Rabaté, *Think, Pig!*, 193.
137 Casanova, *The World Republic of Letters*, 41.

138 Ibid.
139 Maurice Blanchot, *The Infinite Conversation*, trans. Susan Hanson (Minneapolis: University of Minnesota Press, 1992), 299.
140 Ibid.
141 Ibid.
142 Rabaté, *Think, Pig!*, 193.
143 Daniel Katz, 'What remains of Beckett: Evasion and history', in *Beckett and Phenomenology*, ed. Ulrika Maude and Matthew Feldman (New York: Routledge, 2009), 145.
144 Jacques Derrida, *Of Grammatology*, trans. Gayatri Chakravorty Spivak (Baltimore: Johns Hopkins University Press, 1998), 151.
145 Adorno, *Aesthetic Theory*, 6.
146 In this instance, I am influenced by Jacques Derrida's *The Monolingualism of the Other; or, The Prosthesis of Origin*, trans. Patrick Mensah (Stanford: Stanford University Press, 1998). In that autobiographical text concerning the relationship between language and an origin which would lend it stable meaning, Derrida demonstrates, through his methodological deployment of aporias, that language is both alienation itself and that it does not alienate anything. In this autobiographical text, he writes of himself as a monolingual French speaker that

> speaks a language of which he is *deprived*. The French language is not his. Because he is therefore deprived of *all* language, and no longer has any other recourse ... because this monolingual is in a way *aphasic* ... he is thrown into absolute translation, a translation without a pole of reference, without an originary language, and without a source language. For him, there are only target languages, if you will, the remarkable experience being, however, that these languages just cannot manage to reach themselves because they no longer know where they are coming from, what they are speaking *from* and what the sense of their journey is. (61)

Thus, for Derrida, language 'is never purely natural, nor proper, nor inhabitable. ... There is no possible habitat without the difference of this exile and this nostalgia' (ibid., 61). As with Beckett's narrators – who have been 'thrown into absolute translation, a translation without a pole of reference' – language 'lacks nothing that precedes or follows it, it alienates no ipseity, no property and no self' (ibid., 25). Thus, for Derrida, language constitutes 'only arrivals, and therefore only events without arrival' (ibid., 25).
147 Beckett, *The Unnamable*, 1.
148 Ibid.
149 Ibid.
150 Ibid.
151 Ibid., 36.

152 Ibid., 1.
153 Theodor Adorno, *Negative Dialectics*, trans. E. B. Ashton (London: Routledge, 1973), 380–2.
154 Beckett, *The Unnamable*, 1.
155 Ibid, 127.
156 Ibid., 97.
157 Ibid., 92.
158 McNaughton, *Samuel Beckett and the Politics of Aftermath*, 112.
159 Alysia E. Garrison, '"Faintly struggling things": Trauma, testimony, and inscrutable life' in Beckett's *The Unnamable*', in Kennedy, *Samuel Beckett: History, Memory, Archive*, 98.
160 Ibid., 105.
161 Bixby, for example, reads this predicament as 'a dilemma often voiced in postcolonial writing' but resists making a deterministic argument concerning *The Unnamable* and Ireland's postcolonial condition. He suggests that, ultimately, the narrator 'denies all origins, all grounding identities or grounded subjectivities' (*Samuel Beckett and the Postcolonial Novel*, 199).
162 Stephen Spender, 'Lifelong suffocation', *New York Times*, 12 October 1958.
163 Mark Quigley, 'Unnaming the subject: Samuel Beckett and colonial alterity', *Samuel Beckett Today/Aujourd'hui* 15 (2005): 94.
164 Jude R. Meche, '"A country that called itself his": Molloy and Beckett's estranged relationship with Ireland', *Colby Quarterly* 36, no. 3 (2000): 228.
165 Declan Kiberd, *Inventing Ireland* (London: Vintage, 1995), 535.
166 Beckett, *The Unnamable*, 121.
167 Marx Nixon, *Samuel Beckett's German Diaries 1936–1937* (London: Bloomsbury, 2011), 117–18.
168 Ibid.
169 For more on Beckett's relationships with Pelorson and Stuart, see Knowlson's *Damned to Fame* and Morin's *Beckett's Political Imagination*. Particularly, Morin notes that, after the war, 'Beckett only ever alluded to Pelorson's role in the Vichy administration in covert terms. His correspondence with Belmont evidences a warm friendship and is punctuated by attempts to assist him in getting his work published under his new identity' (ibid., 139). As Morin continues, 'Among common acquaintances Beckett seems to have been the only one willing to engage with Pelorson-Belmont after the War' (ibid.).
170 Beckett, *The Unnamable*, 120.
171 Ibid., 9.
172 Ibid., 8.
173 Concerning the same lack of origin prevalent to the novel, David Houston Jones, in *Samuel Beckett and Testimony* (Basingstoke: Palgrave Macmillan, 2011), reads the

'shearing-off of enunciation from context as characteristic of Beckettian testimony' where the 'impossibility of reference ... creates the possibility of testimony, which is understood here not through representation but rather in the anguished and problematic entry of the speaker into language' (20). It is as such for Houston Jones that the translatorial effects of the writing – 'the deployment of a variety of signatures which may or may not account for the creation of the narrative' (21) – establish a complex account of what constitutes a definition of Beckettian testimony.

2 Brian, Flann, Myles and the origins of Irish modernism

1 Rónán McDonald and Julian Murphet, 'Introduction', in *Flann O'Brien and Modernism*, ed. Rónán McDonald, Julian Murphet and Sascha Morell (London: Bloomsbury, 2014), 1.
2 Terence Brown, *Ireland: A Social and Cultural History 1922–2002* (London: Harper Perennial, 2004), 180.
3 Joe Cleary, *Literature, Partition and the Nation State* (Cambridge: Cambridge University Press, 2002), 73.
4 Diarmaid Ferriter, *The Transformation of Ireland 1900–2000* (London: Profile, 2005), 376, 409, 468.
5 Rónán McDonald, 'An astonishing parade of nullity? Nihilism', in McDonald, Murphet and Morell, *Flann O'Brien and Modernism*, 136.
6 Joseph Brooker, 'Myles' Tones', in *Flann O'Brien in the Twenty-First Century*, ed. Jennika Baines (Dublin: Four Courts, 2011), 31.
7 Carol Taaffe, *Ireland through the Looking-Glass: Flann O'Brien, Myles na gCopaleen and Irish Cultural Debate* (Cork: Cork University Press, 2008), 32.
8 Maebh Long, *Assembling Flann O'Brien* (London: Bloomsbury, 2014), 7.
9 Jennika Baines, 'Introduction', in Baines, *Flann O'Brien in the Twenty-First Century*, 12.
10 Richard Kearney, *Transitions: Narratives in Modern Irish Culture* (Manchester: Manchester University Press, 1988), 88.
11 Paul Fagan, '"I've got you under my skin": "John Duffy's Brother," "Two in One," and the Confessions of Narcissus', in *Flann O'Brien: Contesting Legacies*, ed. Ruben Borg, Paul Fagan, and Werner Huber (Cork: Cork University Press, 2014), 61.
12 Long, *Assembling Flann O'Brien*, 160.
13 McDonald and Murphet, 'Introduction', 2.
14 Ibid., 1–2.
15 Ibid., 5.
16 Ibid.

17 Thierry Robin, 'Tall tales or "petites histoires": History and the void in "The Martyr's Crown" and *Thirst*', in Borg, Fagan and Huber, *Flann O'Brien: Contesting Legacies*, 91.
18 McDonald and Murphet, 'Introduction', 1.
19 R. W. Maslen, 'Flann O'Brien's bombshells: *At Swim-Two-Birds* and *The Third Policeman*', *New Hibernia Review* 10, no. 4 (2006): 85.
20 Taaffe, *Ireland through the Looking Glass*, 39.
21 McDonald and Murphet, 'Introduction', 2.
22 Astrid Erll, *Memory in Culture*, trans. Sara B. Young (London: Palgrave Macmillan, 2011), 152.
23 Adam Meehan, *Modernism and Subjectivity: How Modernist Fiction Invented the Postmodern Subject* (Baton Rouge: Louisiana State University Press, 2020), 6. See also Marjorie Perloff's *Radical Artifice: Writing Poetry in the Age of Media* (Chicago: University of Chicago Press, 1991), 243. Meehan demonstrates that understandings of postmodernism revelling in and celebrating ambiguity and fragmentation, against a supposed modernism 'limited by writers' desire to restore some notion of a lost order', are built on a straw-man argument (*Modernism and Subjectivity*, 6). Like Perloff, Meehan notes, in a critique of the dominant accounts of postmodernism that have become conventional since the 1980s, that this straw man modernism has had the dual effect of legitimizing postmodernism as a descriptive aesthetic category while simultaneously minimizing modernism's heterogeneity and intellectual sophistication' (ibid., 6). If we accept this view, writes Meehan, 'modernism resembles a nascent form of postmodernism that has not yet reached its full potential' (ibid., 10). Against this position, Meehan suggests that if we allow modernism to speak for itself, then we realize that it in fact already speaks the language of postmodernism. Thus, 'the theoretical work done by postmodern critics has already been done by modernist authors' (ibid., 13).
24 Long, *Assembling Flann O'Brien*, 4.
25 Paul Saint-Amour, 'The medial humanities: Toward a manifesto for meso-analysis', *Modernism/modernity Print Plus* 3, no . 4 (2019). Available online: https://modernismmodernity.org/forums/posts/medial-humanities-toward-manifesto-meso-analysis (accessed 11 December 2019) .
26 Taaffe, *Ireland through the Looking Glass*, 32.
27 For more on the question of postmodernism in relation to this oeuvre, see Keith Hopper, *Flann O'Brien: A Portrait of the Artist as a Young Post-Modernist* (Cork: Cork University Press, 2009).
28 Adrian Oţoiu, '"Compartmentation of personality for the purpose of literary utterance": Pseudonymity and heteronymity in the various lives of Flann O'Brien', *Word and Text: A Journal of Literary Studies and Linguistics* 1, no. 1 (2011): 134.

29 Ibid.
30 Maebh Long, 'Plagiarism and the Politics of Friendship: Brian O'Nolan, Niall Sheridan and Niall Montgomery', in *Flann O'Brien: Acting out*, ed. Paul Fagan and Dieter Fuchs (Cork: Cork University Press, 2022, forthcoming).
31 Walter Benjamin, 'The destructive character', in *Reflections: Essays, Aphorisms, Autobiographical Writings* (New York: Random House, 1995), 301.
32 Niall Montgomery, 'An aristophanic sorcerer', *Irish Times*, 2 April 1966, 7.
33 Ibid., 7.
34 Ibid.
35 Benjamin, 'The destructive character', 301.
36 Ibid., 303.
37 Flann O'Brien, *The Third Policeman* (London: Flamingo, 1967), 110.
38 Walter Benjmain, 'The work of art in the age of mechanical reproduction', in *Illuminations* (London: Pimlico, 1999), 215.
39 Ibid.
40 Friedrich Nietzsche, *Beyond Good and Evil*, trans. R. J. Holingdale (London: Penguin, 2003), 69.
41 Ibid.
42 Ibid., 69–70.
43 W. B. Yeats, *Memoirs*, ed. Denis Donoghue (New York: Macmillan, 1972), 191.
44 Ibid.
45 W. B. Yeats, 'The Mask', in *The Poems*, ed. Daniel Albright (London: Everyman, 1994), 144.
46 See Louis MacNeice, *The Poetry of W. B. Yeats* (Oxford: Oxford University Press, 1948); and Richard Ellmann, *The Man and the Masks* (New York: Macmillan, 1948).
47 Margaret Mills Harper and Warwick Gould, eds., *Yeats's Mask: Yeats Annual No. 19* (Cambridge: Open Book, 2013).
48 Daniel Keith Jernigan, '"Simulat Ergo Est": Brian O'Nolan's Metaperformative Simulations', *New Hibernia Review* 20, no. 1 (2016): 93.
49 Taaffe, *Ireland through the Looking Glass*, 32.
50 For a complete account of the intricacies of these methodologies, see John Brannigan's *New Historicism and Cultural Materialism* (Basingstoke: Macmillan Press, 1998).
51 Giordano Vintaloro, 'Brian O'Nolan, the conspirator', *Studi Irlandesi* 7 (2017): 262.
52 Ibid.
53 Flore Coulouma, 'Tall tales and short stories: "Cruiskeen Lawn" and the dialogic imagination', *Review of Contemporary Fiction* 31, no. 3 (2011): 163.
54 Diarmaid Ferriter, *Transformation of Ireland 1900–2000*, 409, 468.
55 Taaffe, *Ireland through the Looking Glass*, 32.
56 Nietzsche, *Beyond Good and Evil*, 70.
57 Taaffe, *Ireland through the Looking Glass*, 32.

58 Nietzsche, *Beyond Good and Evil*, 69.
59 Yeats, 'The Mask', 144.
60 In *No Laughing Matter: The Life and Times of Flann O'Brien* (Boulder: Paladin Press, 1990), Anthony Cronin gives an account of Sheridan's and Montgomery's involvement in the writing of *Cruiskeen Lawn* (199); in contrast to Montgomery's contributions, however, Sheridan's involvement remains unsubstantiated.
61 Long, *Assembling Flann O'Brien*, 160.
62 Roland Barthes, 'From work to text', in *Image, Music, Text*, ed. and trans. Stephen Heath (London: Fontana, 1977), 161.
63 Ibid., 159, 161.
64 Taaffe, *Ireland through the Looking Glass*, 40.
65 Ibid., 61.
66 Long, *Assembling Flann O'Brien*, 22.
67 Flann O'Brien, *At Swim-Two-Birds* (London: Penguin, 2000), 9.
68 Ibid.
69 Ibid.
70 Ibid.
71 Ibid., 25.
72 Long, *Assembling Flann O'Brien*, 32.
73 Ibid.
74 Ibid.
75 O'Brien, *At Swim-Two-Birds*, 25.
76 Ibid., 13.
77 Jacques Derrida, *Of Grammatology*, trans. Gayatri Chakravorty Spivak (Baltimore: Johns Hopkins University Press, 1997), 145.
78 Alana Gillespie explores this issue further in 'In defence of "gap-worded" stories: Brian O'Nolan on authority, reading and writing', in *Flann O'Brien: Problems with Authority*, ed. Ruben Borg, Paul Fagan and John McCourt (Cork: Cork University Press, 2017), 204–18.
79 O'Brien, *At Swim-Two-Birds*, 73.
80 Ibid.
81 Ibid., 61.
82 Paul Ricoeur, *Memory, History, Forgetting*, trans. Kathleen Blamey and David Pellauer (Chicago: University of Chicago Press, 2004), 85.
83 O'Brien, *At Swim-Two-Birds*, 101.
84 M. Keith Booker, *Flann O'Brien, Bakhtin, and Menippean Satire* (New York: Syracuse University Press, 1995), 38.
85 T. S. Eliot, '*Ulysses*, Order and Myth', in *Selected Prose of T. S. Eliot*, ed. Frank Kermode (London: Faber and Faber, 1975), 177.
86 Declan Kiberd, *Irish Classics* (London: Granta Books, 2000), 502.

87 Ibid.
88 Ibid.
89 Gilles Deleuze and Félix Guattari, *Anti-Oedipus*, trans. Robert Hurley, Mark Seem and Helen R. Lane (London: Bloomsbury, 2013), 16–17.
90 Long, *Assembling Flann O'Brien*, 14.
91 Maebh Long, ed., *The Collected Letters of Flann O'Brien* (Champaign: Dalkey Archive Press, 2018), 8.
92 Rebecca Walkowitz, *Born Translated: The Contemporary Novel in an Age of World Literature* (New York: Columbia University Press, 2015), 25.
93 Emily Apter, *Against World Literature: On the Politics of Untranslatability* (New York: Verso, 2013), 15.
94 Deleuze and Guattari describe Proust's *À la recherche du temps perdu* in such terms in *Anti-Oedipus*, 46–7.
95 Taaffe, *Ireland through the Looking Glass*, 34–5.
96 Gregory Dobbins, 'Constitutional Laziness and the Novel: Idleness, Irish Modernism, and Flann O'Brien's *At Swim-Two-Birds*', *NOVEL: A Forum on Fiction* 42, no. 1 (2009): 94.
97 Derrida, *Of Grammatology*, 145.
98 Jean-Michel Rabaté, *The Pathos of Distance: Affects of the Moderns* (London: Bloomsbury, 2016), 51.
99 Long, *Assembling Flann O'Brien*, 87.
100 Ondřej Pilný, '"Did you put charcoal adroitly in the vent?" Brian O'Nolan and pataphysics', in Borg, Fagan and Huber, *Flann O'Brien: Contesting Legacies*, 161.
101 McDonald, 'An astonishing parade of nullity?', 139–40.
102 Taaffe, *Ireland through the Looking Glass*, 78–81.
103 John Attridge, 'Nonsense, ordinary language philosophy, and Flann O'Brien's *The Third Policeman*', *Modern Fiction Studies* 60, no. 2 (2014): 309.
104 Michael Rubenstein, *Public Works: Infrastructure, Irish Modernism and the Postcolonial* (Notre Dame: University of Notre Dame Press) 105–6.
105 Flann O'Brien, *The Third Policeman* (London: Flamingo, 1967), 3.
106 Ibid., 10.
107 Ibid., 4.
108 Ibid., 6.
109 Ibid., 10.
110 Ibid., 3.
111 Ibid., 18.
112 See Gilles Deleuze and Félix Guattari, *A Thousand Plateaus*, trans. Brian Massumi (London: Bloomsbury, 2013), 178–80. Deleuze and Guattari describe two types of 'bodies without organs' that lend themselves to thinking about the narrator's reality in *The Third Policeman*. They write that pleasure, for the drugged and

masochist body, 'is something that must be delayed ... because it interrupts the continuous process of positive desire' (*A Thousand Plateaus*, 180). 'There is', then, 'a joy that is immanent to desire as though desire were filled by itself ..., a joy that implies no lack or impossibility' (ibid.). Thus, both the drugged and masochist body use 'suffering as a way of constituting a body without organs and bringing forth a plane of consistency of desire' so as to experience a joy that is immanent to uninterrupted desire (ibid.).

113 McDonald, 'An astonishing parade of nullity?', 140.
114 O'Brien, *The Third Policeman*, 19.
115 Ibid., 52.
116 Ibid., 101–2.
117 Ibid., 35.
118 Hopper, *Flann O'Brien*, 155.
119 Robert Lumsden, 'Voidence in *The Third Policeman*', *Review of Contemporary Fiction*, no. 31 (2011), 55.
120 Hopper, *Flann O'Brien*, 77.
121 O'Brien, *The Third Policeman*, 39.
122 Tamara Radak explores the issue of multiple realties in *The Third Policeman* in '"Walking forever on falling ground": Closure, hypertext and the textures of possibility in *The Third Policeman*', in Borg, Fagan and McCourt, *Flann O'Brien: Problems with Authority*, 242–54.
123 O'Brien, *The Third Policeman*, 30.
124 Deleuze and Guattari, *A Thousand Plateaus*, 180.
125 O'Brien, *The Third Policeman*, 30.
126 Ibid., 66.
127 Deleuze and Guattari, *A Thousand Plateaus*, 180.
128 Ibid.
129 O'Brien, *The Third Policeman*, 39–40.
130 Terence Brown, *The Literature of Ireland: Culture and Criticism* (Cambridge: Cambridge University Press, 2010), 117.
131 Gilles Deleuze and Guattari, *A Thousand Plateaus*, 342.
132 Ibid., 118, 342.
133 O'Brien, *The Third Policeman*, 84.
134 Ibid., 64.
135 Ibid., 90.
136 Ibid., 64.
137 Ibid., 94.
138 Ibid., 105.
139 Ibid., 93.
140 Ibid., 139.

141 Ibid., 147.
142 Ibid., 149.
143 Ibid., 104.
144 Ibid., 150.
145 Derrida, *Of Grammatology*, 145.
146 Barthes, 'From work to text', 159.
147 Derrida, *Of Grammatology*, 151.
148 Jacques Derrida, 'Who or what is compared? The concept of comparative literature and the theoretical problems of translation', trans. Eric Prenowitz, *Discourse* 30, nos 1 and 2 (2008): 36.
149 Ibid., 50.
150 Neil Murphy and Keith Hopper, 'Introduction', in *The Short Fiction of Flann O'Brien*, ed. Keith Hopper and Neil Murphy (Champaign: Dalkey Archive Press, 2013), ix–x.

3 Elizabeth Bowen's modernist history

1 Roy Foster, 'Irish and regional: Locale in Elizabeth Bowen's writing', in *Elizabeth Bowen Remembered: The Farahy Address*, ed. Eibhear Walshe (Dublin: Four Courts, 1998), 21. Foster writes, 'In a strange way, there is an aspect of her work that is "regional". I say strange, because she seems to have been a highly sophisticated metropolitan operator, much fêted on the international circuit, and the students who write theses about her do not, actually, deal with her primarily as an Irish writer' (ibid.).
2 Seán Ó Faoláin, 'A reading and remembrance of Elizabeth Bowen', *London Review of Books* 4, no. 4 (1982): 15.
3 Or, more broadly, as Heather Laird suggests, 'amongst the Elizabeth Bowens figured in literary and cultural criticism is the "Anglo-Irish Bowen", "the modernist Bowen", "the postmodernist Bowen", "the bisexual Bowen", "the woman writer", "the British wartime author", and "the writer of the Irish Protestant Gothic"'. See Laird, 'The "placing" and politics of Bowen in contemporary Irish literary and cultural criticism', in Elizabeth Bowen, ed. *Eibhear Walshe* (Dublin: Irish Academic Press, 2009), 193.
4 See Chris Hopkins, 'Elizabeth Bowen: Realism, modernism and gendered identity in her novels of the 1930s', *Journal of Gender Studies* 4, no. 3 (1995): 271–9.
5 Quoted in Heather Bryant Jordan, *How Will the Heart Endure: Elizabeth Bowen and the Landscape of War* (Michigan: University of Michigan Press, 1992), xvi.
6 Pound develops such terminology when editing T. S. Eliot's 'The Wasteland'. See T. S. Eliot, *The Waste Land: A Facsimile and Transcript of the Original Drafts Including the Annotations of Ezra Pound*, ed. Valerie Eliot (Boston: Mariner Books, 1993).

7 Feminist revisions of the modernist canon have brought Bowen to its fore. Particularly, Nicola Humble, in *The Feminine Middlebrow Novel, 1920s to 1950s* (Oxford: Oxford University Press, 2001), has addressed a (previously) gendered dichotomy between modernism (read as masculine) and the middlebrow (read as feminine), a category to which Bowen and other women writers were made relative based on their gender and apparent aesthetic strategies. Collapsing this distinction through analysis of the formal autonomy of a host of supposedly middlebrow writings, such feminist revisions of the remit of modernism have made Bowen one of its integral writers.
8 Late modernism – occurring from the late 1920s and suggesting a mode of modernism concerned with formal self-consciousness while suspicious of, and critically revising, the central tenets of high modernism, particularly in terms of the supposed autonomy of the work of art – has catered for Bowen's previously shy modernism becoming central to modernist discussion over the last two decades. As Sian White and Pamela Thurschwell suggest in 'Introduction to Elizabeth Bowen and modernity', *Textual Practice* 27, no. 1 (2013), 'much of Bowen's work engages with the questions of subjectivity and form that attracted the high modernists, while simultaneously registering directly and obliquely a changing political, historical and cultural landscape' (1–2).
9 Joe Cleary, 'Introduction', in *The Cambridge Companion to Irish Modernism*, ed. Joe Cleary (Cambridge: Cambridge University Press, 2014), 4.
10 Lauren Arrington, 'Irish modernism', *Oxford Research Encyclopedia of Literature*, 27 February 2017. Available online: https://oxfordre.com/view/10.1093/acrefore/9780190201098.001.0001/acrefore-9780190201098-e-237.
11 Maud Ellmann, *Elizabeth Bowen: The Shadow across the Page* (Edinburgh: Edinburgh University Press, 2003), 17.
12 'Interview with Elizabeth Bowen', *The Bell* 4, no. 6 (1942).
13 Brendan Clifford and Jack Lane, eds, *A North Cork Anthology: 250 Years of Writings from the Region of Millstreet, Duhallow, Slieve Luachra, and Thereabouts* (Cork: Aubane Historical Society, 1999).
14 Maria Di Battista, 'Elizabeth Bowen's troubled modernism', in *Modernism and Colonialism: British and Irish Literature, 1899–1939*, ed. Richard Begam and Michael Valdez Moses (Durham: Duke University Press, 2007), 227.
15 Ibid., 232.
16 Or as Vera Kreilkamp describes, the novel is ambivalent concerning past and future. 'Bowen: Ascendency modernist', in *Elizabeth Bowen*, ed. Eibhear Walsh (Dublin: Irish Academic Press, 2009).
17 In a manner symptomatic of the modernist novel following the exploits of James Joyce and Virginia Woolf, history has, Ann Banfield suggests, 'receded to such an incomprehensible distance, become an impersonal force'. 'Remembrance and

tense past', in *The Cambridge Companion to the Modernist Novel*, ed. Morag Shiach (Cambridge: Cambridge University Press, 2009), 50.
18 Quoted in Ellmann, *The Shadow across the Page*, 166.
19 Susan Osborn, '"How to measure this unaccountable darkness between the trees": The strange relation of style and meaning in *The Last September*', in *Elizabeth Bowen: New Critical Perspectives*, ed. Susan Osborn (Cork: Cork University Press, 2009), 55. As Osborn writes, 'the infiltration of the monstrous discomfits the absoluteness of the natural order represented in the manifest plot and of most historical and thematic interpretations of *The Last September*, exposing them as uneasy intellectual impositions' (ibid.).
20 Ibid.
21 Andrew Bennett and Nicholas Royle, *Elizabeth Bowen and the Dissolution of the Novel* (London: Palgrave MacMillan, 1995), xvii.
22 Ibid., 18.
23 Ibid.
24 Jed Esty, *Unseasonable Youth, Modernism, Colonialism and the Fiction of Development* (Oxford: Oxford University Press, 2011), 179.
25 Ibid.
26 Neil Corcoran, *Elizabeth Bowen: The Enforced Return* (Oxford: Oxford University Press, 2008) 13.
27 Ibid., 18.
28 Ibid., 46.
29 Ibid.
30 Or as Osborn suggests, 'Bowen's inconsistent and unsystematic employment of representational and formal irregularities … threaten the stability of conventionally conceived historical interpretations" ('"How to measure this unaccountable darkness between the trees"', 42).
31 Victoria Glendinning writes that *The Last September*, 'while centred on the doomed world of Danielstown and on Lois, has everything to say about the English-Irish relationship in the Troubles'. See Glendinning, *Elizabeth Bowen: Portrait of a Writer* (London: Weidenfeld and Nicolson, 1977), 66. Renée C. Hoogland writes that 'the sense of dislocation Laurence and Lois have in common is placed at the centre of the narrative by being reflected in the novel's sociohistorical setting, metaphorically foregrounded by the violence of the Troubles'. See Hoogland, *Elizabeth Bowen: A Reputation in Writing* (New York: New York University Press, 1994), 50. Eibhear Walshe writes that 'times of violence were also times of intense creativity for Bowen, as witnessed by her Irish War of Independence novel, The *Last September*'. See Walshe, 'A time for hard writers', in *Elizabeth Bowen*, ed. Eibhear Walshe (Dublin: Irish Academic Press, 2009), 101. Kelly Sullivan writes that '*The Last September* … takes place during the War of Independence'. See Sullivan, 'Elizabeth

Bowen and 1916: An architecture of suspense', *Modernism/modernity* 4, no. 3 (2020). Available online: https://modernismmodernity.org/articles/sullivan-1916-architecturesuspense (accessed 16 December 2020).
32 Corcoran, *The Enforced Return*, 13.
33 Ellmann, *The Shadow across the Page*, 20.
34 Matt Eatough, 'Bowen's court and the Anglo-Irish world-system', *Modern Language Quarterly* 73, no. 1 (2012), 74.
35 Ibid.
36 See Jonathan Culler, 'Omniscience', *Narrative* 12, no. 1 (2004): 22–34; Nicholas Royle, *The Uncanny* (Manchester: Manchester University Press, 2003).
37 Culler, 'Omniscience', 31.
38 Shlomith Rimmon-Kenan, *Narrative Fiction: Contemporary Poetics* (London: Methuen, 1983), 94.
39 Ibid., 95.
40 Ibid.
41 Ibid.
42 Ibid.
43 Gérard Genette, *Narrative Discourse: An Essay in Method*, trans. Jane E. Lewin (Ithaca: Cornell University Press, 1983), 189.
44 Ibid.
45 Ibid.
46 Ibid., 192.
47 Rimmon-Kenan, *Narrative Fiction*, 108.
48 Seymour Chatman, *Coming to Terms: The Rhetoric of Narrative in Fiction and Film* (Ithaca: Cornell University Press, 1990), 116.
49 Genette, *Narrative Discourse*, 189.
50 Elizabeth Bowen, *The Last September* (London: Vintage, 1998), 7–8.
51 Ibid., 7.
52 Ibid., 8.
53 Ibid.
54 Ibid.
55 See note 31 above.
56 Bowen, *The Last September*, 23.
57 Ibid.
58 Ibid., 24.
59 Ibid.
60 Ibid.
61 Ibid., 24–5.
62 Ibid., 25.
63 Ibid.

64 Ibid., 24.
65 Ibid.
66 Ibid., 25.
67 Ibid.
68 Ibid.
69 Ibid.
70 Ibid.
71 Ibid., 26.
72 Ibid., 25.
73 Ibid., 26.
74 Ibid., 38.
75 Ibid.
76 Ibid., 46.
77 Ibid., 47.
78 Ibid.
79 Ibid.
80 Ibid., 47–8.
81 Ibid., 48.
82 Ibid.
83 Ibid.
84 Ibid.
85 Ibid., 47.
86 Ibid., 49.
87 Ibid., 62.
88 Ibid., 63.
89 James Wurtz, 'Elizabeth Bowen, modernism and the spectre of Anglo-Ireland', *Estudios Irlandeses* 5 (2010): 123.
90 Shannon Wells-Lasagne, '"He Believed in Empire"', *Irish Studies Review* 15, no. 4 (2007): 452.
91 Esty, *Unseasonable Youth*, 189.
92 Ibid., 82.
93 Ibid.
94 See Corcoran, *The Enforced Return*, 51.
95 Bowen, *The Last September*, 125.
96 Ibid.
97 Ibid.
98 Ibid., 126.
99 Ibid.
100 Ibid.
101 Ibid.

102 Ibid.
103 Ibid., 129.
104 J. Hillis Miller, *Topographies* (Stanford: Stanford University Press, 1995), 77.
105 Ibid., 124–5.
106 Ibid., 127.
107 Pascale Casanova, *The World Republic of Letters*, trans. M. B. Debevoise (Cambridge: Harvard University Press, 2007), 86.
108 Peter Kalliney, *Modernism in a Global Context* (New York: Bloomsbury, 2015), 43.
109 Ibid., 44.
110 Ibid.
111 Esty similarly uses the stage metaphor in his analysis of the novel in *Unseasonable Youth* (180).
112 See Jacques Derrida, *The Gift of Death and Literature in Secret*, trans. David Wills (Chicago: University of Chicago Press, 2008).
113 Bowen, *The Last September*, 126.
114 Corcoran, *The Enforced Return*, 40.
115 Bowen, *The Last September*, 198.
116 Ibid., 199.
117 Ibid., 200.
118 Ibid., 199.
119 Ibid., 200.
120 Ibid., 201.
121 Ibid., 203.
122 Ibid., 206.
123 Ellmann, *The Shadow across the Page*, 42.
124 Bowen, *The Last September*, 206.
125 Such is perhaps the reason why Bowen's critical position has always been so fraught: the temptation to read Bowen as a social realist and mimetically representing historical realities is inviting, but her narrative operations always thwart this potentiality. Similarly, because of the apparent sheen of social realism which her texts seemingly display, it has proved difficult for critics to place her writing directly in a category of high modernism.
126 Beth Wightman, 'Geopolitics and the sight of the nation: Elizabeth Bowen's *The Last September*', *Literature Interpretation Theory* 18, no. 1 (2007): 41.
127 Di Battista similarly makes this point when she writes that Bowen was a writer of 'conservative instincts, but radical imagination', and thus should not 'be suspected of disingenuous ideological alibis for the cultural and politial dominance of their class before the Treaty of 1922' ('Elizabeth Bowen's troubled modernism', 227).
128 Bowen, *The Last September*, 166.

129 My thinking in this instance is influenced by Gary Wilder's *Freedom Time: Negritude, Decolonization and the Future of the World* (Durham: Duke University Press, 2015).
130 Dawn Miranda Sherratt-Bado, 'Endgame', *Dublin Review of Books* 126 (2020).

4 Kate O'Brien's 'flawed' modernism

1 Michael Cronin, *Impure Thoughts: Sexuality, Catholicism and Literature in Twentieth-Century Ireland* (Manchester: Manchester University Press, 2012).
2 Gerardine Meaney, 'Territory and transgression: History, nationality and sexuality in Kate O'Brien's fiction', *Irish Journal of Feminist Studies* 2 (1997): 81.
3 Roland Barthes, 'From work to text', in *Image, Music, Text*, ed. and trans. Stephen Heath (London: Fontana, 1977), 158.
4 Anne Fogarty, '"The business of attachment": Romance and desire in the novels of Kate O'Brien', in *Ordinary People Dancing: Essays on Kate O'Brien*, ed. Eibear Walshe (Cork: Cork University Press, 1993), 101.
5 Evelyn Waugh, 'The Irish bourgeoisie', in *The Essays, Articles and Reviews of Evelyn Waugh*, ed. Donat Gallagher (London: Metheun, 1983), 230.
6 Ibid.
7 Ibid.
8 Adele M. Dalsimer, *Kate O'Brien: A Critical Study* (Dublin: Gill and Macmillan, 1990), 47.
9 Eibhear Walshe, 'Introduction', in Walshe, Ordinary People Dancing, 2.
10 See Terry Eagleton's 'Form and ideology in the Anglo-Irish novel', in *Literary Relations: Ireland, Egypt and the Far East* (Gerrards Cross: Colin Smythe, 1996), 135–46: Eagleton writes, 'That the novel never flourished as vigorously as its English counterpart is surely no mystery. For culture demands a material base; and a society as impoverished as Ireland was hardly in a position to provide one' (145).
11 Eibhear Walshe and Mary Breen in their respective essays in *Ordinary People Dancing* explicitly write about O'Brien's writing as radical. In his essay, 'Lock Up Your Daughters: From Ante-Room to Interior Castle', Walshe writes, 'in *That Lady* … O'Brien finally create[s] a narrative wherein a female protagonist actualises radical dissent and achieves vital contradistinction from patriarchal control' (151). Mary Breen writes that *The Land of Spices* is a 'radical and subversive critique of patriarchal ideology' (167).
12 Eibhear Walshe, *Kate O'Brien: A Writing Life* (Dublin: Irish Academic Press, 2006) 2.
13 Ailbhe Smyth, 'Counterpoints: A note (or two) on feminism and Kate O'Brien', in Walshe, *Ordinary People Dancing*, 33.

14 Cronin, *Impure Thoughts*, 89.
15 Aintzane Legarreta Mentxaka, *Kate O'Brien and the Fiction of Identity: Sex, Art and Politics in Mary Lavelle and Other Writings* (Jefferson: McFarland, 2011), 12.
16 Ibid., 140.
17 Mary Breen, '"Something understood?": Kate O'Brien and *The Land of Spices*', in Walshe, *Ordinary People Dancing*, 171.
18 Legarreta Mentxaka, *Kate O'Brien and the Fiction of Identity*, 42.
19 Culler, 'Omniscience', 31.
20 Jacques Derrida, *Spectres of Marx: The State of the Debt, the Work of Mourning and the New International*, trans. Peggy Kamuf (New York: Routledge, 1994), 18.
21 Ibid.
22 Roland Barthes, *The Pleasure of the Text*, trans. Richard Miller (New York: Hill and Wang, 1998), 47.
23 Fogarty, '"The business of attachment"', 101.
24 Kate O'Brien, 'UCD as I forget it', *University Review* 3, no. 2 (1963): 6.
25 Ibid., 132.
26 Kate O'Brien, *Mary Lavelle* (London: Virago Press, 1984), 88.
27 Ibid.
28 Ibid., 12.
29 Ibid.
30 Legarreta Mentxaka, *Kate O'Brien and the Fiction of Identity*, 139.
31 Ibid., 29–30.
32 Ibid., xv.
33 Ibid.
34 Derrida, *Spectres of Marx*, 48.
35 Legarreta Mentxaka, *Kate O'Brien and the Fiction of Identity*, 63.
36 O'Brien, *Mary Lavelle*, 27.
37 Ibid., xiii.
38 Ibid., 19.
39 Ibid., 28.
40 Ibid., 27.
41 Ibid., 27–8.
42 Derrida, *Spectres of Marx*, 5.
43 For a detailed analysis of the politics of *Mary Lavelle* as a self-development novel, see Michael Cronin's *Impure Thoughts*.
44 Legarreta Mentxaka, *Kate O'Brien and the Fiction of Identity*, 95–100.
45 Fogarty, '"The business of attachment"', 101.
46 O'Brien, *Mary Lavelle*, 12, 88.
47 Ibid., 112.

48 See Legarreta Mentxaka's *Kate O'Brien and the Fiction of Identity* for a full account of O'Brien's incorporation of anarchist and Marxist politics into *Mary Lavelle*.
49 Paige Reynolds, 'Spectacular nostalgia: Modernism and dramatic form in Kate O'Brien's *Pray for the Wanderer*', *Irish University Review* 48, no. 1 (2018): 58.
50 Anthony Roche, '"The devil era": The presence of Éamon de Valera in three novels by Kate O'Brien', *Irish University Review* 48, no. 1 (2018): 113.
51 Kate O'Brien, *Pray for the Wanderer* (New York: Doubleday, Doran & Company, 1938), 44–5.
52 Ibid.
53 Ibid.
54 Ibid.
55 Ibid., 159.
56 Ibid., 44.
57 Waugh, 'The Irish bourgeoisie', 230.
58 O'Brien, *Pray for the Wanderer*, 51.
59 Ibid.
60 Ibid.
61 Ibid.
62 Ibid., 56.
63 The narrative strategy of *Pray for the Wanderer* perhaps establishes a metacritical forewarning of its own unreliability in another of Matt's concessions. In a later conversation with Tom in chapter two, after Tom recounts the story of his relationship with Nell, it is suggested that Matt concedes that 'memory is random and irresponsible in every heart … Some of our most vividly retained impressions seem to bear no significant relation to any existent feeling' (ibid., 84).
64 Roche, '"The devil era"', 114.
65 Brad Kent, 'An argument manqué: Kate O'Brien's *Pray for the Wanderer*', *Irish Studies Review* 18, no. 3 (2010): 287.
66 O'Brien, *Pray for the Wanderer*, 135.
67 Ibid., 137.
68 Ibid., 138. Indeed, the omniscient narration in this instance signals another narrative perspective as it contrasts with the previous use of free-indirect narration for the representation of Matt's thoughts.
69 Ibid., 154.
70 Ibid., 159.
71 Ibid.
72 Ibid., 225.
73 Ibid., 221.
74 Ibid., 263.

75 Gérard Genette, *Narrative Discourse: An Essay in Method*, trans. Jane E. Lewin (Ithaca: Cornell University Press, 1983), 189.
76 Shlomith Rimmon-Kenan, *Narrative Fiction: Contemporary Poetics* (London: Methuen, 1983), 108.
77 Kate O'Brien, *The Land of Spices* (London: Virago Press, 1988), 10.
78 Ibid., 20.
79 Ibid., 11.
80 Ibid., 10–11.
81 Kelly Sullivan, "'An absolutely private thing": Letters in Kate O'Brien's *The Land of Spices*', *Irish University Review* 48, no. 1 (2018): 87
82 Breen, "'Something understood?'", 182.
83 O'Brien, *The Land of Spices,* 15.
84 Ibid., 152.
85 Ibid.
86 Ibid., 156.
87 Ibid., 163.
88 Ibid., 163–5.
89 Ibid., 165.
90 Ibid., 168.
91 Anne Fogarty, "'The gentle thread of the little voice:" Silence, sexuality, and subjectivity in Kate O'Brien's *The Land of Spices*', in *Silence in Modern Irish Literature*, ed. Michael McAteer (Leiden: Brill, 2017), 154.
92 Ibid., 242.
93 Ibid., 254.
94 Ibid., 155.
95 Ibid., 154.
96 Anne Fogarty, 'Women and modernism', in *The Cambridge Companion to Irish Modernism*, ed. Joe Cleary (Cambridge: Cambridge University Press, 2014), 157.

5 John McGahern and the limits of Irish modernism

1 See Joe Cleary, *Outrageous Fortune, Capital and Culture in Modern Ireland* (Dublin: Field Day, 2007). Cleary includes McGahern in a group of 1960s naturalists including Brian Moore, Tom Murphy and Edna O'Brien (ibid., 165). See James Whyte, *History, Myth and Ritual in the Fiction of John McGahern: Strategies of Transcendence* (New York: Edwin Mellen, 2002). Whyte writes that 'McGahern's starting point is realism' and that 'after engagement with experimental forms …, his later work provides evidence of a circling back, as he returns to more "traditional" realistic forms' (ibid., 57). See Eamon Grennan, "'Only what happens": Mulling

over McGahern', *Irish University Review* 35, no. 1 (2005): 13–27. Grennan writes, 'By mixing his realist-naturalist mode of story with the symbolist mode of fable, McGahern creates his own peculiar kind of novel' (ibid., 19).
2. See Eamon Maher, *John McGahern: From the Local to the Universal* (Dublin: Liffey Press, 2003). Maher writes, 'When we read his books and short stories, we are transported back in time to a rural Ireland that is very close to extinction' (ibid., 2). In *The Transformation of Ireland* (London: Profile, 2005), Diarmaid Ferriter writes that McGahern's work 'remains both an indictment of the failures of Irish independence and a celebration of Ireland's distinctiveness. It is difficult for the historian to disagree with his assessment' (759).
3. Joe Cleary, *Literature, Partition and the Nation State* (Cambridge: Cambridge University Press, 2002), 73.
4. Ibid.
5. Kristin Bluemel, 'Introduction: What is intermodernism?', in *Intermodernism: Literary Culture in Mid-Twentieth Century Britain*, ed. Kristin Bluemel (Edinburgh: Edinburgh University Press, 2009), 1.
6. Ibid., 5.
7. Kristin Bluemel and Michael McCluskey, 'Introduction: Rural modernity in Britain', in *Rural Modernity in Britain: A Critical Intervention*, ed. Kristin Bluemel and Michael McCluskey (Edinburgh: Edinburgh University Press, 2018), 3.
8. Ibid., 2.
9. John McGahern, *Creatures of the Earth* (London: Faber and Faber, 2006), vii.
10. Maher expresses this tacitly throughout both *From the Local to the Universal* and *The Church and Its Spire* (Dublin: Columba Press 2011).
11. Grennan, '"Only what happens"', 26.
12. Grace Tighe Ledwidge, 'Death in marriage: The tragedy of Elizabeth Reegan in *The Barracks*.' *Irish University Review* 35, no. 1 (2005): 90.
13. For examples of those who read McGahern's life story through his fiction, see Maher (above) and Dermot McCarthy, *John McGahern and the Art of Memory* (Oxford: Peter Lang, 2010); in the latter, McCarthy sees McGahern's fiction as the writer's working through of the personal traumas of his own childhood.
14. John McGahern, *The Barracks* (London: Faber and Faber, 2003), 50: 'Did it matter where they went, whether one thing happened more than another? It seemed to matter less and less. An hour ago she'd been on the brink of collapse and if she finally collapsed did anything matter?'
15. See Paul Ricoeur, *Memory, History, Forgetting*, trans. Kathleen Blamey and David Pellauer (Chicago: University of Chicago Press, 2004). Ricoeur writes that habit memory constitutes a form of memory in which 'what is acquired is incorporated into the living present, unmarked, unremarked as past' (ibid., 24). Habit memory is employed 'when we recite the lesson without evoking one by one each of the

successive readings of the period of learning' (ibid., 25). Importantly, habit memory is that form of memory in which the past 'adheres to the present', and, as a result, it is opposed to memory that imagines because it repeats (ibid., 25). Examples of habit memory are, as Ricoeur suggests, walking and writing in the sense that both involve the performance of an action which does not require a process of recall for the action to happen (ibid., 25). What is accentuated in these examples 'is the set to which recitation belongs, that of knowing-how' (ibid., 26).

16 As Elizabeth says: 'What was her life? … Had it achieved anything or been given any meaning? … What was it all about? Where was she going? What was she doing?' (*The Barracks*, 85).

17 By evocative memory in this instance, I am again citing Ricoeur who implies an understanding of evocation in relation to memory as the 'unexpected appearance of a memory', that is to say, 'evocation is an affection, therefore, in contrast to the search' (*Memory, History, Forgetting*, 26).

18 McGahern, *The Barracks*, 85.

19 Ibid.

20 Moreover, at this point in the novel, the process of memory has thus shifted from memory as evocation to memory as searching. Memory as searching, as Ricoeur explains, is the search or 'relearning of what has been forgotten … [the] recollection of what one fears having forgotten, temporarily or for good' (*Memory, History, Forgetting*, 27). More precisely, in this instance it would seem that Elizabeth is engaging in what Ricoeur calls 'spontaneous recollection' in the sense that it is the 'zero-degree of searching in comparison to laborious recollection which is its purposeful form' (ibid.). The details, in this instance, come easy to Elizabeth; she is not presented as suffering any struggle to recall.

21 McGahern, *The Barracks*, 93.

22 Ibid., 92.

23 Ibid., 94.

24 Whyte writes, 'There is a dichotomy in McGahern studies to date. Much of the criticism, of his earlier work takes McGahern's fiction as social documentary and focuses upon its representation of Irish society.' 'On the other hand', for Whyte, 'there is a body of criticism which concentrates on McGahern's art' (*History, Myth, Ritual*, 9).

25 See Denis Sampson, *Outstaring Nature's Eye* (Dublin: Lilliput Press, 1993). Sampson performs a study which explores McGahern's poetics and locates his 'work among the writers of the past hundred years' (ibid., xii, 247).

26 Stanley van der Ziel, *John McGahern and the Imagination of Tradition* (Cork: Cork University Press, 2015), 23.

27 Richard Robinson, *John McGahern and Modernism* (London: Bloomsbury, 2016), 239.

28 Niamh Campbell, *Sacred Weather: Atmospheric Essentialism in the Work of John McGahern* (Cork: Cork University Press, 2019), 2.
29 Patrick Crotty, '"All toppers": Children in the fiction of John McGahern', *Irish University Review* 35, no. 1 (2005): 42.
30 See John McGahern, 'The Image', in *Love of the World* (London: Faber and Faber, 2010). McGahern writes,

> Art is an attempt to create a world in which we can live: if not for long or forever, still a world of the imagination over which we can reign, and by reign I mean to reflect purely on our situation through this created world of ours, this Medusa's mirror, allowing us to see and to celebrate even the totally intolerable. (ibid., 7)

31 van der Ziel, *John McGahern and the Imagination of Tradition*, 13–14.
32 Frank Shovlin, *Touchstones* (Liverpool: Liverpool University Press, 2016), 3.
33 Peter Murphy, 'John McGahern', *Hotpress*, 7 March 2002.
34 See Robinson's chapter on the *The Dark* in *John McGahern and Modernism* for a detailed account of the broad critical reception of the novel's narrative strategy.
35 McCarthy, *John McGahern and the Art of Memory*, 81.
36 For a detailed account of the *The Dark* as a *bildungsroman*, see the second chapter of Richard Robinson's *John McGahern and Modernism* and Chapter 6, 'Arrested development: sexuality, trauma and history in Edna O'Brien and John McGahern', of Michael Cronin's *Impure Thoughts: Sexuality, Catholicism and Literature in Twentieth Century Ireland* (Manchester: Manchester University Press, 2012).
37 McCarthy, *John McGahern and the Art of Memory*, 81.
38 Ibid., 101.
39 Ibid., 100.
40 Robinson, *John McGahern and Modernism*, 46.
41 John McGahern, *The Dark* (London: Faber and Faber, 2006), 11.
42 See Cathy Caruth, 'Introduction', in *Trauma*, ed. Cathy Caruth (Baltimore: Johns Hopkins University Press, 1995). Caruth writes, 'For a history to be a history of trauma means that it is referential precisely to the extent that it is not fully perceived as it occurs; or to put it somewhat differently, that a history can be grasped only in the very inaccessibility of its occurrence' (ibid., 8).
43 McGahern, *The Dark*, 17.
44 Ibid., 17.
45 'There was nothing else to say, it was better not to think or care, and the hands – the rhythmic words – were a kind of pleasure if thought and loathing could be shut out' (ibid., 20).
46 Patricia Harty, 'An interview with Seamus Heaney', *Irish America*, 13 April 1996.
47 Roland Barthes, *The Pleasure of the Text*, trans. Richard Miller (New York: Farrar, Straus & Giroux, 197), 6.

48 McGahern, *The Dark*, 189.
49 Ibid., 31.
50 Derrida, *Of Grammatology*, 151–2.
51 Ibid., 153.
52 McGahern, *The Dark*, 31.
53 Derrida, *Of Grammatology*, 152.
54 McGahern, *The Dark*, 32.
55 Ibid., 33.
56 Derrida, *Of Grammatology*, 153.
57 Ibid.
58 Ibid., 151.
59 McGahern, *The Dark*, 33.
60 Ibid.
61 Ibid.
62 Derrida, *Of Grammatology*, 151.
63 McGahern, *The Dark*, 141.
64 Ibid., 142.
65 Derrida, *Of Grammatology*, 151.
66 Saint Augustine, quoted in James Knowlson, *Damned to Fame: The Life of Samuel Beckett* (New York: Grove Press, 1996), 379.
67 McGahern, *The Dark*, 35.
68 Ibid., 36.
69 Ibid., 37.
70 Ibid., 35.
71 Ibid.
72 Ibid., 37.
73 Ibid.
74 'You went, asking, when you weren't sure, across the Corrib, two swans against withering October reeds in the distance, stone buttresses alone in the water, remnants of a railway that crossed the river to Clifden once. You didn't think. You were excited. You had the university to see' (ibid., 166).
75 Pascale Casanova, *The World Republic of Letters*, trans. M. B. Debevoise (Cambridge, MA: Harvard University Press, 2007), 86.
76 McCarthy, *John McGahern and the Art of Memory*, 81.
77 Similarly, this reading differs from van der Ziel's suggestion that *The Dark* is McGahern's 'triumph rather than failure' considering that the 'pronouns that were the only thing left to Beckett's Unnamable can ultimately be discarded by McGahern's narrator, for whom there is life beyond pronouns'. See van der Zeil '"All this talk and struggle": John McGahern's *The Dark*', *Irish University Review* 35, no. 1 (2005): 116. As van der Ziel writes in *John McGahern and the Imagination of Tradition*, 'after spending

the whole novel uncertainly shifting between the first-, second- and third-person pronoun, Young Mahoney's narrative voice is finally allowed the detachment of a dispassionate, god-like Flaubertian narrator ... the newfound stability of the point-of-view in the final chapter reads like a prologue to a future retrospect' (208). Yet, if the rationale in the reading tended here is followed – and it is recognised that *The Dark* ends (though in a more content tone than before) with free indirect narration – then there is little reason to see the novel as ending on a note of hope given that that narrative trope is deployed for reasons of non-identification.

78 Robinson, *John McGahern and Modernism*, 47.
79 David Malcolm, *Understanding John McGahern* (Columbia: University of South Carolina Press, 2007), 43.
80 See John McGahern, *The Leavetaking* (London: Faber and Faber, 2009). In the scene referred to in *The Leavetaking*, Patrick, in remembering a moment in which his mother and father argue over the economic affairs of the family, recalls a story his father told him and his siblings as children. Patrick recounts the story of how his father's childhood was made difficult by economic instability. Patrick begins the story in his own voice and denotes the characters (his grandfather, his grandmother, his father) which comprise it. As the presentation of the story moves into dialogue, Patrick is identifiably narrating the first sentence of a passage which begins, "'Has Patrick come into sight?', she'd ask, I heard him tell' (ibid., 53). He quotes his grandmother through the memory of his father recounting the story to him. The second sentence, however, is not as clear. Without warning, or without notification of a change in speaker, the voice of narration seems to switch to the first person of the father: "'No. Not yet, mother'" (ibid., 53). In one sense, this passage and the remainder of this story could be read as a dialogue between Patrick's father and Patrick's grandmother. Such a reading, though, would accept a shift in narration and the reader would be introduced to a new 'I' for the first and only time in the novel. What disrupts the introduction of a new 'I' is that this 'I' has no name – Patrick's father is referred to as daddy, sergeant, father; he is never referred to by his first name. The reader does know, however, that Patrick's grandfather's name is Patrick, and they are left to interject that his father's name may also be Patrick Moran. Patrick Moran, then, would be the narrator of the passage quoted above, thereby creating the effect of father speaking within son, or son speaking within father. Moreover, because no signal of a change in narrator has been made, this passage can be reread as consistent with the first-person narration of the rest of the novel. This passage then becomes a story not from Patrick's father's childhood but from Patrick's own childhood. Patrick would take the story of economic hardship experienced in his father's childhood and retell it in his voice. If the passage is considered in this manner, what becomes pertinent is not the moral lesson of providing for a family, but the fact that Patrick infuses the story with details that

we know belong to his childhood: waiting with a mother for a father who is absent; witnessing his mother vomit as a result of severe stress; and, at the end of the scene, making promises to his mother regarding his future profession in accordance with the situation of her life. This narration of the promise suggests that there never has been a shift in narrative voice: '"When I grow up we'll never be poor, mother," I said to her, and though she is gone I'm not going to be poor now either, and "we'll have to make a serious effort to save" he said to my mother smoothing out the two fivers as they went back to his bicycle that leaned against the wall of the house' (ibid., 56).

81 As Sampson notes, the voice of the earlier novels is left behind for an 'objectivity of presentation'. 'In contrast to the method used to present Elizabeth Reegan … Moran is presented objectively, with the narrative voice rarely entering his consciousness, or … the consciousness of any other character' (*Outstaring Nature's Eye*, 216–17).

82 John McGahern, *Amongst Women* (London: Faber and Faber, 2009), 145.

83 Gérard Genette, *Narrative Discourse: An Essay in Method*, trans. Jane E. Lewin (Ithaca: Cornell University Press, 1983), 33.

84 Ibid., 49.

85 Ibid., 66.

86 Ibid.

87 McGahern, *Amongst Women*, 177.

88 Ibid., 177–8.

89 McGahern, quoted in van der Ziel, *John McGahern and the Imagination of Tradition*, 13–14.

90 John McGahern, *That They May Face the Rising Sun* (London: Faber and Faber, 2010), 10.

91 Ibid.

92 Ibid., 10–11.

93 Ibid., 11.

94 Ibid., 12.

95 Ibid.

96 Ibid.

97 Ibid., 13.

98 Gilles Deleuze and Félix Guattari, *A Thousand Plateaus*, trans. Brian Massumi (London: Bloomsbury, 2013), 342.

99 In this instance, I am referring to what Deleuze and Guattari in *A Thousand Plateaus* describe as the effect of 'a line of becoming' (ibid., 342). The analeptic memory which occurs between Ruttledge and Bill Evans can be likened to what Deleuze and Guattari call a line of becoming in the sense that it

> is not defined by points that it connects, or by points that compose it; on the contrary it passes between points, it comes up through the middle, it runs perpendicular to the points first perceived, transversally to the localizable

relation to distant or contiguous points. But a line of becoming has neither beginning nor end, departure nor arrival, origin nor destination, ... If becoming is a block (a line-block), it is because it constitutes a zone of proximity and indiscernibility, a no-man's land, a nonlocalizable relation sweeping up the two distant or contiguous points, carrying one into the proximity of the other. (341–2)

100 McGahern, *That They May Face the Rising Sun*, 12.
101 Genette, *Narrative Discourse*, 66.
102 John McGahern, *Memoir* (London: Faber and Faber, 2006), 261.
103 Ibid., 241.
104 For more on this aspect of McGahern's writing see Joe Cleary, 'McGahern's rages', in *Essays on John McGahern*, ed. Derek Hand and Eammon Maher (Cork: Cork University Press, 2019), 162–80.
105 Peter Brooks, *Reading for Plot: Design and Intention in Narrative* (Cambridge: Harvard University Press, 1992), 33.
106 Barbara Cassin and Emily Apter, eds, *Dictionary of Untranslatables: A Philosophical Lexicon* (Princeton: Princeton University Press, 2014), xvii. Or as Cassin later writes, 'we began with the many (our plural form indicates this: "dictionary of untranslatables"), and we remain with the many: we have addressed the question of the untranslatable without aiming at unity, whether it is placed at the origin or at the end' (ibid., xix).

Epilogue

1 Ross Chambers, *Room for Maneuver: Reading Oppositional Narrative* (Chicago: University of Chicago Press, 1991), 17.
2 Jacques Derrida, *The Gift of Death & Literature in Secret*, trans. David Wills (Chicago: University of Chicago Press, 2008), 130–3.
3 J. Hillis Miller, *The Ethics of Reading* (New York: Columbia University Press, 1987), 8.
4 Ibid.
5 J. Hillis Miller, *Topographies* (Stanford: Stanford University Press, 1995), 77
6 Paul de Man, *The Resistance to Theory* (Manchester: Manchester University Press, 1986), 11.
7 Hillis Miller, *The Ethics of Reading*, 8.
8 Deaglán Ó Donghaile and Gerry Smyth, 'Introduction: Remapping Irish modernism', *Irish Studies Review* 26, no. 3 (2018): 298.

Bibliography

Ackerley C. J., and S. E. Gontarski, eds. *The Grove Companion to Samuel Beckett*. New York: Grove Press, 2004.

Adorno, Theodor. *Aesthetic Theory*. Translated by Robert Hullot-Kentor. London: Bloomsbury, 2013.

Adorno, Theodor. *Negative Dialectics*. Translated by E. B. Ashton. London: Routledge, 1973.

Apter, Emily. *Against World Literature: On the Politics of Untranslatability*. New York: Verso, 2013.

Apter, Emily. *The Translation Zone: A New Comparative Literature*. Princeton: Princeton University Press, 2006.

Attridge, John. 'Nonsense, ordinary language, and Flann O'Brien's *The Third Policeman*'. *Modern Fiction Studies* 60, no. 2 (2014): 298–319.

Arrington, Lauren. 'Irish modernism'. *Oxford Research Encyclopedia of Literature*, 27 February 2017. Available online: https://oxfordre.com/view/10.1093/acrefore/9780190201098.001.0001/acrefore-9780190201098-e-237.

Baines, Jennika, ed. *Flann O'Brien in the Twenty-First Century*. Dublin: Four Courts, 2011.

Bal, Mieke. *Narratology: Introduction to the Theory of Narrative*. 3rd edn. Toronto: University of Toronto Press, 2009.

Barber, Fionna. 'Irish modernism'. *Routledge Encyclopedia of Modernism*, 1 October 2016. Available online: https://www.rem.routledge.com/articles/irish-modernism (accessed 4 February 2020).

Barry, Elizabeth. 'Translating nationalism: Ireland, France and military history in Beckett's *Merier et Camier*'. *Irish Studies Review* 13, no. 4 (2005): 505–15.

Barthes, Roland. *Image, Music, Text*. Translated by Stephen Heath. London: Fontana Press, 1987.

Barthes, Roland. *The Pleasure of the Text*. Translated by Richard Miller. New York: Hill and Wang, 1998.

Barthes, Roland. *Writing Degree Zero and Elements of Semiology*. Translated by Annette Lavers and Colin Smith. London: Vintage, 2010.

Beckett, Samuel. *Malone Dies*. London: Faber and Faber, 2009.

Beckett, Samuel. *Malone Meurt*. Paris: Minuit, 1951.

Beckett, Samuel. *Mercier and Camier*. London: Faber and Faber, 2010.

Beckett, Samuel. *Mercier et Camier*. Paris: Editions du Minuit, 1970.

Beckett, Samuel. *Molloy*. London: Faber and Faber, 2009.

Beckett, Samuel. *More Pricks Than Kicks*. London: Faber and Faber, 2010.

Beckett, Samuel. *Murphy*. London: Faber and Faber, 2009.

Beckett, Samuel. *Texts for Nothing and Other Shorter Prose, 1950–1976*. London: Faber and Faber, 2010.

Beckett, Samuel. *The Unnamable*. London: Faber and Faber, 2010.

Beckett, Samuel. *Waiting for Godot: A Tragicomedy in Two Acts*. London: Faber and Faber, 2010.

Beckett, Samuel. *Watt*. London: Faber and Faber, 2009.

Begam, Richard, and Michael Valdez Moses, eds. *Modernism and Colonialism: British and Irish Literature, 1899–1939*. Durham: Duke University Press, 2007.

Behan, Brendan. *Borstal Boy*. London: Cornerstone, 1994.

Benjamin, Walter. *Illuminations*. London: Pimlico, 1999.

Benjamin, Walter. *Reflections: Essays, Aphorisms, Autobiographical Writings*. New York: Random House, 1995.

Bennett, Andrew, and Nicholas Royle. *Elizabeth Bowen and the Dissolution of the Novel*. London: Macmillan, 1995.

Berman, Jessica. *Modernist Commitments: Ethics, Politics, and Transnational Modernism*. New York: Columbia University Press, 2015.

Bixby, Patrick. *Samuel Beckett and the Postcolonial Novel*. Cambridge: Cambridge University Press, 2009.

Blanchot, Maurice. 'Où maintenant? Qui maintenant?'. *La Nouvelle Nouvelle Revue Française* 10 (1953): 678–86.

Blanchot, Maurice. *The Infinite Conversation*. Translated by Susan Hanson. Minneapolis: University of Minnesota Press, 1992.

Bluemel, Kristin, ed. *Intermodernism: Literary Culture in Mid-Twentieth Century Britain*. Edinburgh: Edinburgh University Press, 2009.

Bluemel, Kristin, and Michael McCluskey, eds. *Rural Modernity in Britain: A Critical Intervention*. Edinburgh: Edinburgh University Press, 2018.

Booker, M. Keith. *Flann O'Brien, Bakhtin, and Menippean Satire*. New York: Syracuse University Press, 1995.

Borg, Ruben, Paul Fagan and Werner Huber, eds. *Flann O'Brien: Contesting Legacies*. Cork: Cork University Press, 2014.

Bourke, Richard, and Ian McBride, eds. *The Princeton History of Modern Ireland*. Princeton: Princeton University Press, 2016.

Bowen, Elizabeth. *A World of Love*. London: Vintage, 1998.

Bowen, Elizabeth. *The Last September*. London: Vintage, 1998.

Brannigan, John. *New Historicism and Cultural Materialism*. Basingstoke: Macmillan Press, 1998.

Brooks, Peter. *Reading for Plot: Design and Intention in Narrative*. Cambridge: Harvard University Press, 1992.

Brown, Terrence. *Ireland: A Social and Cultural History 1922–2002*. London: Harper Perennial, 2004.
Brown, Terrence. *The Literature of Ireland: Culture and Criticism*. Cambridge: Cambridge University Press, 2010.
Burns, Anna. *Milkman*. London: Faber and Faber, 2018.
Campbell, Niamh. *Sacred Weather: Atmospheric Essentialism in the Work of John McGahern*. Cork: Cork University Press, 2019.
Caruth, Cathy, ed. *Trauma*. Baltimore: Johns Hopkins University Press, 1995.
Caruth, Cathy. *Unclaimed Experience: Trauma, Narrative and History*. Baltimore: Johns Hopkins University Press, 2017.
Casanova, Pascale. *Samuel Beckett: Anatomy of a Literary Revolution*. Translated by Gregory Elliott. New York: Verso, 2009.
Casanova, Pascale. *The World Republic of Letters*. Translated by M. B. Debevoise. Cambridge: Harvard University Press, 2007.
Cassin, Barbara, and Emily Apter, eds. *Dictionary of Untranslatables: A Philosophical Lexicon*. Princeton: Princeton University Press, 2014.
Castle, Gregory, and Patrick Bixby, eds. *A History of Irish Modernism*. Cambridge: Cambridge University Press, 2019.
Chatman, Seymour. *Coming to Terms: The Rhetoric of Narrative in Fiction and Film*. Ithaca: Cornell University Press, 1990.
Chambers, Ross. *Room for Maneuver: Reading Oppositional Narrative*. Chicago: University of Chicago Press, 1991.
Cleary, Joe, ed. *The Cambridge Companion to Irish Modernism*. Cambridge: Cambridge University Press, 2014.
Cleary, Joe. *Literature, Partition and the Nation State*. Cambridge: Cambridge University Press, 2002.
Cleary, Joe. *Outrageous Fortune, Capital and Culture in Modern Ireland*. Dublin: Field Day, 2007.
Connor, Steven. *Beckett, Modernism and the Material Imagination*. Cambridge: Cambridge University Press, 2014.
Connor, Steven. *Samuel Beckett: Repetition, Theory, Text*. Cambridge: Blackwell, 1988.
Conrad, Kathryn, Cóilín Parsons and Julie McCormick Weng, eds. *Science Technology and Irish Modernism*. New York: Syracuse University Press, 2019.
Coulouma, Flore. 'Tall tales and short stories: "Cruiskeen Lawn" and the dialogic imagination'. *Review of Contemporary Fiction* 31, no. 3 (2011): 162–77.
Corcoran, Neil. *Elizabeth Bowen: The Enforced Return*. Oxford: Oxford University Press, 2004.
Cronin, Michael. *Impure Thoughts: Sexuality, Catholicism and Literature in Twentieth-Century Ireland*. Manchester: Manchester University Press, 2012.
Culler, Jonathan. 'Omniscience'. *Narrative* 12, no. 1 (2004): 22–34.
Dalsimer, Adele M. *Kate O'Brien: A Critical Study*. Dublin: Gill and Macmillan, 1990.

Deane, Seamus, ed. *Nationalism, Colonialism and Literature*. Minnesota: Minnesota University Press, 1990.

Deleuze, Gilles. *Desert Islands*. Translated by Michael Taormina. New York: Semiotext(e), 2004.

Deleuze, Gilles, and Félix Guattari. *Anti-Oedipus*. Translated by Robert Hurley, Mark Seem and Helen R. Lane. London: Bloomsbury, 2013.

Deleuze, Gilles, and Félix Guattari. *A Thousand Plateaus*. Translated by Brian Massumi. London: Bloomsbury, 2013.

De Man, Paul. *The Resistance to Theory*. Manchester: Manchester University Press, 1986.

Derrida, Jacques. *The Gift of Death and Literature in Secret*. Translated by David Wills. Chicago: University of Chicago Press, 2008.

Derrida, Jacques. *Monolingualism of the Other; or, The Prosthesis of the Origin*. Translated by Patrick Mensah. Stanford: Stanford University Press, 1998.

Derrida, Jacques. *Of Grammatology*. Translated by Gayatri Chakravorty Spivak. Baltimore: Johns Hopkins University Press, 1998.

Derrida, Jacques. *Spectres of Marx: The State of the Debt, the Work of Mourning and the New International*. Translated by Peggy Kamuf. New York: Routledge, 1994.

Derrida, Jacques. *Speech and Phenomena*. Translated by David B. Allison. Evanston: Northwestern University Press, 1973.

Derrida, Jacques. 'Who or what is compared? The concept of comparative literature and the theoretical problems of translation'. Translated by Eric Prenowitz, *Discourse* 30, nos 1 and 2 (2008): 22–53.

Derrida, Jacques. *Writing and Difference*. Translated by Alan Bass. New York: Routledge, 2001.

Dobbins, Gregory. 'Constitutional laziness and the novel: Idleness, Irish modernism, and Flann O'Brien's *At Swim-Two-Birds*'. *NOVEL: A Forum on Fiction* 42, no. 1 (2009): 86–108.

Dow Feshenfeld, Martha, and Lois More Overbeck, eds. *The Letters of Samuel Beckett, 1929–40*, vol. 1. Cambridge: Cambridge University Press, 2009.

Eagleton, Terry. 'Form and ideology in the Anglo-Irish novel'. In *Literary Relations: Ireland, Egypt and the Far East*, edited by Mary Massoud, 135–46. Gerrards Cross: Colin Smythe, 1995.

Eliot, T. S. *The Waste Land: A Facsimile and Transcript of the Original Drafts Including the Annotations of Ezra Pound*. Edited by Valerie Eliot. Boston: Mariner Books, 1993.

Eliot, T. S. '*Ulysses*, Order and Myth'. In *Selected Prose of T. S. Eliot*, ed. Frank Kermode. London: Faber and Faber, 1975.

Ellmann, Maud. *Elizabeth Bowen: The Shadow across the Page*. Edinburgh: Edinburgh University Press, 2003.

Ellmann, Richard. *The Man and the Masks*. New York: Macmillan, 1948.

Erll, Astrid. *Memory in Culture*. Translated by Sara B. Young. London: Palgrave Macmillan, 2011.

Esty, Jed. *Unseasonable Youth, Modernism, Colonialism and the Fiction of Development*. Oxford: Oxford University Press, 2011.

Fagan, Paul, John Greaney and Tamara Radak, eds. *Irish Modernisms: Gaps, Conjectures, Possibilities*. London: Bloomsbury, 2022.

Ferriter, Diarmaid. *The Transformation of Ireland 1900–2000*. London: Profile, 2005.

Flatley, Jonathan. *Affective Mapping: Melancholia and the Politics of Modernism*. Boston: Harvard University Press, 2008.

Flaubert, Gustav. *Bouvard et Pécuchet*. Paris: Gallimard, 1999.

Foster, Roy. 'Irish and regional: Locale in Elizabeth Bowen's writing'. In *Elizabeth Bowen Remembered: The Farahy Address*, edited by Eibhear Walshe, 21–7. Dublin. Four Courts, 1998.

Frawley, Oona, ed. *Memory Ireland Volume 1: History and Modernity*. New York: Syracuse University Press, 2011.

Frawley, Oona, ed. *Memory Ireland Volume 4: James Joyce and Cultural Memory*. New York: Syracuse University Press, 2014.

Genette, Gérard. *Narrative Discourse: An Essay in Method*. Translated by Jane E. Lewin. Ithaca: Cornell University Press, 1983.

Gibson, Andrew. 'Samuel Beckett: History, memory, archive (review)'. *Modernism/modernity* 18, no. 4 (2011): 926–8.

Glendinning, Victoria. *Elizabeth Bowen: Portrait of a Writer*. London: Weidenfeld and Nicolson, 1977.

Graham, Colin. *Deconstructing Ireland: Identity, Theory, Culture*. Edinburgh: Edinburgh University Press, 2001.

Greenblatt, Stephen. *Renaissance Self-Fashioning: From More to Shakespeare*. Chicago: University of Chicago Press, 2005.

Grennan, Eamon. '"Only what happens": Mulling over McGahern'. *Irish University Review* 35, no. 1 (2005): 13–27.

Hand, Derek, and Eamon Maher, eds. *Essays on John McGahern*. Cork: Cork University Press, 2019.

Heidegger, Martin. *Hölderlin's Hymn 'The Ister'*. Bloomington: Indiana University Press, 1996.

Hill, Leslie. 'Up the Republic: Beckett, writing, politics'. *Modern Language Notes* 112, no. 5 (1997): 909–28.

Hoogland, Renée C. *Elizabeth Bowen: A Reputation in Writing*. New York: New York University Press, 1994.

Hopkins, Chris. 'Elizabeth Bowen: Realism, modernism and gendered identity in her novels of the 1930s'. *Journal of Gender Studies* 4, no. 3 (1995): 271–9.

Hopper, Keith. *Flann O'Brien: A Portrait of the Artist as a Young Post-Modernist*. Cork: Cork University Press, 2009.

Houston Jones, David. *Samuel Beckett and Testimony*. Basingstoke: Palgrave Macmillan, 2011.

Humble, Nicola. *The Feminine Middlebrow Novel, 1920s to 1950s*. Oxford: Oxford University Press, 2001.
James, David, ed. *Modernism and Close Reading*. Oxford: Oxford University Press, 2020.
Jameson, Frederic. 'Modernism and imperialism'. In *Nationalism, Colonialism, and Literature*, edited by Seamus Deane, 43–66. Minnesota: University of Minnesota Press, 1990.
Janvier, Ludovic. *Samuel Beckett par lui-meme*. Paris: Seuil, 1969.
Jernigan, Daniel Keith. '"Simulat ergo est": Brian O'Nolan's metaperformative simulations'. *New Hibernia Review* 20, no. 1 (2016): 87–104.
Jordan, Heather Bryant. *How Will the Heart Endure: Elizabeth Bowen and the Landscape of War*. Michigan: University of Michigan Press, 1992.
Joyce, James. *Dubliners*. London: Penguin, 2000.
Joyce, James. *Finnegans Wake*. London: Penguin, 2001.
Joyce, James. *A Portrait of the Artist as a Young Man*. London: Penguin, 2000.
Joyce, James. *Ulysses*. London: Penguin, 2001.
Kalliney, Peter. *Modernism in a Global Context*. New York: Bloomsbury, 2015.
Kavanagh, Patrick. *The Green Fool*. London: Penguin, 2001.
Kearney, Richard. *Transitions: Narratives in Modern Irish Culture*. Manchester: Manchester University Press, 1988.
Kennedy, Séan, ed. *Beckett and Ireland*. Cambridge: Cambridge University Press, 2010.
Kennedy, Séan, ed. *Samuel Beckett: History, Memory, Archive*. Basingstoke: Palgrave Macmillan, 2009.
Kent, Brad. 'An argument manqué: Kate O'Brien's *Pray for the Wanderer*'. *Irish Studies Review* 18, no. 3 (2010), 285–98.
Keown, Edwina, and Carol Taaffe, eds. *Irish Modernism: Origins Contexts, Publics*. Oxford: Peter Lang, 2009.
Kiberd, Declan. *Inventing Ireland*. London: Vintage, 1995.
Kiberd, Declan. *Irish Classics*. London: Granta Books, 2000.
Kirkland, Richard. *Identity Parades: Northern Irish Culture and Dissident Subjects*. Liverpool: Liverpool University Press, 2002.
Knowlson, James. *Damned to Fame: The Life of Samuel Beckett*. New York: Grove Press, 1996.
Laird, Heather. 'The "placing" and politics of Bowen in contemporary Irish literary and cultural criticism'. In *Elizabeth Bowen*, edited by Eibhear Walshe, 193–207. Dublin: Irish Academic Press, 2009.
Latham, Sean, and Gayle Rodgers. *Modernism: Evolution of an Idea*. London: Bloomsbury, 2015.
Legarreta Mentxaka, Aintzane. *Kate O'Brien and the Fiction of Identity: Sex, Art and Politics in Mary Lavelle and Other Writings*. Jefferson: McFarland, 2011.
Lewis, Cara L. *Dynamic Form: How Intermediality Made Modernism*. Ithaca: Cornell University Press, 2020.

Lloyd, David. *Anomalous States: Irish Writing and the Post-Colonial Moment*. Durham: Duke University Press, 1993.
Loomba, Ania. *Colonialism/Postcolonialism*. New York: Routledge, 2015.
Long, Maebh. *Assembling Flann O'Brien*. London: Bloomsbury, 2014.
Long, Maebh, ed. *The Collected Letters of Flann O'Brien*. Champaign: Dalkey Archive Press, 2018.
Love, Heather. 'Close but not deep: Literary ethics and the descriptive turn'. *New Literary History* 41, no. 2 (2010): 371–91.
Lumsden, Robert. 'Voidence in *The Third Policeman*'. *Review of Contemporary Fiction* 31 (2011): 49–61.
MacNeice, Louis. *The Poetry of W. B. Yeats*. Oxford: Oxford University Press, 1948.
Maher, Eamon. *John McGahern: From the Local to the Universal*. Dublin: Liffey Press, 2003.
Maher, Eamon. *The Church and Its Spire*. Dublin: Columba Press, 2011.
Malcolm, David. *Understanding John McGahern*. Columbia: University of South Carolina Press, 2007.
Mao, Douglas. 'The new critics and the text-object'. *ELH* 63, no. 1 (1996): 227–54.
Mao, Douglas, and Rebecca Walkowitz, eds. *Bad Modernisms*. Durham: Duke University Press, 2006.
Mao, Douglas, and Rebecca Walkowitz. 'The new modernist studies'. *PMLA* 123, no. 3 (2008): 737–8.
Marshik, Celia, and Allison Pease. *Modernism, Sex and Gender*. London: Bloomsbury, 2019.
Maslen, R.W. 'Flann O'Brien's bombshells: *At Swim-Two-Birds* and *The Third Policeman*'. *New Hibernia Review* 10, no. 4 (2006): 84–104.
Maude, Ulrika, and Matthew Feldman, eds. *Beckett and Phenomenology*. New York: Routledge, 2009.
McAteer, Michael, ed. *Silence in Modern Irish Literature*. Ledien: Brill, 2017.
McBride, Eimear. *A Girl is a Half-Formed Thing*. London: Faber and Faber, 2014.
McCarthy, Dermot. *John McGahern and the Art of Memory*. Oxford: Peter Lang, 2010.
McCormack, Mike. *Solar Bones*. Dublin: Tramp Press, 2016.
McDonald, Rónán, Julian Murphet and Sascha Morell, eds. *Flann O'Brien and Modernism*. London: Bloomsbury, 2014.
McElhattan Williams, Julia. '"Fiction with the texture of history": Elizabeth Bowen's *The Last September*'. *Modern Fiction Studies* 41, no. 2 (1995): 219–42.
McGahern, John. *Amongst Women*. London: Faber and Faber, 2009.
McGahern, John. *The Barracks*. London: Faber and Faber, 2003.
McGahern, John. *Creatures of the Earth*. London: Faber and Faber, 2006.
McGahern, John. *The Dark*. London: Faber and Faber, 2006.
McGahern, John. *The Leavetaking*. London: Faber and Faber, 2009.
McGahern, John. *Love of the World*. London: Faber and Faber, 2010.
McGahern, John. *Memoir*. London: Faber and Faber, 2006.

McGahern, John. *That They May Face the Rising Sun*. London: Faber and Faber, 2010.
McHugh, Roger, ed. *Jack B. Yeats: A Centenary Gathering*. Dublin: Doleman Press, 1971.
McNaughton, James. *Samuel Beckett and the Politics of Aftermath*. Oxford: Oxford University Press, 2018.
Meaney, Gerardine. 'Territory and transgression: History, nationality and sexuality in Kate O'Brien's fiction'. *Irish Journal of Feminist Studies 2* (1997): 77–92.
Meehan, Adam. *Modernism and Subjectivity: How Modernist Fiction Invented the Postmodern Subject*. Baton Rouge: Louisiana State University Press, 2020.
Miller, J. Hillis. *The Ethics of Reading*. New York: Columbia University Press, 1987.
Miller, J. Hillis. 'Presidential address 1986: The triumph of theory, the resistance to reading, and the question of the material base'. *PMLA* 102, no. 3 (1987): 281–91.
Miller, J. Hillis. *Topographies*. Stanford: Stanford University Press, 1995.
Mills Harper, Margaret, and Warwick Gould, eds. *Yeats's Mask: Yeat's Annual No. 19*. Cambridge: Open Book, 2013.
Montgomery, Niall. 'An aristophanic sorcerer'. *Irish Times*, 2 April 1966.
Mooney, Sinéad, *A Tongue Not Mine: Beckett and Translation*. Cambridge: Cambridge University Press, 2009.
Moretti, Franco. *Distant Reading*. New York: Verso, 2013.
Morin, Emilie. *Beckett's Political Imagination*. Cambridge: Cambridge University Press, 2018.
Morin, Emilie. *Samuel Beckett and the Problem of Irishness*. Basingstoke: Palgrave Macmillan, 2009.
Murphy, Neil, and Keith Hopper, eds. *The Short Fiction of Flann O'Brien*. Champaign: Dalkey Archive Press, 2013.
Nietzsche, Friedrich. *Beyond Good and Evil*. Translated by R. J. Holingdale. London: Penguin, 2003.
Nixon, Mark. *Samuel Beckett's German Diaries 1936–1937*. London: Bloomsbury, 2011.
Nolan, Emer. *James Joyce and Nationalism*. New York: Routledge, 1994.
O'Brien, Edna. *The Country Girls*. London: Orion, 2007.
O'Brien, Flann. *At Swim-Two-Birds*. London: Penguin, 2000.
O'Brien, Flann. *The Dalkey Archive*. London: Picador, 1976.
O'Brien, Flann. *The Third Policeman*. London: Flamingo, 1967.
O'Brien, Kate. *Mary Lavelle*. London: Virago Press, 1984.
O'Brien, Kate. *Pray for the Wanderer*. New York: Doubleday, Doran, 1938.
O'Brien, Kate. *The Land of Spices*. London: Virago Press, 1988.
O'Brien, Kate. 'UCD as I forget it'. *University Review* 3, no. 2 (1963): 6–11.
Ó Donghaile, Deaglán, and Gerry Smyth. 'Introduction: Remapping Irish modernism'. *Irish Studies Review* 26, no. 3 (2018): 297–303.
Ó Faoláin, Seán. 'A reading and remembrance of Elizabeth Bowen'. *London Review of Books* 4, no. 4 (1982): 15–16.

Oțoiu, Adrian '"Compartmentation of personality for the purpose of literary utterance": Pseudonymity and heteronymity in the various lives of Flann O'Brien'. *Word and Text: A Journal of Literary Studies and Linguistics* 1, no. 1 (2011): 128–38.

Osborn, Susan, ed. *Elizabeth Bowen: New Critical Perspectives*. Cork: Cork University Press, 2009.

Perloff, Marjorie. *Radical Artifice: Writing Poetry in the Age of Media*. Chicago: University of Chicago Press, 1991.

Piette, Adam. *Imagination at War: British Fiction and Poetry, 1939–1945*. Michigan: University of Michigan Press, 1995.

Pilný, Ondřej. '"Did you put charcoal adroitly in the vent?" Brian O'Nolan and pataphysics'. In *Flann O'Brien: Contesting Legacies*, edited by Ruben Borg, Paul Fagan and Werner Huber, 156–68. Cork: Cork University Press, 2014.

Proust, Marcel. *In Search of Lost Time: The Way by Swann's*. Translated by Lydia Davis. London: Penguin, 2003.

Quigley, Mark. 'Unnaming the subject: Samuel Beckett and colonial alterity'. *Samuel Beckett Today/Aujourd'hui* 15 (2005): 87–100.

Rabaté, Jean-Michel. 'Editor's Introduction'. *Journal of Modern Literature* 38, no. 2 (2015): v–vi.

Rabaté, Jean-Michel, ed. *A Handbook of Modernism Studies*. Oxford: Wiley-Blackwell, 2013.

Rabaté, Jean-Michel. *The Pathos of Distance: Affects of the Moderns*. London: Bloomsbury, 2016.

Rabaté, Jean-Michel. *Think, Pig!: Beckett at the Limit of the Human*. New York: Fordham University Press, 2016.

Rancière, Jacques. *Mute Speech*. Translated by Gabriel Rockhill. New York: Columbia University Press, 2009.

Read, Forrest, ed. *Pound/Joyce: The Letters of Ezra Pound to James Joyce, with Pound's essays on Joyce*. New York: New Directions Books, 1967.

Reynolds, Paige. 'Spectacular nostalgia: Modernism and dramatic form in Kate O'Brien's *Pray for the Wanderer*'. *Irish University Review* 48, no. 1 (2018): 54–68.

Ricoeur, Paul. *Memory, History, Forgetting*. Translated by Kathleen Blamey and David Pellauer. Chicago: University of Chicago Press, 2004.

Rimmon-Kenan, Shlomith. *Narrative Fiction: Contemporary Poetics*. London: Methuen, 1983.

Robinson, Richard. *John McGahern and Modernism*. London: Bloomsbury, 2016.

Roche, Anthony. '"The devil era": The presence of Éamon de Valera in three novels by Kate O'Brien'. *Irish University Review* 48, no. 1 (2018): 113–26.

Rousseau, Jean-Jacques. *Confessions*. Translated by Angela Scholar. Oxford: Oxford University Press, 2008.

Rousseau, Jean-Jacques. *Émile; or on Education*. Translated by Barbara Foxley. London: Penguin, 2007.

Royle, Nicholas. *The Uncanny*. Manchester: Manchester University Press, 2003.

Rubenstein, Michael. *Public Works: Infrastructure, Irish Modernism and the Postcolonial*. Notre Dame: University of Notre Dame Press, 2010.

Saint-Amour, Paul. 'The medial humanities: Toward a manifesto for meso-analysis', *Modernism/modernity Print Plus* 3, no. 4 (2019). Available online: https://modernismmodernity.org/forums/posts/medial-humanities-toward-manifesto-meso-analysis (accessed 11 December 2019).

Saint-Amour, Paul. *Tense Future: Modernism, Total War, Encyclopaedic Form*. Oxford: Oxford University Press, 2015.

Sampson, Denis. *Outstaring Nature's Eye*. Dublin: Lilliput Press, 1993.

Sartre, Jean-Paul. *Qu'est-ce que la littérature?* Paris: Gallimard, 1964.

Sheils, Barry. *W. B. Yeats and World Literature: The Subject of Poetry*. New York: Routledge, 2015.

Shovlin, Frank. *Touchstones*. Liverpool: Liverpool University Press, 2016.

Stanford Friedman, Susan. *Planetary Modernisms: Provocations on Modernity across Time*. New York: Columbia University Press, 2015.

Sullivan, Kelly. '"An absolutely private thing": Letters in Kate O'Brien's *The Land of Spices*'. *Irish Studies Review* 48, no. 1 (2018): 84–96.

Sullivan, Kelly. 'Elizabeth Bowen and 1916: An architecture of suspense'. *Modernism/modernity* 4, no. 3 (2020). Available online: https://modernismmodernity.org/articles/sullivan-1916-architecture-suspense (accessed 16 December 2019).

Taaffe, Carol. *Ireland through the Looking-Glass: Flann O'Brien, Myles na gCopaleen and Irish Cultural Debate*. Cork: Cork University Press, 2008.

Taylor, Julie, ed. *Modernism and Affect*. Edinburgh: Edinburgh University Press, 2015.

Tighe Ledwidge, Grace. 'Death in marriage: The tragedy of Elizabeth Reegan in *The Barracks*'. *Irish University Review* 35, no. 1 (2005): 90–103.

van der Ziel, Stanley. *John McGahern and the Imagination of Tradition*. Cork: Cork University Press, 2015.

Vintaloro, Giordano. 'Brian O'Nolan, the conspirator'. *Studi Irlandesi* 7 (2017): 261–82.

Walker, Tom. 'The culture of art in 1880s Ireland and the genealogy of Irish modernism'. *Irish Studies Review* 26, no. 3 (2018): 304–17.

Walshe, Eibhear, ed. *Elizabeth Bowen*. Dublin: Irish Academic Press, 2009.

Walshe, Eibhear. *Kate O'Brien: A Writing Life*. Dublin: Irish Academic Press, 2006.

Walkowitz, Rebecca. *Born Translated: The Contemporary Novel in an Age of World Literature*. New York: Columbia University Press, 2015.

Warren Friedman, Alan. *Surreal Beckett: Samuel Beckett, James Joyce, and Surrealism*. New York: Routledge, 2017.

Waugh, Evelyn. *The Essays, Articles and Reviews of Evelyn Waugh*. Edited by Donat Gallagher. London: Metheun, 1983.

Weller, Shane. *Language and Negativity in European Modernism*. Cambridge: Cambridge University Press, 2019.

Wells-Lasagne, Shannon. '"He believed in empire"'. *Irish Studies Review* 15, no. 4 (2007): 451–63.
Wightman, Beth. 'Geopolitics and the sight of the nation: Elizabeth Bowen's *The Last September*'. *Literature Interpretation Theory* 18, no. 1 (2007): 37–64.
Wilder, Gary. *Freedom Time: Negritude, Decolonization and the Future of the World*. Durham: Duke University Press, 2015.
Williams, Raymond. *Culture and Materialism*. London: Verso, 2005.
Wolfson, Susan J., and Marshall Brown, eds. *Reading for Form*. Seattle: University of Washington Press, 2006.
Wollaeger, Mark, ed. *The Oxford Handbook of Global Modernisms*. Oxford: Oxford University Press, 2012.
Whyte, James. *History, Myth and Ritual in the Fiction of John McGahern: Strategies of Transcendence*. New York: Edwin Mellen, 2002.
Wurtz, James F. 'Elizabeth Bowen, modernism and the spectre of Anglo-Ireland'. *Estudios Irlandeses* 5 (2010): 119–28.
Yeats, W. B. *The Autobiography of William Butler Yeats*. New York: Collier, 1965.
Yeats, W. B. *The Poems*. Edited by Daniel Albright. London: Everyman, 1994.

Index

absent presence 20–1, 29, 69, 83, 95, 109, 112, 122, 138
Adorno, Theodor 27–8, 34, 53–7, 60–1
affect 5, 8–9, 15
ambiguity of the mask 69–74
Apollinaire, Guillaume 52
Apter, Emily 22–3
  'deowned literature' 82
  Dictionary of Untranslatables: A Philosophical Lexicon 212 n.106
Arrington, Lauren 6, 17, 92
Attridge, John 84

Baines, Jennika 65
Barber, Fionna 9
Barry, Elizabeth 37
Barthes, Roland 12, 28, 29, 37, 53–7, 70, 76, 115, 120, 187 n.131
  writing degree zero 46–53, 60–1
Battista Di, Maria 201 n.127
Baudelaire, Charles 172
Beckett, Samuel 15, 18, 26, 30, 31–62, 115, 141, 169, 182 n.22, 185 n.105, 186 n.111, 188 n.146, 189 n.169
  Dream of Fair to Middling Women 187 n.118
  écrire sans style 37
  Malone Dies/Malone Meurt 28, 32, 35, 37, 41, 46, 49–51, 53–4, 60
  Mercier and Camier/Mercier et Camier 32, 37–8, 41–5
  Molloy 28, 32, 35, 37, 41, 46, 48, 51, 54, 60
  More Pricks Than Kicks 31–2, 41
  Murphy 31–2, 42, 59
  'Recent Irish Poetry' 31–2
  Texts for Nothing 32
  translation 50–3
  The Unnamable/L'Innomable 2, 4, 12, 28, 32, 34, 37, 41, 46, 52–4, 57–61, 189 n.161
  Waiting for Godot 2, 4, 32, 41, 46, 155

Watt 32
writing degree zero 50–3
Behan, Brendan
  Borstal Boy 172
Benjamin, Walter 29, 70–2, 76
Bennett, Andrew 94
Berman, Jessica
  Modernist Commitments 6
Bixby, Patrick 6, 9, 33, 48, 185 n.105, 189 n.161
  A History of Irish Modernism 3
Blanchot, Maurice 45, 53–7
  The Infinite Conversation 56
Booker, M. Keith 80
Bowen, Elizabeth 9, 26, 28, 30, 91–113, 115, 196 n.3, 201 n.125
  Elizabeth Bowen Remembered: The Farahy Address 196 n.1
  A History of Irish Modernism 92
  Irish modernism 111–13
  The Last September 10, 12, 29, 91, 93–4, 98–111, 124, 130, 169, 198 n.31
  omniscient narration 96–8
  A World of Love 92, 111
Boydell, Brian 4
Brannigan, John
  New Historicism and Cultural Materialism 192 n.50
Breen, Mary 118, 134
Bréton, Andre 52
Brooker, Joseph 65
Brooks, Cleanth 2, 97
Brooks, Peter 165
Brown, Terrence 64, 86
Burns, Anna
  Milkman 173

The Cambridge Companion to Irish Modernism 8–9, 92
Campbell, Niamh 147, 207 n.28
Cape, Jonathan 94

Caruth, Cathy
  Trauma 208 n.42
Casanova, Pascale 19–22, 23, 45, 55, 109, 184 n.84
  The World Republic of Letters 20
Cassin, Barbara 22–23, 166
  Dictionary of Untranslatables: A Philosophical Lexicon 212 n.106
  Vocabulaire européen des philosophies 22
Castle, Gregory 6, 9
  A History of Irish Modernism 3
cause-and-effect analysis 20
Celan, Paul 172
Celine, Louis Ferdinand 53–4
Celtic Twilight 33
Chambers, Ross 170
Char, René 52
Chatman, Seymour 98
Cixous, Hélène 27
Cleary, Joe 64, 92, 141, 173
  Outrageous Fortune: Capital and Culture in Modern Ireland 205 n.1
Clifford, Brendan 93
Coffey, Brian 31
Connor, Steven 35, 51, 184 n.71
  Samuel Beckett and the Material Imagination 185 n.101
  Samuel Beckett: Repetition, Text, Theory 186 n.110
Corcoran, Neil 94–5
Cronin, Michael 115, 117
Crowley, Ronan 66
Culler, Jonathan 96–8, 119, 123
cultural materialism 74
cultural studies 7, 35
Cunard, Nancy 49
  Authors Take Sides on the Spanish War 49
  Negro 52–3

Dalsimer, Adele M. 116–17
Damrosch, David 7
dangerous supplement 18, 21, 88, 153–4
Deane, Seamus 177 n.39, 179 n.69
Decade of Centenaries 2012–2022 2, 174
deconstruction 5, 35, 172
Deleuze, Gilles 82, 86–7
  A Thousand Plateaus 194 n.112, 211 n.99
De Man, Paul 27, 171
Derrida, Jacques 12, 18, 24, 27, 57, 79, 83, 89, 109, 120, 125, 151, 153–5, 170–1, 172, 196 n.148
  Of Grammatology 11, 21, 153
  The Monolingualism of the Other; or, The Prosthesis of Origin 23, 188 n.146
  Spectres of Marx 119–20
de Saint-Ruhe, Charles Chalmot 38, 43
désœuvrement 16, 28
Devlin, Denis 31
distance 17–19
  impersonal 65
  of Irish modernism 24–7, 173
  irreducible vii, 4, 29–30, 42, 45, 49–50, 109, 157, 161, 164, 167, 169, 186 n.108
  of literature 5
  and meso-analysis 17–19
  proximity and 7, 16, 21, 33, 95
  untranslatable 29
distant reading 19
Donghaile, Deaglán Ó 9
Duffy, Enda 8–9
Duthuit, Georges
  Transition 52, 56

Eagleton, Terry 117
  Literary Relations: Ireland, Egypt and the Far East 202 n.10
Eatough, Matt 95–6
Edgeworth, Maria
  Castle Rackrent 111
Eliot, George 97
Eliot, T. S. 3, 31, 81
Ellmann, Maud 92, 95
Ellmann, Richard 14–15, 73
Eluard, Paul 52
Engels, Friedrich 22
Erll, Astrid 16
  Memory in Culture 178 n.65
Esty, Jed 94, 106
ethics 53–7
ethics of reading vii, 25, 30, 108, 170–2
Eurocentrism 5
extratextual
  allusions 41

denial of the 21
realities/events vi–vii, 7, 16, 40, 52, 94, 113, 178 n.65
referent 157
traumatic experience 152
world 5, 16, 67

Ferriter, Diarmaid
  The Transformation of Ireland 1900–2000 64
First World War 39, 40, 93, 106, 111
Flatley, Jonathan
  Affective Mapping 6
Flaubert, Gustav 42, 44
  Bouvard et Pécuchet 41
Fogarty, Anne 15, 116, 137
form
  epistolary 122
  estranged 106
  of ethical testimony 59
  fragmentary 78
  literary 19, 26, 157
  of mimesis 132, 144
  mnemonic 16
  morality of 57, 187 n.131
  narrative 81, 96
  novelistic 15
  omniscient 146
  recoiling 28, 37, 56–8, 60
  refracted 20
  self-knowing 93
  and style 36, 59, 118
formalism 6, 15–16, 26–7, 180 n.98
Forster, E. M. 18
Foster, Roy 93
Frawley, Oona 5
French Revolution 55
Freud, Lucian 175 n.7
Freud, Sigmund 120

Garrison, Alysia E. 58
Genet, Jean 76
Genette, Gérard 97–8, 132, 160
Gibson, Andrew 33, 36
Gillespie, Alana 193 n.78
Glendinning, Victoria 198 n.31
Gloria SMH 38, 40
Graham, Colin
  Deconstructing Ireland 13

Gray, Eileen 4
Greenblatt, Stephen 74
Grennan, Eamon
Guattari, Félix 82, 86–7
  A Thousand Plateaus 194 n.112, 211 n.99

Heaney, Seamus 152
Heidegger, Martin 23
  Hölderlin's Hymn 'The Ister' 22
Higgins, F. R. 31
Hill, Leslie 186 n.108
A History of Irish Modernism 3, 63, 92
Holocaust 33–4, 57–8
Hoogland, Renée C. 198 n.31
Hopper, Keith 85–6
Humble, Nicola
  The Feminine Middlebrow Novel, 1920s to 1950s 196 n.7

intermodernism 142
Irish Literary Revival 14–15, 36, 92
Irish studies 2–3, 10, 28, 115
Irish Studies Review 173
Irish Times 64–5, 70

James, David 25–6
Jameson, Frederic 7, 17–18
Johnston, Jennifer 141
Jolas, Eugene 52
Jones, David Houston
  Samuel Beckett and Testimony 189–90 n.173
Joyce, James 1, 2, 4, 18, 23, 41, 77, 95, 115, 141, 172, 197 n.17
  achievements of 1
  Finnegans Wake 2–4, 12–13, 15, 52
  A Portrait of the Artist as a Young Man 23
  Ulysses 2, 4–5, 10, 12, 15, 118

Katz, Daniel 56
Kavanagh, Patrick
  The Green Fool 172
Kearney, Richard 65
Kennedy, Seán 33
  Beckett and Ireland 34
Kenner, Hugh 2, 14–15
Kent, Brad 129

Kiberd, Declan 9, 59, 81
  Inventing Ireland 8, 177 n.37
Knowlson, James 59
  Damned to Fame 189 n.169

Lacan, Jacques 18, 27
Laird, Heather 196 n.3
Lane, Jack
  The North Cork Anthology 93
late modernism 28, 54, 92, 115, 141, 197 n.8
Latham, Sean 5
Lawrence, D. H. 1
Le Fanu, Sheridan
  Uncle Silas 111
Legarreta Mentxaka, Aintzane 118, 122–3, 125–6
Lemass, Noel 32, 38, 44
Lewis, Cara L.
  Dynamic Form 26
Lloyd, David 35
  Anomalous States 13
Long, Maebh 82
Loomba, Ania
Lumsden, Robert 85

MacGreevy, Thomas 31, 45, 50
MacNeice, Louis 73
Maher, Eamon
  John McGahern: From the Local to the Universal 205 n.2
Malcolm, David 158
Mao, Douglas 25
Marx, Karl 22
Marxism/Marxist 24, 126, 203 n.48
Massumi, Brian 194 n.112
material base 8, 11, 117
McBride, Eimear 173, 175 n.7
  A Girl is a Half-Formed Thing 173
McCarthy, Dermot 149, 157
  John McGahern and the Art of Memory 206 n.13
McCluskey, Michael 142
McCormack, Mike 173, 175 n.7
  Solar Bones 173
McDonald, Rónán 35, 63–6, 85
McElhattan Williams, Julia
McGahern, John 15, 26–8, 141–67, 170, 172–3

  Amongst Women 143, 158–64, 166
  The Barracks 30, 143–8, 158, 161, 165–6, 206 n.14
  Creatures of the Earth 143
  The Dark 30, 148–58, 161, 165–6, 209 n.77
  Irish modernism 164–7
  The Leavetaking 158, 165, 210 n.80
  Love of the World 207–8 n.30
  Memoir 148, 164–5
  The Pornographer 158
  That They May Face the Rising Sun 30, 143, 158–66
McNaughton, James 34, 58
  Samuel Beckett and the Politics of Aftermath 181 n.7
Meaney, Gerardine 15, 115
Meche, Jude R. 59
Meehan, Adam 67
  Modernism and Subjectivity 191 n.23
memory
  analeptic 163, 211 n.99
  conceptualization of literature as 178 n.65
  cultural vi–vii, 2, 12, 16, 25, 36, 63, 67, 80, 88, 113, 118–19
  evocative 145, 207 n.17
  habit 206 n.15
Memory Ireland 2
memory studies 2, 10, 16, 59
meso-analysis 17–19, 68
metafiction 26, 29, 63, 67, 69, 169
metalepsis 83–8
methodological nationalism 13, 15, 19, 29, 112
Miller, J. Hillis 11–12, 171
  Topographies 108, 171
moderately symbolic 12, 25, 28–9, 89, 116, 137, 141, 172
Modernism and Colonialism 8
modernist studies vi–vii, 3, 16, 26, 63
  'distance' in 24
  diversification of 3
  dominant trends of 5
  expansion of 66
  Irish modernist studies and 68
  and literary studies 34

modernity as integral to 7
modernist aesthetic practice 6
study of modernist art and literature 4
temporal expansion of 5, 143
Montgomery, Niall 65, 70, 73, 76
Mooney, Sinéad 51
A Tongue Not Mine 186 n.110
Moretti, Franco 5, 19–22
Morin, Emilie 36–7, 51
Beckett's Political Imagination 181 n.7, 182 n.22, 189 n.169
Samuel Beckett and the Problem of Irishness 186 n.108
Murphet, Julian 63–6

narratology vii, 97–8
New Criticism 2, 14, 25
new formalist studies 25–6
new historicism 74
Nietzsche, Friedrich 29, 70, 73, 75, 76
Beyond Good and Evil 72
Nixon, Mark 59
Nolan, Emer 9
James Joyce and Nationalism 8, 177 n.38
Nouveau Roman 46, 149

O'Brien, Edna 141, 173
The Country Girls 172
O'Brien, Kate 15, 26, 28, 115–39, 129, 172
The Land of Spices 29, 116, 118–20, 133–8
Mary Lavelle 29, 116, 118–20, 121–6, 129, 133, 138–9
Pray for the Wanderer 29, 116, 118–20, 126–8, 130, 132–4, 137–9, 204 n.63
Ó Donghaile, Deaglán 173
Ó Faoláin, Seán 91
omniscient narration 96–8, 112, 119, 132, 146–7, 204 n.68
O'Nolan, Brian 26, 63, 64–7, 68–9, 70–1, 73–5, 77, 82, 90, 169
Barnabas, Brother 68, 74
An Béal Bocht 64
Broc, An 68
Comhthrom Féinne 74
Cruiskeen Lawn 63–5, 64–5, 68, 75, 89
The Dalkey Archive 64

Doe, John James 68
The Hard Life 64
Knowall, George 68
metafictions 26
modernism 27, 30
na gCopaleen, Myles 64–7, 70, 74–6, 169
O'Blather, Count 68
O'Brien, Flann 15, 28, 64–7, 68, 70, 74–6, 89–90, 115, 118
O'Donnell, John Shamus 90
The Poor Mouth 64
The Short Fiction of Flann O'Brien 90
At Swim-Two-Birds 10, 27, 29, 63–7, 68–70, 76–83, 88–9, 132
The Third Policeman 10, 27, 29, 63–4, 66–7, 68–71, 77, 83–4, 88–9, 194 n.112, 195 n.122
Osborn, Susan 10, 94
Oțoiu, Adrian 69–70
O'Toole, Tina 15

Pellauer, David 206 n.15
Pelorson, Georges 59–60, 189 n.169
Belmont, Georges 59
Perloff, Marjorie 67
Radical Artifice: Writing Poetry in the Age of Media 191 n.23
Péron, Afred 40, 52, 59
phenomenology 5
Pilný, Ondřej 83
postcolonial 8, 10, 13, 48, 59, 66, 170
discourse 92
frameworks 34
identity 35
linguistic heritage 68
studies 2–3, 10
theory 13, 16, 29, 58
postmodernism 67–9
poststructuralist/poststructuralism 5, 33
Pound, Ezra 1, 2, 3, 31, 91, 95, 115, 175 n.1
The Cantos 12
position on literary modernism 2
Proust, Marcel 42, 76
À la recherche du temps perdu (In Search of Lost Time) 160
pseudonyms 26, 64–70, 74, 89, 169
metacommentary 71

and metafictional strategies 63
  as text 74–7

Quigley, Mark 59

Rabaté, Jean-Michel 7, 13, 17, 37, 53, 55–6, 83, 113, 187 n.131
  The Pathos of Distance 24
  Think, Pig! 35
Radak, Tamara 195 n.122
radically symbolic 10–13, 28, 76, 89, 95, 172
Ramazani, Jahan 7
Rancière, Jacques 37
  modern literature 42–5
Ransom, John Crowe 2
Reynolds, Paige 15, 127
Ricoeur, Paul 16, 207 n.17, 207 n.20
  Memory, History, Forgetting 80, 206 n.15
Rimbaud, Arthur 31
Rimmon-Kenan, Shlomith 97, 98, 132
  Narrative Fiction 97
Robin, Thierry 66
Robinson, Richard 147, 157, 167
Roche, Anthony 127, 129
Rogers, Gayle 5
Ross, Patience 82
Rousseau, Jean-Jacques 153–4
Royle, Nicholas 94, 96, 98, 119, 123
Rubenstein, Michael 84
rural modernity 142

Saint-Amour, Paul 18, 68
  Tense Future 14
Sampson, Denis 147, 211 n.81
  Outstaring Nature's Eye 207 n.25
Sarsfield, Patrick 39, 43
Sartre, Jean-Paul 53–6
  Qu'est-ce que la littérature? 182 n.22
Second World War 33, 34, 37, 40, 54, 58, 60, 93
Sheils, Barry 21, 179 n.75
Sheridan, Niall 65, 70, 76
Shoah. *See* Holocaust
Shovlin, Frank 148
Smyth, Gerry 9, 173
Spanish Civil War 50
Spender, Stephen 58–9

Spivak, Gayatri Chakravorty 7
Stanford Friedman, Susan 9
Stephens, James 31
Stuart, Francis 59, 189 n.169
Sullivan, Kelly 134
surrealism 53, 187 n.118
Swanzy, Mary 4
Synge, J. M.
  modernisms of 2
  The Playboy of the Western World 1

Taaffe, Carol 77, 84
Taylor, Julie 6
Thurschwell, Pamela 197 n.8
Tighe Ledwidge, Grace 144
translation 19, 30, 37, 42–3, 50–3, 59, 88, 148, 165, 188n.146
  dilemma of 20
  and literary technique 21
  problematics of 46
  studies 20
  untranslatability 22–4, 30, 45, 52, 157, 169
  untranslatable 4, 22–4, 29, 61, 88, 112, 165–6, 169–70, 212 n.106
  and writing degree zero 50–3
trauma 149–52, 155, 157, 206 n.13
  cultural 28
  European 33, 35, 45
  extratextual 152
  historical 28, 44, 55–6, 58, 113
  postcolonial 45
  referential representation of 148
Trevor, William 141
Trollope, Anthony 97

UNESCO
  Anthology of Mexican Poetry 52

V21 Collective 26, 180 n.98
van der Ziel, Stanley 147, 167, 209 n.77
  John McGahern and the Imagination of Tradition 209 n.77
Victorian studies 26, 180 n.98
von Goethe, Johann Wolfgang 22

Walker, Tom 4, 10
Walkowitz, Rebecca 51, 186 n.111
  Born Translated 20

Walshe, Eibhear
   Elizabeth Bowen Remembered: The Farahy Address 196 n.1
   Ordinary People Dancing 117, 202 n.11
War of Independence 10, 96, 100, 106, 110, 111, 112
Warren, Robert Penn 2, 97
Warren Friedman, Alan 187 n.118
Waugh, Evelyn 116, 119
weak theory 14–15
Weller, Shane
   Language and Negativity in European Modernism 182 n.22
White, Sian 197 n.8
Whyte, James 205 n.1, 207 n.24
Wilder, Gary 201 n.129
Williams, Moretti 5, 7, 19–21
Williams, Raymond 7, 74
Wolfson, Susan J. 26
Wollaeger, Mark 176 n.22
Woolf, Virginia 3, 91, 197 n.17
world literary space 20–1, 23, 45
world literature 19–22
writing degree zero 28, 37, 46–57, 60–1, 169, 187 n.131

Yeats, Jack B. 31
Yeats, W. B. 15, 27, 29, 70, 72, 75, 76, 172
   'The Mask' 73
   poetry of 1
   The Tower 2, 4, 12
   A Vision 2, 4

www.ingramcontent.com/pod-product-compliance
Lightning Source LLC
Chambersburg PA
CBHW062214300426
44115CB00012BA/2063